Performing Ethics through Film Style

Levinas with the Dardenne Brothers, Barbet Schroeder and Paul Schrader

Edward Lamberti

EDINBURGH
University Press

Edinburgh University Press is one of the leading university presses in the UK. We publish academic books and journals in our selected subject areas across the humanities and social sciences, combining cutting-edge scholarship with high editorial and production values to produce academic works of lasting importance. For more information visit our website: edinburghuniversitypress.com

© Edward Lamberti, 2020, 2021

Edinburgh University Press Ltd
The Tun – Holyrood Road
12 (2f) Jackson's Entry
Edinburgh EH8 8PJ

First published in hardback Edinburgh University Press 2020

Typeset in Ehrhardt MT Pro by
Manila Typesetting Company

A CIP record for this book is available from the British Library

ISBN 978 1 4744 4400 2 (hardback)
ISBN 978 1 4744 4401 9 (paperback)
ISBN 978 1 4744 4402 6 (webready PDF)
ISBN 978 1 4744 4403 3 (epub)

The right of Edward Lamberti to be identifed as author of this work has been asserted in accordance with the Copyright, Designs and Patents Act 1988 and the Copyright and Related Rights Regulations 2003 (SI No. 2498).

Contents

List of Figures iv
Acknowledgements vi

Introduction: Textual Performances in Levinas and Film 1

Part I The Dardenne Brothers: An Ethics without Rest
Part I Introduction 29
1. *Je Pense à Vous* and *La Promesse*: From Describing to Performing 33
2. Levinasian Responsibility in *Le Fils* 50
3. *The Kid with a Bike* and the Reframing of Ethics 69

Part II Barbet Schroeder: Devoted to the Other
Part II Introduction 85
4. *Maîtresse*: Direction without Domination 89
5. The Ethical and the Juridical in *Reversal of Fortune* and *Terror's Advocate* 105
6. *Our Lady of the Assassins* and Levinas's Ethics as First Philosophy 129

Part III Paul Schrader: An Unexpected Ethics
Part III Introduction 147
7. *American Gigolo* and the Ethics of Falling in Love 151
8. Levinasian Limits of Performativity in *Mishima: A Life in Four Chapters* 170
9. Passivity and Responsibility in *The Comfort of Strangers*, *Dominion: Prequel to the Exorcist* and *Adam Resurrected* 187

Conclusion: Levinasian Films in the World 204

Notes 209
Bibliography 231
Index 241

Figures

1.1	The opening shot of *Je Pense à Vous* shows Seraing	35
1.2	Igor hears Assita being attacked; Roger intervenes; Roger pays the assailant	40
1.3	Hamidou thanks Igor for his help with the gas	42
2.1	Olivier reads the form announcing Francis's arrival at the centre	53
2.2	Olivier turns as he hears Francis's question; Francis pauses as he walks past	62
2.3	Olivier and Francis: from half a meal each to matching sustenance	65
3.1	Cyril rides his bike away, having been rejected by his father again	74
3.2	Cyril clings to Samantha in the doctor's surgery	77
4.1	Olivier discovers the noose in Ariane's den	93
4.2	Olivier looks down in the direction of Mario's departure . . . and looks up towards Ariane's apartment	94
4.3	'The distance of love': Ariane interacts with clients in her den	99
4.4	Ariane and Olivier drive along at the film's climax	104
5.1	Sunny in her hospital bed is shown from above	109
5.2	Claus romances Alexandra on a spacious yacht	109
5.3	Alan is surrounded by his students at Harvard	110
5.4	Symmetry: Christmas at Clarendon Court; Sunny walking towards her bathroom; Claus and Alan at the club; Clarendon Court in the snow	115
5.5	Jeremy Irons made up to play Claus von Bülow	117
5.6	Jacques Vergès brandishes his cigar	122
5.7	The film's information onslaught	125
6.1	Fernando cries at the table in the bar; Alexis attends to him	133
6.2	The two old friends hug and Fernando is shown in a classic first close-up	139
7.1	Julian hangs upside down, exercising and learning Swedish	153
7.2	Julian's ties and shirts	154
7.3	Julian and Michelle talk in the bar on their first meeting	158

7.4	Julian drives along, in his utter self-containment	159
7.5	Julian accepting Michelle's love	167
8.1	Making the structure clear from the outset: the four chapters	174
8.2	*American Gigolo* and *Mishima*: laying out clothes on a bed	177
8.3	*American Gigolo* and *Mishima*: getting dressed in the mirror	178
8.4	*American Gigolo* and *Mishima*: Venetian blinds	179
8.5	Mishima as an adult, as a boy, as an adolescent, as a young man; Mizoguchi; Osamu; Isao	182
9.1	Colin and Mary are unaware that a stranger is photographing them	190
9.2	Colin and Mary wonder whether to go up to Robert and Caroline's apartment	192
9.3	Stellan Skarsgård as the melancholy Father Merrin	195
9.4	Merrin goes out to do the Lord's work	197
9.5	David looks out from under his sheet; Adam looks back at him	199
9.6	Adam contemplates the future	203

Acknowledgements

My first thanks go to Mrs Goddard, who, when I was about ten, read my short story 'The Curse of Blue' out to the class. Teachers like that change your life.

I came to the ethical philosophy of Emmanuel Levinas and the films of Jean-Pierre and Luc Dardenne, Barbet Schroeder and Paul Schrader via separate routes. My engagement with Schrader's work began in the early 1990s, when I first saw *American Gigolo* on TV. I remember enjoying it but I wasn't quite sure what to think about it. A few years later, I encountered it again, as an undergraduate studying Film and Literature at the University of Warwick. With the benefit of two screenings of the film in two days and Colin McArthur's lecture and seminar, I found myself really getting into it. It was Colin's seminar that sealed the deal. His comments on Schrader's work opened my mind to this fascinating filmmaker. From then on, I was conscious of wanting to seek out films written and/or directed by Schrader.

It was in about the early 2000s that it dawned on me that every time I watched a film directed by Barbet Schroeder, I seemed to like it. I ran back through the films of his that I had seen up to that point: *Single White Female*, *Reversal of Fortune*, *Before and After* and *General Idi Amin Dada: A Self Portrait*. I had indeed liked them all – and if the same name keeps cropping up on films that you have liked without thinking about it, you're surely a fan. From that point on, Schroeder, like Schrader, was someone whose work I was consciously seeking out.

With the Dardennes, it was the release of *Le Fils* in UK cinemas in March 2003 that got me hooked. I had read the reviews out of Cannes and was intrigued by its premise, but when I saw the film, it astounded me. Within a few weeks I had also seen *La Promesse* and *Rosetta*. I was an instant fan of the Dardennes.

Over the next few years, something started to form in my mind about the work of these different filmmakers. Then when I was studying for an MA at King's College London in the late 2000s, Sarah Cooper's module 'Thinking Cinema' introduced us to Levinas's ethical philosophy and its burgeoning impact on film scholarship. And I realised that Levinas's work was enabling me to see connections between some of the films of the Dardennes, Schroeder and Schrader. At the same time, the films were helping me to understand more about Levinas and to appreciate crucial aspects of his ethics.

I should therefore like to thank Colin and Sarah for the different ways in which they sparked my thoughts on these filmmakers and on ethics. Sarah was also my PhD supervisor, and I feel so fortunate to have had the benefit of her expertise, her encouragement and her support. Thank you also to Martin O'Shaughnessy and Libby Saxton, my thesis examiners, whose encouraging words spurred me on to think that I could develop my research further. On a more general note, I want to say thank you to the Department of Film and Television Studies at Warwick and the Department of Film Studies at King's for all their teaching and for being so friendly and supportive over the years. V. F. Perkins taught me at Warwick and became a dear friend; his death in 2016 was a huge loss, but his influence lives on through all who were inspired by his teaching, his writing and his kindness. And I want to mention two people who, like Victor, taught me and whose friendship means a lot to me: Richard Dyer and Edward Gallafent. With regard to this project, my thanks to Richard for his thought-provoking advice at the start and my thanks to Edward for his invaluable feedback on the draft manuscript.

I have presented aspects of my research at a number of institutions. I should like to say thanks to Robert Sternberg and Stephen Webster at Imperial College London for inviting me to give a talk on *Terror's Advocate*; to Alan Bernstein, Jonathan Hourigan and Sophia Wellington at the London Film School for inviting me to give classes on Levinas and *Le Fils*; to Catherine Constable at Warwick for inviting me to talk about *Reversal of Fortune*; and to the department at King's for inviting me to present my research more generally. Also, I was very grateful for the opportunity to give a talk on *American Gigolo* at the 2013 Society for Cinema and Media Studies conference in Chicago and to the department and the Faculty of Arts & Humanities at King's for their financial support for the trip. My thanks to the attendees on those days: their support and their comments were invigorating. Thanks also to Sonia Mullett for inviting me to appear in the British Film Institute's documentary 'Domestic Masochism: Barbet Schroeder's *Maîtresse*'.

I should also very much like to thank Edinburgh University Press, especially Gillian Leslie, Richard Strachan and Eddie Clark, for their enthusiastic support for the project and for being such a pleasure to work with, and the readers for their encouraging comments. My heartfelt thanks to all my friends, for variously helping me engage with my work and helping me take my mind off it. My colleagues at the British Board of Film Classification have accommodated my research and writing interests and have kindly asked how it's all going: thank you to every single one of them. And thank you to the Institut français du Royaume-Uni, including the admin staff, my teachers – especially Cécile Alais and Annie Vengeant – and all my fellow students, past and present.

Finally, much love to my parents, Bruno and Rosalind Lamberti; my brothers, Richard and David, and their families; and Uncle Barry, Auntie Pam, Auntie Teresa and all my cousins and their families. They all know how much I love books, films and writing and I'm proud to be able to share this work with them.

Introduction: Textual Performances in Levinas and Film

One of the defining characteristics of Emmanuel Levinas's ethical philosophy is the emergence of a prose style that seeks not just to describe but to *perform* his ethics. This performative quality is vital in that it strives to communicate the struggle to express something that, for Levinas, exists outside of reason or choice – namely, the self's inescapable responsibility for the Other. This book will argue that this performativity adds an important new dimension to how we can read films in terms of Levinasian ethics. To demonstrate this, I will focus on a range of films directed by Jean-Pierre and Luc Dardenne, Barbet Schroeder and Paul Schrader. These directors have all made films that contend with Levinasian concerns, and of primary significance to this study is how we can understand these films to be performing Levinasian ethics through their styles.

I shall start with an observation from Schrader. Before he became a filmmaker, he was a critic, and in 1972 he published a book entitled *Transcendental Style in Film: Ozu, Bresson, Dreyer*. His book seeks to define a common style prevalent in the films of those three geographically and industrially distinct filmmakers, a style that expresses the Transcendent. At one point, discussing the difference between an experience and a form, Schrader says 'a form can express the Transcendent, an experience cannot'.[1] For Schrader, experience is local and individual – it changes from person to person and from place to place – but a clear and successful deployment of form is something that can be perceived by all and that all can benefit from. Schrader illustrates this with an everyday example:

> [A] certain form (the mass, transcendental style) expresses the Transcendent. A viewer, perceiving and appreciating that form, undergoes the experience of transcendence. He then seeks to evoke that same feeling in his friend. He tells his friend exactly how he felt; his friend is curious and faintly amused, but does not share the speaker's transcendent feelings.[2]

The issue here is that the viewer is not successfully recreating his own experience of the form so that his friend can have a good chance of feeling what he felt. Instead, the viewer is indulging his own feelings, his own experience: he is more invested, even if unintentionally, in the excitement of his own experience and its retelling than he is in conveying that experience to his friend. What should he have done instead? Schrader says, 'In order to successfully induce transcendence in his friend, the viewer would have had to transform his feelings into a form (as transcendental style does) in which his friend could perceive the Transcendent, and then experience transcendence.'[3] Two aspects of Schrader's observation are especially pertinent here. First, if we must turn our experience into a form in order to convey that experience to another person, this is a demanding prospect: we need to deny what we think of as our own enjoyment so that the friend can have an experience. We need to focus on the Other's needs rather than on the gratification of our own. Second, not only is a demand placed on us, we are required to become a form so as to convey what we want to convey. We need to engage performatively; we need to use the tools of communication and performance available to us in order that the friend might benefit. In linking the effectiveness of a film form such as transcendental style to the behaviour of the viewer, Schrader connects discipline in human form – bodily discipline, psychological discipline – with the discipline of a film style. The person and the film communicate successfully in the same way: through a disciplined approach to form.

Similarly, Levinas performs his ethics through a form of language that is designed to give the reader an ethical experience, and part of this experience is the exposure that the self, or subject, undergoes in being ethical:

> The subject is not *in itself*, at home with itself, such that it would dissimulate itself in itself or dissimulate itself in its wounds and its exile, understood as *acts* of wounding or exiling itself. Its bending back upon itself is a turning inside out . . . [I]t becomes a sign, turns into an allegiance.[4]

This stance, from Levinas's 1974 book *Otherwise than Being or Beyond Essence*, shares with Schrader's observation a sense of the selflessness of what Levinas will go on in the same book to articulate as 'substitution', which is his word for when the self takes the place – and thus takes on the burdens – of the Other.[5] In both the Schrader and the Levinas, there is an emphasis on the behavioural state that substitution imposes. Transforming experience into form and 'turning inside out' are descriptions that challenge the reader to understand a process seemingly beyond comfortable, easily achievable everyday actions.

For both film style and Levinas's prose style, there is a set of creative choices involved in conveying experience through form. In Levinas's ethics, however, it is a *lack* of choice that helps to define behaviour as ethical. If to offer oneself to the Other, to stand in the Other's stead and receive the Other's burden, were a conscious decision, it would rob the condition of its ethical dimension. As Levinas says, it 'would then extend forth as an intentionality, out of a subject posited in itself and for itself, disposed to play, sheltered from all ills'.[6] This would be unethical because, for the self, there would be no risk (as the self would be 'sheltered from all ills'), and instead there would be self-centred fun and frivolity (the subject being 'disposed to play'). It would be difficult for the subject to feel ethical while being 'posited in itself and for itself'. Instead, for Levinas, 'giving has meaning only as a tearing from oneself despite oneself'.[7] As ethics happens outside any possibility of there being a choice in the matter, our responsibility for the Other is inescapable. Through the creative choices of its prose style, *Otherwise than Being* attempts to perform the inescapability of the self's responsibility for the Other.

Through my readings of a range of films directed by the Dardennes, Schroeder and Schrader, I will propose that films can perform a Levinasian ethics in ways that enable viewers to experience that inescapable responsibility. The films I am going to discuss do not have a uniform approach to style, and my Levinasian readings of them are also by no means uniform. Rather, the principal connection I make between Levinas's work and these films is via their attempt to perform what Levinas calls the Saying. The Saying is the ethical encounter that happens prior to the conventions of language, which is why Levinas calls it 'pre-original language'.[8] It conveys the newness of the ethical encounter with the Other, 'the proximity of one to the other',[9] which founds the self as ethical prior to the fixity of regular language and its complacent communication. These films reproduce the vitality of the Levinasian Saying, what Levinas refers to as 'the anarchy of responsibility'.[10]

Levinas and Film Studies

Levinas's philosophy has proved to be enticing to Film Studies scholars. There is a strain running through much of Levinas's work, especially in its early years, that is against seeing art as ethical. Levinas does not speak of film as such, but when, for example, in his 1948 essay 'Reality and its Shadow', he denounces the status of time-based arts, claiming that they are unable to exist as a site for ethical engagement and that only criticism can do this work, he implicitly implicates cinema.[11] It is in particular the fixity, the resistance to change or even the inability to change inherent in a work of art to which Levinas objects.[12] As Reni Celeste notes: 'His conclusion is that art is evasion rather than responsibility. Only real time can provide an opening to possibility and change through the existence of the other.'[13] In his early writings, Levinas distinguishes between the fixed, static nature of art and the dynamism of criticism. And while his later philosophy does not really seek to build on such a position, he nevertheless never offers a total retraction. Sarah Cooper, in her introduction to her pioneering work 'The Occluded Relation: Levinas and Cinema', notes how '[t]here is something provocative, then, in wanting to ask what Levinas's philosophy has to say about cinema, if we understand this realm as the location *par excellence* of the moving image'.[14] Thus, in order to discuss Levinas in relation to film, it is important to be willing to engage with the challenge of the pairing.

Much film scholarship on Levinas begins with the *visage*, the Levinasian concept of the face. In his 1961 book *Totality and Infinity: An Essay on Exteriority*, which, along with *Otherwise than Being*, is commonly considered to be one of the two central books in his writing on ethics, the face figures as a key aspect of the ethical relationship between the self and the Other. Levinas describes the face as a purveyor of signification beyond the purely phenomenological. The Levinasian face is enigmatic, providing an opening onto the Other's presence as it arrives unexpectedly, interrupting the self's contented mastery of the immediate environment and placing a demand on the self. The ethics of the encounter happens when the self recognises the Other's demand and responds favourably.[15] This sense of the Levinasian face as being something hard to define, certainly in relation to what we commonly understand a face to be, has proved a fertile site for engagement within Film Studies, as it prompts questions regarding the status of the image. Cooper's early study *Selfless Cinema?: Ethics and French Documentary* focuses on issues pertaining to the filming of human subjects in the work of several French documentary filmmakers and considers the implications for both the face and film itself as surfaces through which a Levinasian sense of alterity can be perceived.[16] Similarly, Libby Saxton has expressed an interest in 'how Levinas's critique of representation as liable to "thematize" and thereby reduce the "visage" to a projection of the Same, may be brought to bear on filmic sounds and images and the ways in which they address, compel and command us as spectators'.[17] Writing on director Claude Lanzmann's Holocaust testimony film *Shoah* (1985), Saxton considers how although the faces of the interviewees express a great deal about what happened, the cinematic face is Levinasian not for what it shows us about the filmed subject but for what it cannot show us:

> The film consistently frustrates our desire to see, know and understand by refusing to allow the other and his or her history to take shape as objects under our gaze. By holding us at a distance the images and voices afford a more intimate encounter with traumatic experience, opening up the possibility of proximity while preserving separation. In so doing, they call Levinas's critique of images and vision as inherently totalising into question.[18]

For Saxton, it is imperative that we consider ourselves both arrested by this filmic encounter with the Other and denied knowledge of that Other: only by recognising the limits of our understanding, and the existence of otherness outside our totalising sphere of comprehension, can we be said to be having a Levinasian response. Cooper makes a comparable observation with regard to the final scene of the Dardenne brothers' film *L'Enfant* (*The Child*, dirs Jean-Pierre and Luc Dardenne, 2005): 'In spectatorial terms, the ability to relate to the characters' suffering depends on our being close to both but identified with neither . . . [T]his positioning firmly outside of the characters' lives is precisely the ethical point.'[19] The implications of the Levinasian face for spectatorship have also been discussed by Michele Aaron, who posits that '[s]pectatorship is not ethically interesting but intrinsically ethical',[20] while Doug Cummings (also on the Dardennes) and John W. Wright (on Steven Spielberg) are two more critics who have discussed the Levinasian face in relation to film.[21] This scholarship acknowledges the Levinasian face as something visible but also beyond our ontological grasp, thus inviting the viewer into a relationship with film that makes of the visible a filmic version of the Levinasian Other, which necessarily for ethical engagement evades comprehension.

This interrogation of the face, and its importance for understanding how film's visual properties can open onto something beyond the ontological, has very much helped shape the discourse on Levinas and film so far. An upshot of this is that many film scholars have remained close to the ideas of the face and the Other as expounded in *Totality and Infinity* and have not yet in general attended in any sustained way to the development (and, in some cases, revision) of the ideas from that book in the later major work *Otherwise than Being*. Arriving thirteen years after *Totality and Infinity*, *Otherwise than Being* presents dramatic ideas of the inescapability of the self's ethical obligation to the Other, such that the self is considered hostage to the Other. It presents these ideas not just through its descriptions but through its own textual practices, and film scholarship on Levinas has so far not included sustained engagement with how the extremely demanding nature of Levinas's staging of his ethics in this text might be rendered in filmic terms. Robert Bernasconi and Simon Critchley, in their introduction to their 1991 collection of (non-film-related) writings on Levinas, suggest that as 'the first generation' of Levinas scholarship was guided by *Totality and Infinity*, their volume will aim to concentrate more on *Otherwise than Being*.[22] Similarly, in this book, I propose that it is time for *Otherwise than Being* to play a more central part in discussions of Levinas and film.

Otherwise than Being and the Inescapability of Responsibility

Otherwise than Being is often thought to have been written in part as an indirect response to Jacques Derrida's critique of *Totality and Infinity*.[23] Derrida's viewpoint is founded on the argument that, while Levinas sets out in *Totality and Infinity* to reconceptualise ethics in terms of what is beyond the self's comprehension so as to open up the possibility of an 'infinite' engagement with the Other, the project ultimately fails, because Levinas ends up falling back on the age-old philosophical language of ontology he has intended to dismantle.[24] For Derrida, '[b]y making the origin of language, meaning, and difference the relation to the infinitely other, Levinas is resigned to betraying his own intentions in his philosophical discourse. The latter is understood, and instructs, only by first permitting the same and Being to circulate within it.'[25] Thus, so it is implied, *Totality and Infinity*, for all its work to establish the unknowability of the Other and the mysteriousness of the ethical relation as expressed through the encounter with the face of the Other, can ultimately be discussed in terms of preserving the primacy of the self as locus of meaning in the world, for the self–Other relation remains reducible to the self's comfortable (and therefore unethical) totality.

Otherwise than Being, however, cannot be so easily reduced or summarised. In this later text, Levinas refines his linguistic approach, taking words to new extremes, 'to near-breaking point',[26] as Colin Davis says, so as to move away from the totalising language of the earlier work. Diane Perpich discusses this move in terms of a narrative that is abandoned: '*Otherwise Than Being* explicitly abandons the narrative commitments of the earlier work and is explicit about the problematic status of its own discourse.'[27] The idea of the 'narrative' of *Totality and Infinity* relates to a sense of the chronology of the self undergoing an ethical transformation through the encounter with the Other, something that *Otherwise than Being* reconfigures in terms of a more problematic relation to chronology, not least through the sense of the self being always already ethical.

Troubling this position, however, is a question that is remarkably persistent in commentaries on Levinas: how do we implement Levinas's demanding ethical philosophy in the real world? The reason this is asked so often is that Levinas's own work does not tell us in any obvious way, and indeed is perhaps not interested in offering ideas for its implementation. There is a good reason for this: to do so may be to violate the Levinasian idea that I cannot expect anyone else to share my ethical responsibility for the Other. As Levinas says, 'Does one have the right to preach to the other a piety without reward? . . . It is easier to tell myself to believe without promise than it is to ask it of the other. That is the idea of asymmetry. I can demand of myself that which I cannot demand of the other.'[28] According to Levinas, I am responsible for all others, and this includes being responsible for their failings. Thus, I cannot demand that others behave ethically, or even how they might do so if they wanted to, because even that might be to impose my view on them and bring them into my totality, rather than accepting their other ways of doing things. Some Levinas scholars, such as Perpich and Adriaan Theodoor Peperzak,[29] have queried whether what Levinas was producing was an ethics at all – especially, says Peperzak, 'if we understand "ethics" as a doctrine about the moral principles, norms, obligations, and interdictions that rule human behavior'.[30] Peperzak thus identifies what we commonly look to ethics to provide: a set of rules instructing us in how to live a more ethical life. Levinas's work avoids, except in fleeting references, any mention of how one might implement his philosophy in the world. Nor does he make more than passing references to real events or situations. He dedicates *Otherwise than Being* primarily to victims of the Nazi persecution that saw more than six million Jews exterminated during the Second World War, and to the countless millions 'of all confessions and all nations, victims of the same hatred of the other man, the same anti-semitism'.[31] But within the book itself there is no discussion or analysis of that genocide.

And yet, on another level, Levinas's work is full of instruction – it is to be found in his writing style, which is indistinguishable from the meanings it generates. If we read Levinas's writing not so much as an ethics, or even as philosophy, but as prose, we can see ways in which his work acquires uses that are very different from prescriptive tenets. I do not mean to suggest that we should not consider Levinas's work to be an ethics – indeed, it is precisely in thinking of it as an ethics that its particularly invigorating qualities come to the fore. But it is in the *ways* in which the texts contain and transmit their meanings – and in particular the efforts we see in *Otherwise than Being* to comment on its process of meaning-making as a crucial part of its argument – that Levinas's contribution to ethics is made especially apparent.

The striking innovation of *Otherwise than Being* is that it reconfigures the terms of *Totality and Infinity* so as to enact or *perform* the unfixed, uncertain, never-satisfied condition of responsibility for the Other. Levinas is trying to describe the indescribably anterior, the otherwise-than-being. The encounter of self and Other is borne not of description or thematisation – the Said – but of an unexpected occurrence – the Saying. The Saying happens prior to the thematisation the Said makes of it, or, as Levinas says, '[a]ntecedent to the verbal signs it conjugates'.[32] It happens prior to reflection, interpretation, or description; it is an unexpected burst of an utterance, 'a foreword preceding languages',[33] a Big Bang that brings into being a world of possible ethics. Levinas's language performs an ever-renewing, never-settling set of propositions that seek, slowly but surely, to school the reader in the primary ethical importance of the Saying, the refusal to settle for the stabilised terms and complacent articulations of the Said. Through paragraph after paragraph and page after page of this linguistic onslaught, the text strives to have us recognise what has always been there within us: our goodness, which is founded on our relation to others and which is unwavering, infinite. This, for Levinas, is ethics as first philosophy, the idea that before anything else – selfhood, thematisation, the conventions of language – there is the ethical relation. If we consider *Otherwise than Being* in its entirety, we can say that the first three chapters lay the groundwork for the adventure of ethical responsibility for the Other, an adventure that will be most expansively expressed in Chapter IV, 'Substitution'. This chapter is the core towards which the book moves and away from which it spins. I do not use the word 'core' accidentally: Levinas has, by this point in the text, discussed '*dénucléation*', the 'coring out' of the ego,[34] as part of the process whereby the self turns towards the Other, and we can see that the central thesis of *Otherwise than Being* is to elucidate how, if the self has a core, it is to be found not in the ego but in the substitution of the self for the Other – the process Levinas names 'the-one-for-the-other'.[35] We may feel that the remaining two chapters that follow 'Substitution' decrease in terms of intensity, but it is precisely for this reason that I believe them to be fascinating: like a course of antibiotics that one sees through to its end long after the symptoms of one's malady appear to have cleared up, *Otherwise than Being* performs its own medicinal ethical work on readers by repeating, restating and, in the process, frustrating anew any understanding of the book's persistent cause – what Peperzak defines as '[t]he pretheoretical responsibility practiced in proximity . . . analyzed by Levinas as *substitution, obsession, accusation, election,* and *persecution*'.[36] By the end of the book, the repeated mentioning of the Saying and the Said achieves two importantly contradictory things: it gives definition to what is apparently impossible to define and it frustrates the definition through recapitulation and revision. In this regard, we might feel that Levinas's prose repeats words such that they begin to lose their effect. This may be especially the case if we were to read *Otherwise than Being* out loud. Indeed, perhaps we are meant to experience it in that way. Reading the prose out loud would accentuate its repetitive qualities, and may even draw out some humour in the writing. Levinas's prose is difficult to read and to absorb, but it is a mistake to approach it with nothing but solemn regard. Whether we read it out loud or silently, we need to wrestle with the prose – to *live* it – if we are to unlock its ethical power.

Thus, *Otherwise than Being* is not only a presentation of Levinas's ethical philosophy regarding the self's responsibility for the Other but also a performance of the restlessness of that responsibility. Levinas says of *Otherwise than Being*, '[t]his book interprets the subject as a hostage and the subjectivity of the subject as a substitution breaking with being's essence'.[37] Hostage status is prisoner-like – we are held by another and the situation robs us of control. For Levinas, the self's status as hostage to the Other is the status of the self in the world – and this particular hostage situation is life-long. It is, one might say, for the self simply a fact of life. And what we see in *Otherwise than Being* is a continual, and continually dissatisfied, attempt not just to describe the self's status as hostage to the Other but to *perform* it.

In order to talk about the notion of performance both in Levinas's writing and in film, this book will draw on performativity theory. The link between performativity theory and film is not obvious – and not unproblematic – but what I aim to do is articulate ways in which certain films perform a Levinasian ethics akin to the performance that Levinas gives through his textual practices in *Otherwise than Being*. That performance places the reader or viewer in the position of being invited to engage with the process of *dénucléation* that leads to the-one-for-the-other, the substitution of the self for the Other. *Otherwise than Being* is recognisably the work of the same man who wrote *Totality and Infinity* and earlier books of ethical philosophy such as *Existence and Existents*[38] – and yet in *Otherwise than Being*, the language becomes its own subject to a greater extent than before. It is because *Otherwise than Being* goes further than *Totality and Infinity* both in detailing the responsibility of the-one-for-the-other and in performing it through its own textual strategy that I believe it proves more instrumental than *Totality and Infinity* in illuminating both the themes and the stylistic strategies of the films in this book.

I present this study in the knowledge that discussions of Levinas's work have sometimes taken place within the context of more general considerations of ethical philosophy and film. For example, Lisa Downing and

Libby Saxton's co-authored volume *Film and Ethics: Foreclosed Encounters* considers Levinas among a number of other philosophers whose work has significance for ethics and film and for discussions of the relative importance of the self and the Other, such as Derrida, Jacques Lacan, Michel Foucault and Slavoj Žižek.[39] Jinhee Choi and Mattias Frey's collection *Cine-Ethics: Ethical Dimensions of Film Theory, Practice, and Spectatorship*, meanwhile, presents a range of debates concerning ethics and film that are attuned to three strands, the 'revisionist perspective' (which includes, among others, Levinas, with his efforts to reorient ethical debates within philosophy), the 'moral perceptionist perspective' (in which, among other pieces, Vivian Sobchack posits a phenomenology of the viewing body and the viewed film) and the 'cognitivist perspective' (which includes such writers as Noël Carroll, Gregory Currie and Carl Plantinga who seek to theorise the emotional aspects of viewer engagement).[40] Robert Sinnerbrink offers a theory of film's capacity for conveying ethical experience aesthetically and a survey of the filmic ethical landscape in his book *Cinematic Ethics: Exploring Ethical Experience through Film*, which encompasses philosophers from Stanley Cavell to Gilles Deleuze and includes a consideration of Levinasian themes through a discussion of the Dardennes' film *La Promesse* (*The Promise*, dirs Luc and Jean-Pierre Dardenne, 1996).[41] These studies, and others besides, show the rich range of approaches to ethics in film, including issues of viewing and spectatorship, ethical aspects in film production, ways in which films dramatise ethical dilemmas or ideas, and debates concerned with how best to bring philosophy to bear successfully on film (and vice versa). In contrast to these recent approaches, my book offers an intense focus on one proposition: an examination of the self's responsibility for the Other as performed by Levinas's prose in *Otherwise than Being* and by the work of the Dardennes, Schroeder and Schrader. This book therefore presents this philosopher and these directors in symbiotic union so as to consider in detail an ethical encounter hitherto under-theorised in studies of ethics and film.

Performativity: J. L. Austin's Speech Act Theory and Beyond

In order to develop the discussion of the way in which Levinas's prose style in *Otherwise than Being* seeks to perform his ethics, it is beneficial to consider the origins and some of the developments of performativity theory. I shall begin with the English philosopher of language J. L. Austin, who developed his work on performativity primarily through a series of twelve lectures he gave at Harvard University in 1955. Austin died young, in 1960, and two years later his lecture notes were prepared for publication and published as *How to Do Things with Words*.[42] This book is the primary text that brought Austin's theory into the philosophical sphere. The lecture series begins with Austin proposing that whereas philosophers of language have typically considered statements to be descriptions and thus verifiable as true or false, for Austin many statements do not describe an action but instead *are* an action in themselves – they *do* what they are saying. Austin presents many examples, such as, 'I bet you sixpence it will rain tomorrow', in which the uttering of the statement does not describe the bet but rather *is* the bet.[43] He suggests calling this type of statement 'a *performative sentence* or a performative utterance, or, for short, "a performative"',[44] in comparison with the constative, which is the statement that purports to be a description.[45] And he explains that '[t]he name is derived, of course, from "perform", the usual verb with the noun "action": it indicates that the issuing of the utterance is the performing of an action – it is not normally thought of as just saying something'.[46] Austin goes on to determine that we can evaluate performative utterances in relation to their contexts. The statement, 'I now pronounce you husband and wife', for example, only has performative success if the person saying the statement is qualified to pronounce the man and woman husband and wife; if the person is not qualified to do so, the statement is said to fail as a performative utterance. Austin classifies such successes and failures as 'happy' and 'unhappy' or 'felicitous' and 'infelicitous' utterances.[47] Austin points out that not all statements are designed simply to record facts: 'for example, "ethical propositions" are perhaps intended, solely or partly, to evince emotion or to prescribe conduct or to influence it in special ways'.[48] As Austin develops his theme, he begins to question the distinction between the constative and the performative. This leads to a new and enduring position in which he complicates and all but abandons the constative-performative distinction in favour of a proposition that more or less *all* utterances are performative in various ways. He refers to these as speech acts,[49] and theorises this claim by breaking down speech acts into their locutionary (grammatical), illocutionary (intended) and perlocutionary (unforeseen) qualities. Austin concludes his final lecture with an invitation to students to take up his work and explore it in new ways.[50]

Austin's work on performativity and speech acts has proved to be very enticing to scholars working in a wide range of contexts and has retained its relevance surely beyond what he may have imagined. One of

Austin's most significant respondents was Derrida, who, in an essay entitled 'Signature Event Context' in 1972,[51] reacted to Austin's work by suggesting, as Jeffrey T. Nealon has noted, how it is not simply the case that a performative utterance is dependent on the context in which it is uttered; instead, the performative utterance is understood also to *influence* the context in which it is said, as it has an effect that carries over into the context that, previously, was being used to define it as performative.[52] Derrida's separate critiques of Austin and Levinas share a sense of how the form, or style, of a work is unavoidably part of its effect.

Performativity has also intersected with literature, notably in the work of Eve Kosofsky Sedgwick, whose queer readings of texts by Herman Melville, Henry James and Marcel Proust, among others, have interrogated society's perceived division of sexualities into the heterosexual and the homosexual.[53] Sandy Petrey, in *Speech Acts and Literary Theory*, carefully charts the development of speech acts from Austin and Derrida to the realm of literature and insists on the fundamental *societal* dimension of performativity.[54] Austin's theories have also been taken into areas of enquiry such as performance theory and identity politics.[55] One of the most significant voices in the latter area is Judith Butler: in her groundbreaking 1990 book *Gender Trouble: Feminism and the Subversion of Identity*, she explores, with the help of performativity theory, ways in which gender can be said to be a construct rather than something innate, while her later book *Excitable Speech: A Politics of the Performative* offers extended engagements with the performative effects of words in social and political arenas.[56] Butler's adaptation of Austin's theory, as Nealon observes, shows how, if what one says does not have a fixed meaning, it means that utterances can not only be deployed to wound and discriminate against certain sectors of society but can also be turned around and, through their performative qualities, deployed to affect relations for the better.[57] Time and again these theorists show us multiple kinds of performativity, from the performance of a character's point of view to the illocutionary and perlocutionary effects of language in social, political and ethical terms. James Loxley draws this sprawling heritage of Austin's work together in his book *Performativity*, offering a lucid account of the key movements in performativity over the past sixty or more years and correcting some of the common misconceptions and generalisations that have arisen.[58]

I shall now discuss two aspects of performativity in Levinas's work: the notion of the ethical encounter being in itself a type of speech act and the ways in which Levinas's writing style seeks to perform his ethics.

Performativity in Levinas: The Ethical Encounter and the Prose Style

In *Totality and Infinity*, the foundational idea, the 'primordial expression', of the face-to-face encounter between self and Other is 'the first word: "you shall not commit murder"'.⁵⁹ In effect, this is what the face of the Other articulates to the self. The self can respond either by killing the Other or by being open to the Other's demand. This encounter happens outside the conventions of everyday language and communication – it is the Saying, and it therefore poses issues for conventional understanding. Michael L. Morgan, for example, asks, '[i]f the face-to-face is a prelinguistic, preconceptual mode of relationship or dimension of everyday interpersonal life, how is it meaningful?'⁶⁰ For Morgan, the Saying is not a speech act, because 'it is not the conversational situation nor the act of speaking. Saying is not what we do with words, the act that we perform in uttering "I promise to meet you at ten o'clock."'⁶¹ In Morgan's reading, the timelessness of the Levinasian face-to-face cannot be pinned to the type of pre-existing social discourse that enables the production and identification of speech acts. After all, Levinas considers 'You shall not commit murder' to be 'the first word'. But an alternative reading to Morgan's could see the speech act at work. 'You shall not commit murder', as a pre-linguistic act of communication between the self and the Other, brings the ethical relationship into being and initiates the self's ethical response. Until the Other says to me that I shall not commit murder, I am open to doing just that, so as to defend my personal universe. Once the Other makes this claim on me, I am constituted as someone who will not commit murder and who will, instead, accept the Other and all the unknowability and responsibility that comes with it. There is therefore perhaps a performative dimension to the moment, which marks out the face-to-face encounter as having value not far removed from that of the speech act proper.

Whether the face-to-face is considered a speech act or not, however, *Totality and Infinity* positions the encounter within a chronology of ethical emergence, which goes something like, 'I was not ethical and now I am.' By contrast, in *Otherwise than Being*, I am *already* hostage to the Other, prior to reason, prior to my own needs, and even, as we have seen, prior to any choice to be ethical. For Perpich, Levinas's work represents 'an arguably original analysis of the performative dimension of language', one that 'think[s] language as providing the formal structure of the possibility of [an ethical] response'.⁶² We can therefore consider the project of *Otherwise than Being* to be one of performing the wrenching demands on the self called to responsibility before the Other. This makes *Otherwise than Being* a difficult book to read initially. But, says Davis, '[t]he difficulty of the work and the problems of understanding that it poses are not tangential to the point; they *are* the point'.[63] When one understands that Levinas's constant desire to redefine terms so as to avoid settling on one fixed meaning is a key aspect of his ethics, one can begin to comprehend the possibilities for new meanings and new understanding made possible by this textual performance. Perpich notes that '[a]s the narrative of the ego coming to moral conscience is abandoned, the conception of responsibility undergoes a correspondingly important shift. The core features of responsibility remain stable between Levinas's two works, but they are rendered in *Otherwise Than Being* in increasingly hyperbolic terms.'[64] Thus, we might say that the language of *Totality and Infinity* is inclined to *state* ideas that the language of *Otherwise than Being* sets out instead to *stage*. This means that while both achievements are textual performatives, *Otherwise than Being* is a more explicitly ethical exploration of words as not just saying but doing.

Attending to Levinas's work, and above all *Otherwise than Being*, in terms of its use of a performative language does, however, come with hazards attached. Paul Davies is one Levinas scholar who has cautioned against a reading of *Otherwise than Being* that would see form and content as working in tandem with each other, as it would 'reintroduc[e] the most conventional conception of a form being appropriate to its content'[65] and would therefore go against Levinas's desire to create a destabilised text, in which the content is a continual surprise that engages with the ethical need to evade fixity of meaning even as it purports to be creating meaning. For Davies, the performative reading – of the text *doing* the ethics – is reductive in that the effect of such a reading is to diminish the sense of alterity that must be felt by the reader. He reminds us that 'the references to nonphilosophical experiences and the empirical event of obligation to another . . . *must* come as a shock'.[66] To do otherwise, he believes, would be to overlook key points that *Otherwise than Being* is making about the difference between the Saying and the Said, about the originary power of language before fixity.[67] Similarly, Sam B. Girgus notes that Levinas's project places him 'in a classic dilemma of using language to escape language',[68] while Hagi Kenaan observes how

> when we try to explain the distinction between Saying and Said through the familiar set of oppositions used in the paradigmatic analysis of speech acts, we are inevitably buying into a dominant metaphysical picture of language that, in principle, cannot make room for the possibility of a transcendental alterity.[69]

And Alphonso Lingis, in his translator's introduction to *Otherwise than Being*, observes how the difficulty of Levinas's task in the book lies in the notion that as soon as you seek to articulate what precedes Being, you turn it into Being, 'just by formulating it in its terms, which are those of theoretical and ontological intelligibility'.[70] These theorists all acknowledge the difficulty of Levinas's project in seeking to convey the Saying through words. Their concern is in support of the book's ethics: they are mindful of any reading of *Otherwise than Being* that risks dulling the effect of its ethical Saying by ascribing to it a formalism that would turn the text into the complacent Said, too easy to understand and therefore, perhaps, too easy to discard.

The issue, then, becomes how to discuss Levinas's approach to language in *Otherwise than Being* without damaging the work's ethical intentions. I should like to address this first by restating something that is widely understood, which is that it is always questionable as to whether form and content can be separated. Theories of performativity testify to this – and so does our understanding of why Levinas has chosen the prose style he uses. All commentary on *Otherwise than Being* has the potential, of course, to elucidate Levinas's work in such a way as to risk robbing his readers of the chance to experience his prose as an example of the Saying in action. But if we do not attempt to account for Levinas's use of language, we risk closing Levinas off to all but the most learned readers of ethical philosophy, those already, in a sense, prepared for the experience. The 'shock' Davies refers to is, surely, only recognisable as a shock if, paradoxically, one knows what one is looking for.

Kenaan offers a solution in noting that '[i]f we find it impossible to encounter the Other's Saying, this is not because the Saying is missing in language, but rather because its turning toward us always precedes any encounter initiated by us'.[71] This means that the Saying is not to be found in any obvious, direct way through the performativity of language; instead it already exists, and it is the hope of language to perform that pre-existence as best it can. Film can do this, too: it is an art form with a visual and aural immediacy even while viewers know that what they are viewing is already in existence. Such immediacy holds always the potential for surprise, as what appears stable can be destabilised in a split second. This makes film an ideal medium for performing the 'shocks' of the Levinasian Saying.

Language, Performativity and Film

If film is going to perform the Saying, however – or to attempt to convey something akin to it – then film needs, first of all, licence to perform. The word 'performativity' has come to assume many different meanings, and the term, and its related theories, have been appropriated in a myriad of ways. A reason for this, Loxley notes, is that performativity 'appears to focus a valuable but not too difficult idea, detachable from the circumstances of its formulation without significant loss and usefully applicable to a wide range of differing intellectual challenges or problems'.[72] Given that Austin began with the linguistic properties of the performative, a logical approach to discussing performativity in relation to film would be to consider film as a language.

Film has been discussed as a language from the earliest days of film theory. To present one influential position, I shall turn to the work of Christian Metz. In his seminal essay 'The Cinema: Language or Language System?', Metz draws on the linguistic analysis of Ferdinand de Saussure in order to raise the question of whether film can be considered a type of language.[73] One of Metz's claims is that Saussure's notion that language has a signifier (for example, a word) and a signified (the idea the signifier represents) is incompatible with the essence of the moving image, because the film image cannot be separated in terms of signifier and signified. Metz notes how '[m]any people, misled by a kind of reverse anticipation, have antedated the language system; they believed they could understand the film because of its syntax, whereas one understands the syntax because one has understood, and only because one has understood, the film'.[74] By this he means that people are mistaken in considering film's properties – such as, for example, montage, shot/reverse shot, continuity editing, or the 180-degree rule – to be in themselves carriers of meaning. For Metz, the opposite is true: it is through having seen these properties at work in specific films, and having understood those specific films, that the properties themselves have come to be intelligible.[75] But, says Metz, film might be considered a type of language more generally through its signifying qualities.[76]

The idea that film is a language has been explored and contested elsewhere, too. Gregory Currie, for example, in 'The Long Goodbye: The Imaginary Language of Film', argues that film cannot be considered language-like.[77] Currie suggests that language works the way it does because it is productive and conventional. It is productive in the sense that 'there is an unlimited number of sentences of English that can be uttered'[78] and conventional in that its meaning is determined 'by adventitious uniformities of practice that are adhered to because they facilitate communication'.[79] Although Currie does not refer to Austin in his chapter, his discussion of language has obvious parallels with Austin's sense of language as rooted in social life – a sense recognised by Petrey in his discussion of the societal dimension of Austin's speech acts. We can therefore draw on Currie's argument to say that words are performative because of agreements regarding usage that have been established within a particular society at a particular time: words have become conventional; their usage is understood conventionally. According to Currie, however, film cannot work in this way, because 'it is not possible to identify any set of conventions that function to confer appearance meaning on cinematic images in anything like the way in which conventions confer (semantic) meaning on language'.[80] Currie notes that films include some standard 'conventions', such as shot/reverse shot editing,[81] but he argues that these are not arrived at through conventionality. For Currie, using the word 'conventionality' to describe something other than the conventionality of language is a failure of rigour. He cautions that

> [t]he distinction between meaning that is determined by convention (and that is therefore convention*al*) and meaning that is merely connected to convention is overlooked by those who appeal to a vague, impressionistic and all-purpose notion of convention to support their claims about the conventionality of images.[82]

Currie's objection echoes an observation from V. F. Perkins, who, in *Film as Film: Understanding and Judging Movies*, also considers the component parts of language to be dissimilar to the material complexity of the image:

> The simplest close-up in the crudest silent film shows much more than can be expressed in one word. Language separates the different aspects of a single phenomenon by its use of nouns, verbs, adjectives and so on; but on film, even edited film, the object (noun) cannot be dissociated from what it does (verb) or how it looks (adjective). The more complex the content of a shot, the less relevant the verbal parallels become.[83]

For both Currie and Perkins, then, the way language works is not akin to the images (and sounds) of film, which present a complex interplay of any number of elements. We may therefore be driven to conclude that the attempt to consider film as performative is futile. More specifically for this study, we may feel that, if *Otherwise than Being* is dependent on the performativity of language to bring its ethics into being, and if film cannot be considered akin to language, then there is no possibility of considering a film as a counterpart to Levinas's textual performance.

This study proposes, however, that if performativity is assessed in terms of conventionality, the conventionality of language is not the only type of conventionality that comes into play. When Currie says that language is conventional because its 'meanings are determined by a co-ordinated practice based on mutual expectation',[84] that could also serve as a definition of, for example, Classical Hollywood Style.[85] As James Monaco observes, the study of signs, semiotics, came into play in film theory as a way of appreciating the systems and signs that film deploys in order to create meaning:

> [F]ilm needs to be considered as a phenomenon very much like language. It has no codified grammar, it has no enumerated vocabulary, it doesn't even have very specific rules of usage, so it is very clearly not a language *system* like written or spoken English; but it nevertheless does perform many of the same functions of communication as language does.[86]

Film, like language, has developed through social practices within particular places and times and is therefore generally understood through a recognition of the conventions that operate within it. To recognise this is to acknowledge the different types of conventionality that determine meaning-making in different contexts within societies. Doing so maintains the fundamental Austinian notion of performativity.

Indeed, while language is a key aspect of the root of performativity theory, it is not inextricable from it, even in Austin's work. For Austin, I would argue, the specifics of language are located in the locutionary, which Austin defines as '[t]he act of "saying something" in [the] full normal sense'[87] and which can be considered a subset of the speech act. There remain, however, the illocutionary and perlocutionary aspects of the speech act, both of which lead away from the words themselves and towards considerations of achievement and response. And it is in the light of these latter considerations that I believe film can be considered as performative. While Austin's theory of performativity is initiated by an investigation into the effects of the spoken word – thus, performative *utterances* – Austin expands this in Lecture V to include written performatives, such as 'Notice is hereby given that trespassers will be prosecuted'.[88] It is only a small step from a written notice warning trespassers to a pictorial sign indicating something similar, by way of, for example, a red line through an illustration of a person walking. And if signs can be speech acts by dint of their conventionally recognisable meanings – locutionary in their textual properties, illocutionary in their functions and perlocutionary in the reactions they inspire by doing what they do – then film is similarly expressive. Because of its emphasis on the moving image (and its accompanying soundtrack), film does not 'say' things the way language does, but it nevertheless has parallels with other aspects of performativity. It is through film's uniqueness, through considering it on its own terms rather than as a poor relation of language, that we are most properly able to discuss film in terms of performativity.

The Performativity *of* a Film and Performativity *in* a Film

Drawing directly on Austin's work, anthropologist Liza Bakewell, in a chapter entitled 'Image Acts', posits the notion that images are just as performative as words.[89] She offers the term 'image acts' as the visual counterpart to the power of the linguistic speech act.[90] For Bakewell, '[i]f images are actions, it follows that images must have an effect on us. From the simplest gesture to the most complex artistic and engineering feat, images do things, and they do these things to us, to our interlocutors, and to our passersby.'[91] She argues persuasively for the importance of giving images their due in studies of language and communication: she notes that calling images 'text' has held us back from seeing images as acts,[92] but she believes nevertheless that humanities scholars are coming to see more and more value in studying not just the artistic importance of images but also their political importance. In pointing out that language systems are symbolic while images are iconic, Bakewell appears to echo the long-held distinction between language, with its signifier and its signified, and film, which has no such easy division. She says, however: 'Rather than emphasize the similarities between verbal and visual forms of communication, a better approach would be to give equal attention to their differences. Among other things, this would broaden both the theoretical and empirical base of language studies.'[93] This assertion – to treat film as film – of course echoes Perkins. Bakewell notes that images do all sorts of things, just as words do, and that we use images when words fail us. Thus, 'a proper theory of speech acts should incorporate images, in the same way that a proper theory of image acts should incorporate language'.[94] Bakewell's chapter therefore inspires engagement with film for its properties as a type of performative just as we engage with the performativity of language.

The 2010 book *Exploring Textual Action*, edited by Lars Sætre, Patrizia Lombardo and Anders M. Gullestad, considers how theories of performativity have an impact on a range of artworks, including films.[95] J. Hillis Miller's chapter in the collection points out a distinction between the performativity *of* a text (Performativity$_1$), which relates to the Austinian sense of a text performing, and performativity *in* a text (Performativity$_2$), which refers to events of a performance nature going on within the text. Thus, in Performativity$_1$ the performative relation is between the film as text and the reader or viewer, while in Performativity$_2$ the performative relation is between the characters within the film's world.[96] Svend Erik Larsen, in the same volume, notes similarly that 'the double orientation of the performance *in* the text and the performance *of* the text has underlined the interaction between text and reader as a particular performative textual dynamics'.[97] My analyses of the films in this book will recognise both levels of performativity, as well as keeping in mind a third level, which is a wider sense of the performativity of film more generally.

Performativity theory has also been important to discussions of documentary film, most notably from Bill Nichols and Stella Bruzzi.[98] Nichols has proposed the 'performative documentary' as a type of documentary film that 'stress[es] subjective aspects of a classically objective discourse'.[99] The performative documentary focuses 'on the evocative quality of the text rather than on its representationalism'.[100] This is suggestive, therefore, of a documentary that deploys style in overtly expressive ways. The result is a film that 'gives priority to the affective dimensions struck up between ourselves and the text'.[101] This prioritising of the viewer's experience suggests a concern with how a film might set about conveying the experience of the documentary's subject rather than depicting it in a more ordered fashion. Bruzzi takes up the notion of the performative documentary by relating it explicitly to the lineage of Austin and Butler. She notes how performative documentaries can 'function as utterances that simultaneously both describe and perform an action'.[102] The idea is that some documentaries can engender understanding of their subjects by drawing attention to the constructiveness of the documentary form itself. Bruzzi derives this notion from 'Austin's radical differentiation between the constative and performative aspects of language'[103] and proposes 'that a documentary only comes into being as it is performed, that although its factual basis (or document) can pre-date any recording or representation of it, the film itself is necessarily performative because it is given meaning by the interaction between performance and reality'.[104] I shall return to the notion of the performative documentary in my discussion of Schroeder's *L'Avocat de la terreur* (*Terror's Advocate*, dir. Barbet Schroeder, 2007). For now, it is significant to note that the idea that a documentary 'only comes into being as it is performed' shows how it is not just fiction films that perform through a complex interplay of style and content. Documentary and fiction film alike can be assessed in terms of Miller's notion of Performativity$_1$ and Performativity$_2$.

Scholarship on Levinas and film has sometimes come close to discussions of performativity. For example, Cooper mentions how 'Levinas's reformulation of ethics as first philosophy creates a fissure at the root of the philosophy of being. The Dardennes' films, in turn, perform a Levinasian-inspired challenge to the being of cinema.'[105] She notes also that 'Levinas's language [in *Otherwise than Being*] performs the very challenge to being that his writing articulates'.[106] This tallies with Dominic Michael Rainsford's assertion, when discussing Levinas in relation to the work of filmmaker Andrei Tarkovsky, that 'Levinas conveys philosophical arguments artistically, in the sense that he goes on reformulating his major concepts, over and over again, finding new words every time, in a process that seems unending: an evasion (as much as this is possible) of fixity and thematisation';[107] thus, we could say that Rainsford is arguing for the performative effects of Levinas's prose in everything but name. Critchley, discussing *Film* (dir. Alan Schneider, 1965), with its screenplay by Samuel Beckett, mentions the 'speech act' in relation to a moment of dialogue in the film, but does not develop this in terms of performativity of the film itself,[108] and he observes how Beckett's textual practice of declarations and withdrawals can be paralleled with the non-fixity of the Levinasian Saying.[109] Asbjørn Grønstad, in his book *Film and the Ethical Imagination*, discusses Levinas as part of his exploration of ethics in film, which is founded on the significant claim that 'images do not dramatize ethics; they are not first and foremost "about" ethical issues. Rather, images perform, or embody, ethics through a process that is considerably more profound and far-reaching than that of a mere thematization of an immediately recognizable issue.'[110] But he develops his claim in ways that do not include discussion of performativity theory. Perhaps most extensively, Kristin Lené Hole's study of the films of Claire Denis alongside the philosophy of both Levinas and Jean-Luc Nancy engages considerably with *Otherwise than Being* and is alert to how its prose style can inform our understanding of film style. She says, for example, that Denis' films 'require the kind of patience and openness that are also necessary for reading Levinas's philosophy, and in this way they point us towards his style itself as a model for film'.[111] In all these examples, there is an acknowledgement of a way in which film can be seen as capable of achieving something similar to Levinas's prose, with similarly ethical effects. At every turn, the performative power of style is implied.

In what follows, I will show how the different uses of film style deployed by the Dardennes, Schroeder and Schrader invite us into an experience of the self's inescapable responsibility for the Other. This is through specific camera angles, such as in *Maîtresse* (dir. Barbet Schroeder, 1975); camerawork and editing, such as the uses of close-ups and long takes in *La Promesse* and *Le Fils* (*The Son*, dirs Jean-Pierre and Luc Dardenne, 2002); or narrative structure, such as the different time frames in *Adam Resurrected* (dir. Paul Schrader, 2008), the ominous, menacing trajectory of *The Comfort of Strangers* (dir. Paul Schrader, 1990) or the juxtapositions of present day, flashbacks and imaginary events in

Mishima: A Life in Four Chapters (dir. Paul Schrader, 1985) and *Reversal of Fortune* (dir. Barbet Schroeder, 1990), delineated through their colour schemes, voiceovers, and other factors. We will also see how film style helps convey ways in which a character puts on a performance, either as part of their job or for an ulterior motive, such as Ariane in *Maîtresse*, Claus von Bülow in *Reversal of Fortune*, Jacques Vergès in *Terror's Advocate*, Julian Kay in *American Gigolo* (dir. Paul Schrader, 1980), Yukio Mishima, and Adam in *Adam Resurrected*. And we will see how conventionality relates to performative power through, for example, the subverting of expectation in *Le Gamin au vélo* (*The Kid with a Bike*, dirs Jean-Pierre and Luc Dardenne, 2011), *La Virgen de los Sicarios* (*Our Lady of the Assassins*, dir. Barbet Schroeder, 2000), and *Dominion: Prequel to the Exorcist* (dir. Paul Schrader, 2005). Through all of this there is an awareness of how creativity and individual expression can have an impact on the wider world, just as Austin was attentive to how we use words in contexts outside the purely philosophical realm.

Selection of Filmmakers and Films

In analysing the work of the Dardennes, Schroeder and Schrader, I do not propose a link between them in terms of overt stylistic commonalities in the manner of, for example, Schrader's *Transcendental Style in Film* with its argument about the commonalities in the film styles of Yasujirô Ozu, Robert Bresson and Carl Theodor Dreyer. The films of the Dardennes have a style in common with one another (although it shifts and modifies from film to film, as I shall discuss) but Schroeder's films do not have what we would call a uniform, recognisable style – Schroeder changes his style according to the film he is making, rather than there being a 'Schroeder style'. As for Schrader, while his preoccupations are often recognisable from film to film, some of his films are more 'stylised' than others. Nor are these directors linked in industrial terms: they spring from different filmmaking circumstances – the Dardennes from a documentary background in southern Belgium in the 1970s and 1980s, Schroeder from the French New Wave in the 1960s and Schrader from the 'Movie Brat' generation of 1970s American filmmaking. What brings the work of these directors together here is a Levinasian dimension to some of their films that plays out not just within the narratives but also through the different approaches to style that the directors deploy.

Notions of style are central to film and to film scholarship: uses of the term often imply or even make overt claims for a distinct stylistic approach that acts as a director's personal signature, a readily identifiable and individualistic deployment of what Alexandre Astruc called '*la caméra-stylo*' ('the camera-pen').[112] Organising a discussion of Levinasian performativity in film around the work of particular directors could therefore prompt readers to infer an auteurist agenda. Reading a film in terms of Levinasian performativity, however, works primarily by seeing style as performative within an individual film rather than as an end in itself across a directorial career. It is the case that the Dardennes have already been characterised – and have characterised themselves – as filmmakers whose work exhibits a Levinasian influence, but to come to each of their films expecting a Levinasian agenda would frustrate engagement both with the stories in the films and with each film's individual stylistic approach to its subject. With Schroeder and Schrader, too, the Levinasian dimensions I identify may come to stand as significant achievements of the bodies of work, but this can only happen by first focusing on the individual films in question.

All that said, I hope that my discussions of the films will shed new light on these directors and contribute to the ongoing study of their work. With regard to the Dardennes, I wish to build on studies that have gone before by developing an analysis of their work in explicitly performative terms. And in discussing their work before that of Schroeder and Schrader, I aim to establish the terms of a Levinasian-performative reading of film that will carry through the rest of the book. In the case of both Schroeder and Schrader, I am reading the Levinasian where the filmmakers have not declared that it is present, in order to draw out the Levinasian dimensions that I believe are there within the films.

It does not escape my attention that all of the directors I have chosen to focus on, as well as Levinas, are white males. I appreciate how their whiteness and maleness could suggest a white and patriarchal dominance, a lack of diversity, in the examples explored. I believe, however, that when it comes to what the films of the Dardennes, Schroeder and Schrader are able to offer viewers in terms of ethics, this includes a lot of diversity – such as in characters, representations, subject matter, and cultures – and that this can transcend issues of the filmmakers' gender and skin colour. With the Dardennes coming from Belgium, Schroeder having been born in Tehran, Iran to parents from Germany and Switzerland and having been brought up in Colombia and France, and Schrader coming from the USA, these directors are diverse in nationality; additionally, Schroeder and Schrader have made films in a number of countries and languages. And performativity theory helps show that these films can be considered to be performing an ethics akin to the anarchic restlessness of the Levinasian Saying, the very point of which is the refusal to coalesce around simple categories and definitions. Therefore, I believe that the ethical dimension of the films is most fruitfully engaged with when considered beyond the 'essence' of identity categories. These filmmakers may enjoy privileged positions within society – but privilege can work in tandem with self-awareness and doesn't preclude ethical engagement.

Another matter relating to my choice of filmmakers also needs to be addressed. Given the fractured nature of Levinas's prose in *Otherwise than Being* and the relatively easy-to-understand styles deployed by Schroeder and Schrader in their films, readers may feel that it would be more fruitful to discuss Levinas and performativity in relation to more 'experimental' filmmakers, such as those of the avant-garde with its explicit and multi-faceted radicalisation of film style, its 'othering' of film. Avant-garde styles might indeed be very well-attuned to attempting to depict the otherness of the Other. But the sense of a Levinasian subject, inescapably responsible for the Other, is performed not just in obvious ways in film but also in subtle and unemphasised ways. Bakewell, in discussing image acts, notes that '[l]anguage does not have to be employed for dramatic purposes to be effective. Even in its most prosaic form it is a powerful political tool.'[113] Language cannot help but be political, simply by dint of its central role in the creation of social discourse. Film, in a similar way, holds perpetual performative power, and analysing the subtleties of a seemingly straightforward moment in a relatively mainstream film for its ethical dimension exposes this power's potential.

With regard to mainstream cinema, there are arguments in favour of discussing directors other than the Dardennes, Schroeder and Schrader in relation to Levinasian ethics and performativity. Many mainstream films tell stories about ethical dilemmas of one kind or another and often use style in ways that draw out the power of the situations. But the films analysed here prove, I believe, to be especially important for a study of how film conveys, through style, the self's responsibility for the Other. This responsibility emerges so effectively in the work of these directors because of their films' particularly judicious combinations of the stylised and the down-to-earth that relate Levinasian ethics on film to the wider world. With the Dardennes' dynamic presentations of character and action through style and the sheer range of subject matter and styles handled with a Levinasian openness to alterity by Schroeder and Schrader, cinema's treatment of the self's responsibility for the Other is presented especially pertinently within the work of these filmmakers.

My chosen films do not just present dramatised examples of Levinasian ethics; they also communicate a Levinasian ethics through their uses of film style. They are examples of the Levinasian Saying on film, with all the restless, anarchic energy that this implies. They greet viewers who are expecting clarity of definition, fixity of meaning, a kind of filmic ontological Said – and they turn those expectations on their heads. I aim to locate in the films a powerful sense of both the inescapability and the vitality of the self's responsibility for the Other.

PART I
The Dardenne Brothers: An Ethics without Rest

Part I Introduction

As we saw in the Introduction, it is not just the subject matter of the films in this study that inspires my Levinasian readings but the film styles through which those topics are treated. Of course, style and content cannot be easily separated – and, indeed, my readings of these films will show how much I believe the style to be an essential measure of the content, because so often the style is affecting the understanding of the world of the film. On a basic performative level, a style helps create a film's fictional world and helps assert its significance. Because of this, a different style would affect our view of the fictional world in a different way – would bring a different film into being – and so there is a distinction to be made between styles. That distinction is crucial to how we understand Levinasian ethics in the films of the Dardenne brothers: their uses of style are vitally important to their work.

The link between Levinas and the Dardennes is not difficult to forge. The filmmakers have declared a debt to Levinas's ethical philosophy. Luc Dardenne, in his diary-form books *Au dos de nos images* and *Au dos de nos images II*, makes several references to Levinas as a philosopher who inspires him and his brother Jean-Pierre in their thinking and in their filmmaking.[1] One of the first mentions of Levinas in *Au dos de nos images* is suggestive of how the Dardennes will approach films and filmmaking as an extension of Levinasian ethics:

> Levinas has written in *Difficult Freedom* that the soul is not the possibility of immortality (mine) but the impossibility of killing (the Other). Art is recognised by many as a demonstration of our possibility of immortality, as an enduring desire to endure, as anti-destiny. Could it be a form of the institution of the impossibility of killing? . . . To look at the screen, the painting, the stage, the sculpture, the page, to listen to singing, music, this would be: not to kill.[2]

For Luc Dardenne, therefore, the encounter we have with art is akin to the directive of the Levinasian Other, the command 'You shall not commit murder'. Levinas's work has influenced both the subject matter and the style of the Dardennes' work. Luc Dardenne says in an interview from 2011, 'I've followed his work and he's someone I continue to read. It was a shock to discover his texts, his consideration of the face as a commandment not to kill.'[3] Levinas's influence is also evident in Luc Dardenne's 2012 book *Sur l'affaire humaine*, a work of philosophical rumination.[4] The book argues that, in order to overcome the fear of death, humans need to be aware of their own mortality, and that this awareness is a prerequisite for a life of shared humanity with others. Dardenne's points of reference in this book include Levinas's work, to which he refers with a sense of inspiration similar to that found in the two parts of *Au dos de nos images*, although here he is not discussing filmmaking per se. It is also worth noting that, in this book, Dardenne writes in a style somewhat redolent of Levinas's style in *Totality and Infinity* and, especially, *Otherwise than Being* in that his argument proceeds not just by reasoned description but also by a textual practice that accumulates power through repetition and recapitulation of phrases and terms. Levinas has evidently proved a lasting inspiration for the brothers. And a number of scholarly works, including chapters by Cooper, Cummings, Martin O'Shaughnessy, Robert Sinnerbrink and Sam B. Girgus, books by Joseph Mai, Philip Mosley and Olivier Ducharme, and an edited collection by Jacqueline Aubenas, have offered engrossing accounts of how various Dardenne films can be read as cinematic exemplars of Levinasian ethics.[5]

And yet, for all the scholarship on the Dardennes that discusses their stylistic choices, the *performative* implications of their cinema have not been explicitly studied. In discussing the Dardennes' work in terms of Levinasian ethics *and* performativity, I am aiming to explain how their films seek to perform the Levinasian ethical work they are purporting to describe. For Mai, the Dardennes' films have a clear ethical project in enabling the viewer to recognise ethical responsibility, through the characters and the styles of the films. This intention is reflected in Mai's bold statement that '[t]he point of their cinema is not to relay the viewer into an imaginary world, but to teach him or her to perceive better than before in order to readjust our views and behavior'.[6] In tandem with Mai's view, Mosley sees in their films a mixture of realistic detail and positive outlook that he describes as a 'subjunctive mood', where 'what may be is more important than simply what is. And this mood elevates their films from the descriptive bounds of observational naturalism to the deeper level of a dynamic realism attuned to a vision of hope and of change for the better.'[7] The sense of a 'subjunctive' mood is suggestive of the pact the films seek to make with audiences, the hope that the films will be able to initiate positive change *beyond* the world of the film. Mosley believes that while the Dardennes' work has often been considered alongside the social realist modes of British filmmakers such as Mike Leigh and Ken Loach, the Belgian brothers are in fact closer to the spirit of the Italian neorealist directors of the 1940s and early 1950s 'in blending a highly observational mode with a distinctive rhetoric of the image to produce an idealist cinema of moral concerns'.[8] When Mosley observes that the films 'allow the possibility of some kind of redemption, reconciliation, or implicit resolution, even as this possibility is not fully realised within the diegesis of the film', this implies performativity *of* the film (Performativity$_1$) as against performativity *in* the film (Performativity$_2$): the events within the diegesis of a Dardenne film do not always show redemption, reconciliation, resolution, but the film itself may prompt such progressive actions.

In the Introduction, I considered Davies' argument about the importance of retaining the 'shock' of the Levinasian Saying, and so I have chosen to discuss a selection of Dardenne films that illustrates the subtle but crucial developments in their style from film to film, developments that, I shall argue, have enabled their work to retain this shock and that have therefore saved their body of work from congealing into a filmic Said that would rob it of its ethical force. I begin by comparing the shifts in Levinas's ethical philosophy between *Totality and Infinity* and *Otherwise than Being* with the evolution of Austin's theories of the constative and the performative into the speech act and the developments in the Dardennes' film style between *Je Pense à Vous* (*I Think of You*, dirs Jean-Pierre and Luc Dardenne, 1992) and *La Promesse*. I then consider *Le Fils* in relation to Derrida's notion of originary performativity so as to explore how the film presents a view of the world that is both grounded and hopeful. From there I discuss more recent developments in the Dardennes' style, especially in *The Kid with a Bike*, and draw on Butler's notion of the resignification of language – her development of Derrida's idea of iterability – to explain why I believe that the brothers' gradual return to various aspects of film style they had avoided using in many of their films can be read as Levinasian in a different way from what has gone before. My discussion of the Dardennes' work will argue that their performative qualities retain the sense of a restless, anarchic Saying and thereby provide audiences with Levinas-inspired encounters of considerable power.

CHAPTER 1

Je Pense à Vous and *La Promesse*: From Describing to Performing

The four-year gap between the release of *Je Pense à Vous* in 1992 and that of *La Promesse* in 1996 is a mysterious period in the Dardennes' career, one in which they consciously retreated in order to rethink their approach to their work, after which they returned with the film that made their names. Although the Dardennes had almost twenty years of documentary filmmaking behind them and had even shot a feature film, *Falsch* (dirs Jean-Pierre and Luc Dardenne, 1987), before *Je Pense à Vous*, *La Promesse* can, for various reasons, be seen as the start of the Dardennes' most characteristic output. It is the first of their films to be shot in the style that has come to be recognisable as their own, a pared-down, gritty, largely handheld style, comprising lengthy shots and scenes and often featuring non-professional actors in leading roles, and it is the first of their films in which the influence of Levinas is explicitly declared (by the Dardennes) and readily analysed (by film scholars).

I shall propose that the stylistic differences between *Je Pense à Vous* and *La Promesse* are comparable with the move that Levinas makes in his ethical philosophy between *Totality and Infinity* and *Otherwise than Being*. I shall do this by drawing initially on Austin's distinction between the constative and the performative.

Je Pense à Vous and *La Promesse*: Constative and Performative

We have seen how Austin begins his analysis of the performative power of language in his lectures published as *How to Do Things with Words* by making a distinction between what he calls constative utterances (which seek to describe, and which can be judged for their truth or falsity) and performative utterances (which perform what they describe, and are therefore neither true nor false). In making this distinction, and as I have noted in the Introduction, Austin posits that language is capable of not just describing but performing an action – thus, language is seen as something that can bring something into being. As we also saw in the Introduction, Levinas's development between *Totality and Infinity* and *Otherwise than Being* involves, among other things, a reconfiguration of the language he uses to express his philosophy, from a language that, despite itself, is still afflicted by the certainties of Being and ontology to one that seeks to fracture and fragment philosophical expression in order to *perform* the ethics he is wanting to convey. For our purposes here, we can say that Levinas's desire to take ethics away from philosophy's privileging of Being and subjectivity and towards an attempt to render the 'beyond essence' of responsibility for the intangible, unknowable Other has a parallel in Austin's concern with the limitations that philosophy had put on speech in restricting it to matters of truth and falsity. For Austin, to restrict speech to statements measurable in terms of truths and falsehoods denies the sense in which speech can also in itself perform an action. For Levinas, any idea of the Other as ultimately knowable by the self reduces the very otherness of the Other to something held within the totality of the self's consciousness, and thus fails to pay respect to the way in which the self is *founded* in the ethical act of responsibility for the Other. Derrida's critique of *Totality and Infinity* was instrumental in developing the view that, in that book, Levinas tried to convey the unknowability of the Other but ended up falling back on the totalising language of Being. *Otherwise than Being*, then, represents an explicit engagement on Levinas's part with the limitations of language, using language to 'perform' the anarchy of the Saying that founds the self as ethical through the encounter with the Other. In a similar way, the Dardennes' filmmaking style undergoes a shift from what I shall begin by defining as the *constative* style of *Je Pense à Vous* to the more *performative* style of *La Promesse*.

The story of *Je Pense à Vous* centres on Fabrice (Robin Renucci), an employee at a steelworks in Seraing, in southern Belgium (Figure 1.1). At the beginning of the film, Fabrice appears to have a very contented life: he is married to a woman he adores, Céline (Fabienne Babe), they have a young son, Martin (Stéphane Pondeville), and they are throwing a party to celebrate their move into a newly built house by the river. But there is a threat to this happy existence: the steelworks is due to be shut down. When Fabrice loses his job, this triggers a personal devastation that affects not only himself but also his family and his wider social circle. His behaviour becomes increasingly erratic, and relations with Céline become strained. Fabrice leaves home, starts to drink heavily, and is barely able to hold down the new job he has managed to secure. Eventually, with the help and patience of his loving wife, Fabrice regains his composure and self-respect, and is reunited with his family during a street carnival in Seraing.

Figure 1.1 The opening shot of *Je Pense à Vous* shows Seraing.

On paper, *Je Pense à Vous* would appear to be a promising project. The brothers co-wrote the film with the veteran screenwriter Jean Gruault, whose other work includes collaborations with such major directors as Jacques Rivette, François Truffaut, Jean-Luc Godard, Roberto Rossellini and Alain Resnais, while the two leading actors, Robin Renucci and Fabienne Babe, were both established actors in French and Francophone cinema. And yet these elements resulted in a film that was deemed an artistic failure, and that also failed to find commercial success. We can see *Je Pense à Vous* afflicted with the concrete sense of knowability that mars the exploration of the self–Other relation in *Totality and Infinity*. The film's classical style renders events and motivations predictable, purports to make characters cohere, and, consequently, lacks space for the viewer to engage in imaginative involvement. The concentration in *Je Pense à Vous* on Fabrice's emotional turmoil resulting from the closure of the plant raises questions that can broadly be called ethical – such as whether he will recover from his dejected state and be able to rejoin his family as a husband and a father, and in the matter of his rescue of a fellow worker from a beating at the hands of the boss – but these emotional 'beats' are presented in a series of conventional narrative manoeuvres that render the outcomes predictable to anyone who has a reasonable knowledge of film narrative. The result is a film that feels stylistically unadventurous on all levels – acting, lighting and framing, story development, editing, and so on.[1] Luc Dardenne has written frankly about the failure of the film,[2] even asking, 'Why have we made this film?',[3] and it remains an obscure entry in the Dardennes' filmography, its value perceived largely in terms of how it illuminated for the brothers the paths they did *not* want to take in their filmmaking output.

After having felt constrained by the filming process of *Je Pense à Vous*, the Dardennes strove to get themselves into a position where they could hand-pick the cast and crew and have total control over all aspects of production.[4] For the cast, they chose largely non-professional actors. Olivier Gourmet, who plays Roger, had had a few small roles in TV films, and Jérémie Renier, playing the central role of Roger's adolescent son Igor, was a *débutant*, found by the Dardennes through the open casting process they still use and which has also yielded other impressive finds, such as Émilie Dequenne in the title role in *Rosetta* (dirs Luc and Jean-Pierre Dardenne, 1999), Morgan Marinne as Francis in *Le Fils*, Déborah François as Sonia in *L'Enfant*, and Thomas Doret as Cyril in *The Kid with a Bike*. The role of Assita, the immigrant worker's wife in *La Promesse*, is played by Assita Ouédraogo, who had acted in several films in Burkina Faso by director Idrissa Ouédraogo, including the internationally recognised *Yaaba* (dir. Idrissa Ouédraogo, 1989) and *Tilaï* (*The Law*, dir. Idrissa Ouédraogo, 1990), but who was relatively unknown in the context of Belgian and wider Francophone cinema. Many of the crewmembers that the Dardennes chose to work with, including cinematographer Alain Marcoen, sound mixer Thomas Gauder and editor Marie-Hélène Dozo, have remained with them on almost all their subsequent films to date. It is with these cast and crew selections that the Dardennes set out to construct a situation in which they had not only total control but also the collaboration of colleagues relatively untouched by the learned behaviours of the film industry.

It is also at about the time of *La Promesse* that Levinas emerges as a declared influence on the Dardennes' work. Luc Dardenne, in an entry from *Au dos de nos images* dated 19 January 1996, writes,

> Emmanuel Levinas died during our filming. The film owes a great deal to the reading of his books. His interpretation of the face-to-face, of the face as first speech. Without these readings, would we have imagined the scenes of Roger and Igor in the garage, of Assita and Igor in the office at the garage and on the stairs at the station? The whole film can be seen as an attempt to arrive finally at the face-to-face.[5]

The adolescent Igor's promise to the dying immigrant worker Hamidou (Rasmané Ouédraogo) that he will look after his wife Assita and their baby, which causes him so much conflict as he becomes torn between his loyalty to his father and his concern for Hamidou's family, dramatises Levinasian concerns regarding the degree to which we are prepared to sacrifice our own comfort and enjoyment in order that we might assume responsibility for another's needs. I am reading Igor's promise as a speech act, in that it seemingly creates him as an ethical being. As Damian Cox and Michael P. Levine posit, Igor does not seem to be ethical before he has made the promise; rather, there are three things that contribute to his growing ethical awareness: the promise he has made to the dying Hamidou, his likely remorse for his involvement in Hamidou's death and the cover-up, and his growing interest in Assita.[6] Igor's speech act, therefore, brings his ethical self into being through a moment of social relation with an Other in which he responds to the Other's ethical call. It is important to note that this reading of Levinas in *La Promesse* is somewhat akin to what Perpich calls the 'narrative' of ethical engagement in *Totality and Infinity*: the Other has interrupted Igor's secure world and called out to him and Igor has responded favourably, thus becoming ethical. But I want to read *La Promesse* not just for its narrative but also for how Igor's growing character is performed by the film's style. This will help locate the film's stylistic emphasis on the experience of Igor as a Levinasian subject held hostage by his ethical commitment to the Other.

The Performativity of *La Promesse*

Something that leads the viewer into Igor's position within the world of the film is that, in its early stages, the dramatic situation is both specific and vague. It is specific in the detail of the transactions involved – there is a lot of money talk and a lot of information, given largely by Roger or Igor to the immigrants, about how their lives as tenants and workers will operate. But it is vague in other ways: it is not made clear, for example, where all of the immigrants have come from (Hamidou, Assita and their child are from Burkina Faso but other characters are not presented with the same level of exposition, although some are evidently from Eastern Europe) or what exactly they are employed to do, or indeed where Roger and Igor have come from, or where Igor's mother might be, or even whether she is alive. It is also not clear how long Igor has been working with or for Roger – whether this is, for example, the only life he knows, or whether it is a more recent state of affairs. When the film opens, Igor has an apprenticeship at a local garage, suggesting he has a chance at being a good student, but it may be that he and Roger are playing the apprenticeship for its legitimacy, as it provides a cover for their illegal scams and allows Igor time to work them in a way that school attendance would not. (An inspector, when visiting the building site, says to Igor, 'You should be in school', and is only pacified when Igor produces his apprentice's contract.) The situation involving the workers being smuggled into the country to live and work outside the detection of the law is not given a great deal of context: the first time the situation becomes apparent, it is when Roger and Igor help a new consignment of workers out of their hiding places in the cars that have arrived on a large transporter.

This establishment of narrative matter is in contrast to the setup in *Je Pense à Vous*, where within minutes the family unit, the troubled steelworks and the wider economic state of the town are all made clear. For Lieve Spaas, the characters in *La Promesse* 'seem to come from nowhere, to have no memories and to live strictly in the present until the moment when Igor makes his promise and finds himself propelled into an ethical system of which he previously knew nothing'.[7] That ethical system into which Igor is propelled is set up almost subliminally in the film. This, though, is another way of saying that, despite its initial obtuseness, the film *does* establish a fictional world that provides the context for Igor's ethical conversion. The effect is of a generalised depiction of an amoral world within the narrative; the lack of specificity is a performative reflection of Roger's and Igor's lack of scrutiny of their actions and motivations. *La Promesse* establishes various kinds of anti-social behaviour that do not get punished or otherwise paid off, such as Igor's theft of the elderly woman's wallet and Roger's jumping of a queue by dishonestly saying that his son has had an accident. And the film depicts unethical behaviour, such as Roger's – and Igor's – exploitation of the vulnerable immigrants for their own financial and material gain and Igor's collusion in the rounding up of four of the illegal immigrants whom Roger sets up to be caught by the authorities in a deal he strikes with a contact working for a political figure who is seeking re-election on the back of such a crackdown. Most impactfully, when Hamidou falls from the building site during a mass panic at the arrival of the inspectors, Roger's decision not to take Hamidou to hospital but to let him die on the ground at the building site, bury him in cement and then deny all knowledge of his whereabouts in effect violates what for Levinas is, as we have seen, the foundational idea: 'you shall not commit murder'. By the end of the film, Igor will have come to recognise the ethical imperative where his father does not.

The film's style comes to express Igor's dilemma, the promise he has made to the dying Hamidou to look after Assita and their child and how this conflicts with his inability to reveal to Assita what has happened to her husband. Narrative structure, camera movements, framing, sound design, editing – indeed, all the elements of film style – combine to convey, for the viewer, the physical and psychological stress of Igor's experience. This is not to suggest, however, that this effect is achieved through obvious artifice or ostentatious aesthetic components. Rather, it is achieved primarily through a style devoted to reflecting the tensions present within Igor's mind and body alike. The progression of events in the story, the length and tempo of each scene, and the way in which the camerawork variously privileges, clarifies, masks or frustrates the desire for information combine to convey Igor's ethical unease. The film's avoidance of extra-diegetic music, predictable framing, foregrounded plot, and so on keeps the viewer from consciously relating what they are seeing to other films, and therefore helps them to stay immersed in the specificity of Igor's dilemma.

It takes a while for Igor's dilemma to emerge as the film's primary ethical focus. This reflects the way in which, for a long time, Igor's agency in his own life is to a large degree suppressed by Roger, who, while promoting an illusion of their being best buddies – for example, giving Igor a ring that matches his own, expecting him to call him Roger, doing a tattoo for him – in fact controls Igor meticulously, keeping him busy with errands, denying him time to ride his go-kart with his friends and discouraging him from being too soft on the tenants. After Hamidou's horrible accident and the burying of his body – where Igor's hesitation and his ethical disquiet are palpable – life carries on almost as normal for Igor and Roger. Igor busies himself with his usual chores, and, on his father's orders, avoids Assita. But a moment comes that is illustrative of the film's performance of Igor's emerging ethical sensibility. Igor hears Assita screaming and realises she is being assaulted. He does not do anything – he continues to obey his father and not get involved, and so he sidles away. As it happens, Roger himself intervenes, throwing the man off Assita. This initially appears to be an impressive act by Roger, although it is undermined by his shifty attempts to talk Assita into leaving: he is even prepared to buy her a plane ticket, thereby buying himself out of trouble; in response, Assita says that if Hamidou does not show up she will go to the police. But it is what happens next that marks this sequence of scenes as being about Igor's emerging ethical sensibility, even though he is absent from the film at this point: Roger leaves Assita and walks into another room, where he meets Assita's assailant, who is his associate Nabil (Hachemi Haddad) – and pays him for a job well done (Figure 1.2). Thus, it becomes immediately apparent that Roger's earlier 'heroic' act of interrupting the assault was nothing of the sort: he had staged the assault, so as to create an opportunity to try to talk Assita into leaving. This plot revelation strengthens the sense that Igor is enmeshed in a world without ethical value, and that if there is going to be any ethical value brought to the situation, he cannot rely on anyone other than himself to bring it.

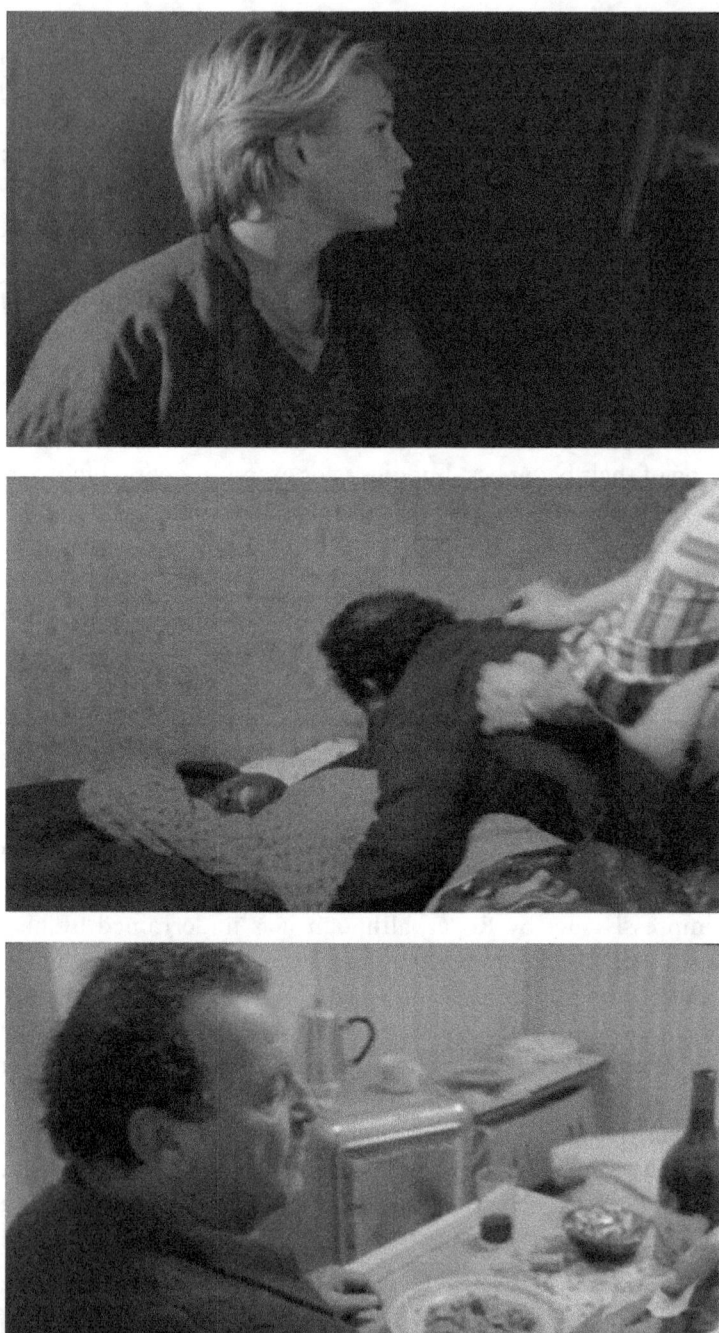

Figure 1.2 Igor hears Assita being attacked; Roger intervenes; Roger pays the assailant.

This sequence of scenes exemplifies what I consider to be the performative qualities of the film's style. Igor is not always present on-screen, and the camera rarely aligns itself with him to the extent that it could be said to be enacting his viewpoint or physical position; point-of-view shots, such as those when he is spying on Assita early in the film, are used sparingly. But because all aspects of the film are related, everything that happens – whether directly or indirectly impacting Igor – relates to his conscience, which, of course, already exists but which is dormant and slowly awakened by the events as they unfold. The film is nimbly depicting a potentially ethical universe in which unethical actions are shown, and so we are aware of ethical alternatives. O'Shaughnessy notes of the Dardennes' technique,

> Working in a socio-political context in which social relations seem condemned to violence and in which there seems no available language with which to name injustice, the fictions nonetheless seek to show a way out of the real that they might otherwise seem merely condemned to inhabit. They do this . . . by creating ethical choices that reopen a fragile sense of alternative possibility.[8]

We can see this principle of 'alternative possibility' in operation earlier in the film, too: Igor is hardly the exclusive focus of attention in the film's first twenty-five minutes (up to the point at which Hamidou has the accident) but the early scenes can still be read as privileging him as protagonist in that they so thoroughly set up the world in which his ethical conversion will take place. The car transporter, for example, looks as though it is bearing down on Roger and Igor's van as it follows it down the road: this can be seen as subtle symbolism when it is revealed that the cars contain the new consignment of illegal immigrant workers, hinting at the burden this situation is already placing on Igor (and Roger, although he is not affected by it in the same way). And the sequence establishing how Roger and Igor manage the workers' accommodation ends on two actions by Igor that hint at a private ethical nature deep within him: his observing of Assita in her room and his permitting Hamidou to have the gas canister without having to pay the 400 Belgian francs (Figure 1.3). It is as if this double act of charity obliges him thenceforth, as if the world of the film has seized on this hope. Throughout the film, the combined dynamics of camera movement, sound, duration of shots, and sequence of events command concentration such that the process of viewing the film becomes an engagement with the tumultuous shifts in will that Igor may be experiencing.

I want to note, however, that I say *may be* rather than *is*. Just as Levinas's project is to convey how the self only exists due to the ethical relation with the Other, it is not necessary for us to feel we 'know' Igor; indeed, it is better if we do not. What the film is performing, I would argue, is not Igor's

Figure 1.3 Hamidou thanks Igor for his help with the gas.

consciousness but an independent filmic consciousness for our benefit. It might be stating the obvious, but Igor is a fictional construct, not a real person; the real people the film is interested in are you and me. What I mean by this is that the ethical power of the film depends on nothing less than a type of narrative trick: *La Promesse* is a highly controlled artwork, and one of the aims of this artwork is to offer to the viewer an experience of tension leading to alleviation, the alleviation potentially accompanied by a kind of ethical epiphany. Mai has called the Dardennes' films 'empathy-producing machines',[9] and while the notion of empathy is in one sense antithetical to a Levinasian ethics – because empathy could be said to eradicate otherness, assimilating the Other into the self's totalising sphere – Mai's description is apt insofar as the word 'machines' draws attention to the constructedness of the Dardennes' film style, its precise calibration enabling the ethical to be the focus of the film as it unfolds. At this point in the narrative of *La Promesse* it is very difficult to foresee how the film is going to end, not least because Igor seems to encounter trouble everywhere he turns. But this is an achievement of the film: in building tension to such a riveting degree, it creates a convincing sense of an inescapable ethical dilemma.

To this end, Jérémie Renier functions in *La Promesse* as an actor but also as an embodiment of the film's physical tensions. Mai has noted how '[o]ver time the brothers have increasingly explored their actors less as mask wearers or characters but as physical bodies. Actors in this state are no longer thinking about their careers, but giving something of themselves.'[10] Thus, Renier and the other actors become devices in the film's project to give a feeling of restrictiveness: the suspense (will Assita discover what has happened? Will she bring in the police? What will Roger ask Igor to do next?) is necessary in order to establish the conditions for Igor's admission to Assita, in the film's final shot, as to what happened to her husband. Subliminally, the film is encouraging us to see Igor's situation as not just an enticing dramatic situation but also an intractable problem that nevertheless demands a release – and the only release on offer requires an admission as to what has happened. When it comes, Igor's confession to Assita surprises partly because it is so sudden – especially in that it comes at a moment when Igor is free, meaning that, in one sense, he need not confess it anymore; Mai notes that '[h]e is no longer hedging: he could easily put her on the train and start his life over'.[11] But it also surprises due to the relief it provides in bringing to a head the anxiety that has been created by both the narrative and the filmmaking style – the relief a 'proof' of the film's illocutionary effects. In *Je Pense à Vous*, the use of style without newness or variance means that Fabrice's story does not feel unique. Rather, it feels as though we could second-guess it. And if we are ahead of the film, we are not experiencing any *emerging* feelings of ethical awareness or engagement. The film's prioritisation of its protagonist over the viewing experience is its weakness. By contrast, the style of *La Promesse* leaves nothing to chance: we are not left on our own to get the point, because, as Igor's feelings of ethical obligation exert their ever more powerful grip on him, the film performs a highly charged energy of suspense and release, not least because it leaves the release until the film's final moments.

Thus, the growth of Igor's ethical consciousness is not just depicted but *initiated* by the film's style, which *performs* – brings into being – the very story and 'character' it purports to describe. Mai has said of this newfound style that 'the forms that the Dardennes searched for so long and hard draw the viewer into the same ethical place from which the films were conceived'.[12] In focusing so closely on the pressure Igor carries with him as a result of his promise – by aligning its camera style with Igor's physical being so as to effect a kind of tunnel vision but also by largely withholding standard pleasures of narrative cinema such as conventional framing and extra-diegetic music – *La Promesse* leaves a lot unspoken and thereby destabilises our sense of orientation within the story, removing the security of the narrative by making the structure of events hard to predict. Cooper observes that '[t]he Dardenne brothers seek permanently to unsettle received ideas of what cinema is. In this, their approach is bound up explicitly, but not exclusively, with the ethical underpinnings of Levinas's thought.'[13] For Spaas, too, both *La Promesse* and the film that followed it, *Rosetta*, 'use a new cinematic language to express a new paradigm, where identity emerges in the present as an ethical awakening in a face-to-face encounter'.[14] Spaas's invocation of the 'face-to-face encounter' clearly indicates a preoccupation with Levinas, even if unstated. For both theorists, the undermining of conventional filmic tropes indicates an attempt to communicate something beyond the essence of faces and easily knowable Others. In this way, says Mai, '[t]he film [*La Promesse*] begins to take root in the spectator's personal life'.[15] By contrast, the sense of the style of *Je Pense à Vous* playing to referents outside the text – dominant ideas of film form, standard narrative tropes, and conventional (fictional) emotional outcomes – is a *constative* quality, a sense that the film is deploying conventional filmic grammar to describe something that exists elsewhere. The implied conventionality here is rooted in Classical Hollywood Style, powerfully conventional by dint of its hegemony within film culture. The classical conventions of style have persisted over the years because, as we see from Metz, audiences have come to understand the devices and effects. But these can suffer from overuse, and we might say that *Je Pense à Vous* fails to find a way of relating them specifically to the situation it depicts. In every scene, the style seems to be referring to the 'conventional' effects of narrative cinema rather than serving as a conduit for the uniqueness of the story being presented. It is, I would argue, much more difficult in *La Promesse* than in *Je Pense à Vous* to predict either the direction the story will take or the outcome it will arrive at, and it is in this way that *La Promesse* performs Igor's uncertainty, and more generally a sense of transformation, of rapid maturity.

It is important, however, not to overplay the distinction between the 'familiarity' of *Je Pense à Vous* and the alignment with Igor's uncertainty in *La Promesse*. For this reason, it is essential now to consider the closeness of the relationship between the Austinian constative and the performative.

The Constative is also Performative

Although, as I have argued, the style of *La Promesse* is surprising in the ways in which it dramatises Igor's plight, there is no cause to see this style as unfamiliar. The film still makes use of many properties intrinsic to the medium – the expressiveness of the close-up, for example, or the clarifying feature-film device of a chronological narrative. Indeed, as with *Je Pense à Vous*, the storyline of *La Promesse* is structured 'conventionally'. It conforms to a standard three-act structure such as is taught by Syd Field and Robert McKee in their paradigmatic approaches to scriptwriting.[16] To follow Field's model from his *Screenplay* books, Act 1 ('setup') sets up the three conventional levels of narrative film: the main character (here, Igor), the character's dramatic need (Igor's need to make his way in life) and the dramatic situation (the tensions inherent in Igor's employment as well as in the relationship between him and his father). Act 1 of *La Promesse* culminates with the 'plot point' in which Hamidou falls from the ladder and Igor makes his promise to the dying man. Act 2 ('confrontation') is a series of tense encounters, principally between Igor and Assita, who is unyielding in her demands to know what has happened to her husband, and between Igor and his father, who, of course, wants, even more than Igor, for the accident to remain hushed up, culminating with the second major plot point, as Igor escapes with Assita and her baby so as to help them travel safely to Italy. In Act 3 ('resolution'), events come to a head as Igor has to fend off his father's efforts to apprehend them and then finally tells Assita what has happened. So it is important to note – here, and with respect to the Dardennes' films in general – that their radical change of style was not accompanied by a radically different narrative structure.

It is therefore important not to presume to forge an easy distinction between a 'constative' style and a 'performative' style. As Austin moves through his twelve lectures, he calls the distinction between the constative and the performative into question, largely through drawing out the ways in which constative utterances can themselves be seen to have performative dimensions. Time and again, his attempts to impose precise rules and criteria for what distinguishes a performative from a constative get broken down.[17] Austin's incisive analyses of many types of utterance show ways in which they can be considered as either constative or performative according to the context in which they are used. For example, in Lecture XI, 'Statements, Performatives, and Illocutionary Force', Austin explains this by questioning the degree to which the test of constatives – that is, whether they are true or false – can hold up. Austin takes the debate towards the question of context, saying, for example, that

> [i]t is essential to realize that 'true' and 'false', like 'free' and 'unfree', do not stand for anything simple at all; but only for a general dimension of being a right or proper thing to say as opposed to a wrong thing, in these circumstances, to this audience, for these purposes and with these intentions.[18]

This relates to something Austin has said earlier – namely, that a performative 'does not by any means necessarily masquerade as a statement of fact, descriptive or constative. Yet it does quite commonly do so, and that, oddly enough, when it assumes its most explicit form.'[19] The suggestion that a performative is a new kind of fact is an enticing claim for the conviction of the speech act; through this, we arrive at a realisation as to how a performative utterance can be a fact and how a constative utterance – historically held, as Austin begins his lecture series by indicating, to be a purveyor of facts, verifiable as true or false – can assume the power of a performative. It is for these reasons that Austin progresses to his theory of speech acts, theorising ways in which language has qualities of locution, illocutionary force, and perlocutionary effects. Petrey explains how this makes the notion of the speech act so vital:

> The punch of speech-act criticism comes less from sensitivity to *certain* kinds of language than from recognition that *all* kinds of language make tangible the network of relationships and agreements in which humans and their signs are always embedded. Whether applied to literary or ordinary language, a speech-act understanding is dense with the commitments and determinants producing the identity of speakers along with the force of speech.[20]

As '*all* kinds of language' have performative power, to sustain an easy distinction between the constative and the performative would be to fail to engage with Austin's matured argument.

And so, to discuss the Dardennes' films in terms of *Je Pense à Vous* being in a constative style and *La Promesse* having a more performative style is too simplistic. The implications of the criticisms levelled at *Je Pense à Vous* are that it is a somewhat conventional film, electing to tell a predictable story and in a predictable style, but as Petrey highlights, conventionality is associated in Austin not with the constative but with the *performative*.[21] Conventionality is the measure of a speech act's performativity because it is through conventionality that the utterance or speech act is contextualised, readable for its effects in society. Without the conventions that a particular society places on a sign at a particular moment in time, it is not possible to assess the illocutionary force of that sign, the effect of the speech act. For example, placing *Je Pense à Vous* side by side with *La Promesse*, it is notable that, despite the latter film's far more obtuse establishment of the terms of its fictional world, expository information has not been reduced or eliminated but rather has simply been *reconfigured*: in *La Promesse*, the absence of standard exposition that would establish Igor's background and his relation to the illegal workers and that would make clear what he 'wants' within the course of the film has been replaced by a new presence, one in which information is synonymous with style and its rhythms. This is one of the key elements that make *La Promesse* the film that established the signature style of the Dardennes. But if we understand the film's expository strategy, we do so by way of convention. Thus, if the expository strategies of *Je Pense à Vous* and *La Promesse* can *both* be assessed in relation to convention, it is not appropriate to attempt to consider one to be constative and the other to be performative. Rather, each film, in its own way, is performing its own particular fictional world, and it is to the viewer to assess the relative degrees of appropriateness and effectiveness of the stylistic choices.

To consider the Dardennes' work in these terms not only helps illustrate the development in their style that *La Promesse* exhibits, it also suggests a path towards rehabilitating the troubled text that is *Je Pense à Vous*. *Je Pense à Vous* is not a disastrous or incompetent film by any means. Mai's comment that it is 'not completely unendurable' may sound as though he is damning it with faint praise, but he also makes a fair assessment of its strengths and difficulties.[22] Mosley, too, is not uncomplimentary, positing that the film 'presents in taut fictional form several themes familiar from [the brothers'] earlier work: the loss of individual and communal identities, the weight of the past and the failure of political resistance'.[23] Wouter Hessels goes further, calling the film 'a strong and visually beautiful call for respect and hope', while also noting that 'the documentary content is more powerful than the supplied fictional elements which sometimes appear too anecdotal',[24] while O'Shaughnessy reads the film as representing a crucial stage in the evolution of the Dardennes' subject matter, moving as it does from a portrait of the collective, historically situated struggles of the post-industrial community to the present-day impact on the individual.[25] In its story of a worker driven to despair by unemployment and its setting of the town of Seraing, where the Dardennes made so many of their documentaries and where they have set all but one of their subsequent feature films – *Le Silence de Lorna* (*The Silence of Lorna*, dirs Jean-Pierre and Luc Dardenne, 2008) being set primarily in Liège – the film is recognisably the work of the brothers. Indeed, one of the Dardennes' achievements in *Je Pense à Vous* is that it seeks to draw mainstream cinematic attention to a stratum of society that, at the time and still today, is underrepresented in film: the European (and here specifically Belgian) industrial worker. To present a conventionally mainstream cinematic story about a character disenfranchised by the closure of the plant in which he works in Seraing and struggling to turn his life around is, at least on paper, a cause for celebration. Therefore, the conventionality of *Je Pense à Vous* demonstrates its own illocutionary force. Its stylistic attributes are conventional by dint of their having come to be accepted *as* conventional due to their widespread acceptability and comprehension within a society of filmgoers. Their ubiquity is testament to their performativity. In its own way, then, *Je Pense à Vous* is just as performative as *La Promesse*.

It remains the case, however, that there is a stylistic shift between *Je Pense à Vous* and *La Promesse*. The proximity the viewer feels to the character of Igor in *La Promesse* comes about because the film is drawing on styles and techniques that relate contrapuntally to styles and techniques used in *Je Pense à Vous*. *La Promesse* shows how a film can use a style that seeks to align the viewer with the subjectivity of a particular character. Every aspect of the film is then seen as directed in the service of suggesting the character's thoughts and feelings, as against presenting that character within classical filmic space. *La Promesse* distinguishes itself in its degree of expressiveness of the ethical encounter, just as in *Otherwise than Being* the textual properties serve to perform the ethics, to demonstrate, through language – typically the domain of the Said – the paradoxically ephemeral nature of the Saying. Levinas conveys the Saying by destabilising the Said long enough for the Saying to be perceptible, giving us access to the ethical relation before the thematisation of the Said dulls its effect. Richard A. Cohen has cited Jacques Rolland's argument that the move between *Totality and Infinity* and *Otherwise than Being* is a development from discussing 'the radical and overwhelming alterity of the Other' to discussing 'the effect of that alterity on the subjectivity of the subject'.[26] The style of *La Promesse* expresses 'the effect of that alterity' on Igor.

If this does not quite return us to Austin's primal distinction between the constative and the performative, what has taken place in the progression from *Je Pense à Vous* to *La Promesse* is a sharpening of the uses of film to draw the Dardennes' filmmaking away from a style of predictable conventionality towards one that trades on its *relation to* conventionality. One way to think about the disappointment of *Je Pense à Vous* is that, because the film's stylistic elements are so familiar as conventional narrative devices, these elements end up initiating only very limited perlocutionary effects. For Luc Dardenne, 'All style is a caricature, a resemblance to itself, a destiny [an end in itself], a mummification, a victory for the necrophiliac who stands always ready to cool down what's hot, does not find its form, its image.'[27] This citation comes from an entry in *Au dos de nos images* dated 14 September 1993, and therefore between the completion of *Je Pense à Vous* and the filming of *La Promesse*. Perhaps Luc Dardenne believed that the style of *Je Pense à Vous* was one such caricature; the references to mummification and the necrophiliac, meanwhile, are redolent of Levinas's assessment in 'Reality and its Shadow' of art as fixed in time. Those words give a strong indication of what the Dardennes are trying, by contrast, to achieve in their films: they want their films to affect viewers positively, to provide an encounter that will enhance ethical interactions in the world.

CHAPTER 2

Levinasian Responsibility in *Le Fils*

We have seen in the previous chapter how it is possible to draw on Austin's work on the constative and the performative to show how, in film, there is no easy distinction to be made between a film that tells or describes its story and themes and a film that performs them. If both *Je Pense à Vous* and *La Promesse* are performing their stories and themes – albeit in different ways – then we may say by extension that *all* films perform. They all perform in the sense that they all exist in the world within a network of social relations: they are all products of the environments from which they stem and they all give back to those environments. Whether it is the blockbuster film seen by millions and which feeds the culture exponentially or the tiny release barely seen or discussed at all, every film has an impact – every film touches *someone*. If, however, all films are performative, then we need a way of assessing the significance of a particular film's performance, so that we can determine what, in the speech-act sense, a particular film is doing.

To address this, it is fruitful to consider Emma Wilson's work on reading literature, in which she posits an argument that, I believe, also proves important for the ethical and performative dimensions of film. In her book *Sexuality and the Reading Encounter*, Wilson notes how the act of reading texts is 'not recreational but experiential'.[1] Wilson asserts that the reading encounter is 'volatile, affective, unknowable, distorting, and transformative'[2] and that the texts she analyses in her book 'testify at once to the freedom of the reader *and* to the formative power of the reading encounter. And in analysis of the reading of these texts, we may be led to reflect further on how far the act of reading might itself redirect reality.'[3] Wilson's stance is redolent of Levinas's idea of 'solicitation'; Davis explains that

> Levinas frequently describes the two-way process between text and reader as *solicitation*: the reader solicits the text with his or her current interests in mind, and is in turn solicited by the text to an exploration of meaning to which those current interests make an indispensable contribution.[4]

Wilson's assertions are also very close to Mai's description, which we have seen, of the intention behind the Dardennes' work – namely, 'to teach [the viewer] to perceive better than before in order to readjust our views and behavior'.[5] As with Wilson's reading encounters, we may therefore say that the viewing of a Dardenne film is 'not recreational but experiential'. The five adjectives Wilson offers to describe the effects of the reading encounter could serve as descriptions of this experience, the ethical encounter between self and Other and between film and viewer. The *volatility* of the encounter with the Other speaks of unpredictability, power, a potential explosion. This is also *affective*, creating an immediate feeling or response (and perhaps not always the desired one). The *unknowability* intrinsic to the encounter is the 'beyond essence' of Levinas's ethical philosophy. The *distortions* created challenge the status quo. And then we arrive at the adjective *transformative*. This, of course, suggests that the encounter has the power to change someone or something. We can therefore consider the films under discussion to be offering 'viewing encounters' akin to Wilson's notion of the reading encounter. If Mai's description of the point of the Dardennes' films is to be borne out, the viewer will change. And it is not a minor change – it is nothing less than an adjustment to 'our views and behavior'.

In the light of this, I shall consider *Le Fils* as performing a Levinasian ethics of inescapable responsibility for the Other. I shall suggest that the film offers us a grounded portrait of the world as it is but also a hopeful sense of the world as it could be. I explore the film's value as performative text, highlighting the participatory role of the viewer in the ethical choices that the film presents. In doing so, I encourage recognition of the film's *transformative* potential.

Beginning with the Ethical Encounter: Our First Moments with Olivier

Le Fils begins with a shot of Olivier (Olivier Gourmet), more specifically of his lower back, barely discernible under the opening credits, while natural sound is heard quietly on the soundtrack. As the credits come to an end, the camera angles up to the back of Olivier's head as he finishes reading a document he is holding (Figure 2.1). Olivier is a carpenter in a facility that provides vocational training to ex-young offenders, and the document is announcing a new arrival, whom we will come to learn is Francis Thirion (Morgan Marinne). The administrator wants to know if Olivier can take the boy into his class. Olivier refuses, saying that he has too many pupils already. What Olivier knows, but what we are not told until later in the film, is that, five years earlier, Francis killed Olivier's young son. From this setup, the Dardennes build the events of the story. Olivier is fascinated by the boy, and decides to accept him into his class, even as Francis's presence clearly affords Olivier great stress. The film dramatises the encounter, or series of encounters, between the two of them (with Francis not knowing that Olivier is the father of the boy he killed), moving towards a climax in which teacher and pupil finally confront each other.

Levinas talks in *Otherwise than Being* about how sociality comes before all else. He refers to 'the excellence, the height and the signification, of responsibility, that is, of sociality, an order to which finite truth – being and consciousness – are subordinate'.[6] As ethics is initiated through sociality, ethics, for Levinas, is first philosophy. To turn such a notion into something cinematic, however, is far from straightforward. It is a question of how a film might set about conveying this foundational moment, the ethical encounter that comes before all other events and existences – before our very 'being and consciousness'. The reading of the document that opens *Le Fils* is the initiation of an ethical encounter between Olivier and (the at this point unseen) Francis as Other, who is placing an ethical demand on Olivier through the document. The incident's performative significance in Levinasian terms is its placement at the start of the film. The opening credits are placed at the exact moment in which the situation kicks off, with Olivier reading the document announcing Francis's arrival. We are reading the credits at the same time that Olivier is reading the document. The film's title appears as the final credit in this opening, and we could say that it appears on-screen just as Olivier's situation dawns on him. In other words, he is thinking about 'le fils', the son, just as we read the film's title. The sequence also equates the film's credits with the document, and our act of reading them with Olivier's act of reading within the film's world. The opening credits sequence thus seals our closeness, our proximity, to Olivier's experience.

A comparison between *Le Fils* and *La Promesse* in relation to this is apt. We have seen how *La Promesse* performs the emerging ethical awareness of Igor as he becomes progressively more responsible to others (the dying Hamidou and then Hamidou's widow Assita and her child). Cox and Levine's comments on the film underline this sense of an emergence when they say that it 'demonstrates the sheer beauty and grace of the creation of a moral identity'[7] and that it 'elicits intuitions about the value of acquiring moral virtues; [i]t works because it shows in a clear and largely unadorned way the transformation of a person'.[8] What is notable here, however, is that *La Promesse* also depicts events happening *prior to* the ethical encounter – events that show Igor as 'a child living a mostly worthless and despicable life'.[9] While Igor's transformation into a more ethical person works plausibly in terms of what Miller would call Performativity$_2$ – performativity within

Figure 2.1 Olivier reads the form announcing Francis's arrival at the centre.

the events of the film – the depiction of an ethical being as having been, to draw on Cox and Levine's description, 'created' or 'transformed', and of moral virtues having been 'acquired', makes of the film's own performance – Performativity$_1$ – a narrative of emerging ethical awareness similar to the sense of emergence that Perpich has seen in *Totality and Infinity*. In *Le Fils*, by contrast, the strategy of *beginning* with the principal ethical encounter – the document announcing to Olivier the arrival of Francis at the institution – means there is no part of the film in which we see Olivier existing without the weight of this ethical obligation. From the outset, the viewer is ensnared by Olivier's status as hostage to the Other. And this is closer to the inescapability of the self's ethical obligation as posited in *Otherwise than Being*.

The film's absence of music – both within the diegesis and extra-diegetically – brings us closer to Olivier's situation as well. In the opening scene, for example, the sound of an off-screen saw in the carpentry workshop introduces a hum into the scene that might initially be mistaken for extra-diegetic music. That it is a non-musical sound emanating from within the diegesis exemplifies the approach to the soundtrack that the film will take: everyday sounds, of workshop, traffic, walking bodies, take the place of a score. The movie will offer us no overt aural commentary on the film's world, no handy musical leitmotifs through which we can interpret events. We must react solely to the sounds of the everyday. But this is not just an absorbing technique – it feels natural in story terms, because an absence of music is in keeping with Olivier's situation: a bereaved father who has also experienced the collapse of his relationship, he exists in a state devoid of spiritual joy. *Le Fils* also consists of handheld camerawork that conveys Olivier's restless enquiry into the new pupil and into his own state of mind. This combines with the film's long takes to convey an unstoppable through-line, unadorned and unedited except to move us from one location to the next.

The film's style is not so much an advance on other filmic styles as a reversal out of them. R. D. Crano says of the Dardennes that 'theirs is a cinema(tography) of subtraction, in which affects are produced only with the removal of aesthetic superfluities and conventional models of individuation'.[10] Just as Levinas's ethical philosophy of the encounter with the Other is predicated on an existence prior to dialogue or discourse, so the film seeks to turn back the theoretical clock, to a time before the aesthetically loaded attributes of editing within scenes, extra-diegetic music, and the 'composed' image. As Cooper observes, '[t]he challenge to cinematic codes, the questioning of the image, and this filming of the body are all stages in the disarticulation of a conventional filmic vocabulary'.[11] Even though the film cannot entirely eliminate these codes, its project of reducing their usage as far as possible is in itself a communication, through its style, of its Levinasian ethical stance. *Le Fils* gives us such a close look at Olivier that it seems to be asking us to respond to him – and, by extension, to the physical form of the film itself. The film prompts us towards a way of looking, a way of scrutinising the world so that we can find the answers in the world around us, without the embellishments of consoling cinematic devices.

Olivier: Character, Teacher, Protagonist

The status of Olivier as Levinasian subject, with Francis the unknowable Other whose presence dramatises the ethical encounter, is refracted through the film's close alignment with Olivier's point of view. Luc Dardenne says, 'The film, it's the character, it's the actor, it's Olivier Gourmet';[12] Gourmet is thus the dominant actor in the film, not least by virtue of being on-screen so extensively – and very often in close-up. Mai writes of the character of Rosetta that 'if she fills the frame of the Dardennes' camera, it is because she is alone in the *mise-en-scène* of her life'[13] – and we could say something similar about Olivier. His ethical burden isolates him. Gourmet embodies this ethical dilemma – we might even say that he carries the film on his shoulders; if ever the phrase were apt to describe an actor's contribution, it is here.

As embodied by Gourmet, Olivier is a physically imposing man. He could physically overpower Francis, who is slight and downcast. None of Olivier's other pupils appear to be a threat: they are well-behaved; about the worst that can be said of them comes from Olivier (who says that the lunch hall is 'too noisy' and who later reminds the boys not to be late on the Monday morning). It is Olivier himself who poses the biggest threat, especially to Francis. This is apparent in the moments in which Olivier sees more than we do. He can see the whole boy through the office door window, but we see only the boy's hand as he signs his name. When the boy buys soup in the canteen, Olivier, stationed deliberately in the kitchen, turns and sees the boy face-on, but we only see, a few seconds later, the boy's back as he walks away from the serving hatch. In each instance it would have been very simple to cut to a shot showing more precisely what Olivier sees, but in maintaining the single take each time, and filtering the view of Francis through that of Olivier, the film encourages us to puzzle out what Olivier is up to. In these moments Olivier is a step ahead of us, and what is fascinating is this inexplicable behaviour. It marks him out as privately minded, solitary, and obsessed.

The fact that Olivier often sees and knows more about Francis than we do illustrates the power Olivier holds over the boy, which increases the sense that he is responsible for the boy's welfare. This suggests a theme of the film, that it is adults who hold the cards, it is adults who must do right by the next generation. After the adolescent protagonists of the Dardennes' two preceding films, *La Promesse* and *Rosetta*, *Le Fils* has an adult as its central figure. It is much more a study of an adult in crisis than an adolescent in crisis. In his role as teacher, and more generally in his professional expertise, Olivier represents authority. He carries the responsibility of being in a position to set an example – the rehabilitation of the pupils depends on him. It is not just the film that rests on his shoulders; it is the future of humanity.

In many shots in the film we are looking partly at the back of Olivier's head. Part of the effect of being behind him is that we can see – over the shoulder, as it were – what he sees. But the back of Olivier's head fills the frame not just so that we can look beyond it but so that we can look at it. We can see something that Olivier cannot see: Olivier himself. The camerawork and the mise en scène allow us to see him in ways not open to him. And his level of self-awareness is a matter of conjecture. Gourmet's performance does not signal thoughts, feelings or motivations overtly, and so we are placed in a position of watching him without being able to read him easily. Richard Rushton suggests a reason for the effectiveness of the ostensibly guarded performances so often seen in Dardenne films:

> If their characters seem to lack expressive depth or to be hiding their thoughts and feelings from us, this does not mean *emotional* depth or content is lacking – quite

the contrary, in fact. Unlike the overt emotional displays typical of many Hollywood films, the constrained expressions of the Dardennes' characters make us think they are bottling up their emotions deep within, so that we do not think these characters are *unemotional* but instead that they must be so *overcome with emotion* that they cannot outwardly express it.[14]

This strong emotion is suggestive of Olivier's burden of ethical responsibility. Where we have so little to go on in terms of a protagonist's exposition or motivations, we are not so much understanding Olivier as *accompanying* him. Daniel Frampton makes a comparable point when he says of the four Dardenne films from *La Promesse* to *L'Enfant* that

> the filmgoer is left no time to assess situations or reflect too much on character actions. This is crucial to the thinkings of the films: we are held by the films, and the films do not want us to dwell. To be is to do; we must understand the characters by their actions; we should feel meanings directly without undue reflection (until the film is over).[15]

In saying 'To be is to do', Frampton takes his analysis close to an Austinian speech act: Olivier *is* what he *does*. Accordingly, we do not get to know what Olivier is thinking because it does not matter: whatever Olivier is thinking, it is his *actions* that will change Francis's world.

An Experience in Rhythm and Duration

The film's alignment with Olivier can be seen partly in the way in which his profession as a carpentry teacher – and thus his position as authority figure and major influence in the lives of Francis and the other pupils – achieves a symbiotic relationship with the film's style. Mai says that '[t]here is a remarkable coherence between these themes of measurement and balance and the evolution of the Dardennes' camera use, which has for this film evolved to a point of utter precision'.[16] This is a key aspect of how the directorial style helps perform the film's ethical stance. Olivier's perfectionism informs his scrupulous behaviour but also helps create, for the viewer, an experience of significance founded in the rhythms of the actors' bodies, the attendant rhythm of the camerawork and the sense of duration provided by the film's single-take scenes and by the judiciously timed edits between them. Crano writes about the properties of rhythm in the Dardennes' films, and invokes music theory in order to assess how this works cinematically:

> Cinema, like music, has the potential to operate in a purely anarchic mode, as a temporal phenomenon comprised of heterogeneous movements and recurring motifs. Continuously variable tempos and time signatures bar all attempts to 'keep' time, which must be experienced as objective affection rather than subjectively possessed.[17]

Crano discusses this primarily in terms of the films' lengthy shots and their capturing of characters' movement, and asserts that '[t]he Dardennes reconfigure perception according to its *affective* rather than *intelligible* capacity'.[18] Cooper, too, suggests a fusion of style and content inherent in the filmic speech act when she says that 'the Levinasian face-to-face encounter relates thought to words in a way that chimes with what we observe in both the movements of the bodies of the Dardennes' characters, and the movements of the films' images'.[19] As with *La Promesse*, it is through the film's style and its rhythms that we can understand the protagonist's dilemma. The Dardennes deploy a non-stop through-line to articulate their belief in the unity of person's physiological and ethical sides. The effect is of a style inviting the viewer to surrender to the film's movements, sounds and rhythms and thereby to experience the events prior to any sense of rational absorption or reflection.

For example, the scene in which Olivier teachers his pupils how to climb a ladder while balancing a plank of wood on their shoulder consists of a single shot (lasting approximately three and a half minutes) in which the handheld camera captures the action from a succession of angles, each following logically from the last, each view adding to the creation of the drama between Olivier and Francis. Crucially, although the specifics of the shot are exacting, the angles and movements arise as if naturally out of the action of the scene. The success of the technique is therefore in its achievement of executing a complex shot with an unostentatious precision so as to dissuade the viewer from spotting how carefully the camera movements have been worked out, as this would spoil the experience.

The film's rhythm conveys both the inescapability and the *constancy* of Levinasian ethical responsibility, by offering to the viewer the sensation of sustaining something without breaking it, without dropping it. This achievement in style is akin to the wire loop game, in which the player holds a stick with a metal loop on the end of it and the object of the game is to manoeuvre the stick from one end of an electrically charged wire to the other without touching the wire. If the player touches the wire with the loop, the contact creates a spark and the player loses the game. If the player gets the stick to the end without touching the wire, the player lifts the loop free of the wire to win the game. It is a game in which victory is the successful completion of a difficult test. The game gives back to the successful player a sense of achievement: the player has done something perfectly. They have sustained something and not dropped it. *Le Fils* is, among other things, akin to a successfully completed wire loop game. The film, when viewed in a single sitting, offers something akin to this sense of achievement. It demonstrates the process a person goes through if they want to implement a change of behaviour – abstention, self-control – all played out with a sense of rhythm and duration. The feat of the sustained rhythm performs an interdependence of the ethical and the physiological that expresses the burden that accompanies the responsibility Olivier feels for Francis. The sum total of Olivier's actions throughout the film represents the film's model for a Levinasian devotion to the Other.

And yet I also believe that the presentation of Olivier in the film prompts us to be conscious of our reading both of the character and of the film. The lengthiness of the takes, the abundance of close-ups that nevertheless resist articulating anything concrete about Olivier's feelings or motivations, and the constant need for the viewer to assess and interpret the radically presented spatiality of the film's world and the unpredictable motions of its narrative all point to a viewing experience that is aware of the film's supreme control over its effects. Supreme control suggests a sense of the fixity of a film's achievement, its awareness of its deliberate choices designed to create effects and its desire to use these effects to help thematise its themes, to capture, solidify and preserve its achievement. Such fixity would seem to run counter to what we have seen Davies consider to be the 'shock' of the Levinasian ethical encounter, what we have seen Levinas call the 'anarchy' of the Saying. It is therefore vital that we interrogate this seeming contradiction between control and anarchy, because it raises questions as to how a film can be considered to be performing a Levinasian ethics founded on language as the anarchic Saying rather than as the controlled Said.

Derrida's Originary Performativity and *Le Fils*

As we have seen, performativity in language is conventional. This means that its effectiveness is due to its drawing on pre-existing conventions of usage: the speaker deploys language to perform the function that it is agreed it will perform given a set of circumstances. Austin considered this to be the 'felicity' of language, its assent to favourable conditions and contexts – the properly qualified person performing the marriage ceremony, the farmer's sign warning of the dangerous bull in the field, and so on. This is how language achieves its illocutionary force. And yet the thrust of Austinian performativity is that something new is brought into being through the 'act' of language. How, then, can language be both conventional and performative? And how can a film hope to convey the non-fixity of the Saying through the use of 'fixed' cinematic conventions? Derrida's notion of 'originary performativity' can shed light on these questions.

In a 1976 lecture at the University of Virginia, Charlottesville, Derrida offered an analysis of the United States Declaration of Independence, the document that, on 4 July 1776, inaugurated the independence of the thirteen American colonies that, until then, had been ruled by the British Empire. Derrida starts by querying the identity of the 'representatives'[20] who are the authors of the document and the identity of the '"good" people'[21] about whom the document speaks and whom the signatories of the document claim to represent. For Derrida, the document speaks of a people who do not yet exist; it is part of the document's effect that these people only come to exist by way of the document itself. Derrida notes,

> One cannot decide – and this is the interesting thing, the force and 'coup de force' of such a declarative act – whether independence is stated or produced by this utterance . . . Is it that the good people have already freed themselves in fact and are only stating the fact of this emancipation in [*par*] the Declaration? Or is it rather that they free themselves at the instant of and by [*par*] the signature of this Declaration?[22]

Derrida thus identifies a duality at the heart of the document between a constative statement of fact – that the American people are free and independent – and a performative utterance – that the document itself is bringing these people into being. For Derrida, this duality is *the* essential aspect of how the document does its work successfully: 'This obscurity, this undecidability between, let us say, a performative structure and a constative structure, is *required* to produce the sought-after effect. It is essential to the very positing or position of a right as such.'[23] Derrida clearly believes that rather than there simply being a constative statement of fact – that the people already exist and that the document is simply describing them – there is a performative dimension at work, the document undertaking a process of subject formation in constituting, first, a group of people and, second, that group of people as being free and independent: 'They do *not* exist as an entity, the entity does *not* exist *before* this declaration, not *as such*. If it gives birth to itself, as free and independent subject, as possible signer, this can hold only in the act of the signature. The signature invents the signer.'[24] As Loxley notes in his discussion of Derrida's analysis,

> [i]nstead of the collective speaker coming first, and then issuing its utterances as the product of its general will or shared intention, the speaker is retroactively constituted by the utterance it appears to authorise. In an uncanny fashion the speech act speaks itself, and in doing so speaks of the speaking 'people' it invents.[25]

This duality manifests itself as an act of political ideology: the Declaration asserts that the new colonies of which it speaks 'are, and of Right ought to be, Free And Independent States'. As Derrida notes, 'the *and* articulates and conjoins here the two discursive modalities, the *to be* and the *ought to be*, the constation and the prescription, the fact and the right'.[26] The Declaration is thus an example of what Derrida elsewhere calls

> the originary performativity that does not conform to preexisting conventions, unlike all the performatives analyzed by the theoreticians of speech acts, but whose force of *rupture* produces the institution or the constitution, the law itself, which is to say also the meaning that appears to, that ought to, or that appears to have to guarantee it in return.[27]

For Derrida, therefore, originary performativity achieves something that other types of performativity do not: rather than producing new work through convention, it breaks with convention in order to effect its change in circumstances.

We can say that *Le Fils* is undertaking an act of originary performativity in using the conventions of film grammar to depart from them, so as to transcend the presentation of the world as it is in order to show us the world as it could be. Mosley, as we have seen, has discussed what he calls 'the subjunctive mood of [the Dardennes'] films: what may be is more important than simply what is'.[28] Taking the 'is/may be' of Mosley's view and relating it to the 'are/ought to be' of the Declaration of Independence, we can see a similar duality at work, a similar desire to recognise and yet also to transcend the status quo in order to assert new conditions on the world. Of course, the Declaration of Independence is a written document, and one that serves an overt political function. But *Le Fils* is another sort of text to encounter, one that, like the Declaration of Independence, has the potential to affect us in transformative ways. When we recall Wilson's assertion that the reading encounter is 'volatile, affective, unknowable, distorting, and transformative', we can see how much that sounds like a summation of the effects of originary performativity, and how *Le Fils* invites us into a similarly powerful viewing encounter. Cooper has noted how '[the brothers'] concern with alterity and the soul incarnates a form of filmmaking that creates an original fissure in the ontology of cinema – an ethical one that gives a different space and time to the lives of others'.[29] This 'original fissure', akin to the Derridean 'rupture', relates to Cooper's observation, which we considered earlier, that 'Levinas's reformulation of ethics as first philosophy creates a fissure at the root of the philosophy of being'.[30] In each case, the fissure makes originary performativity possible.

The film dramatises this by staging interruptions by Francis to Olivier's selfhood and intentions. I mentioned earlier that we can consider ways in which *Le Fils* both recognises and subverts many of the tenets of classic, or standard, film style. The struggle for rhythm, for forward momentum, preoccupies the whole film. Just as we can only measure the performative dimensions of Levinas's language – and its performative success – in relation to convention, so we can only measure the effectiveness of *Le Fils* in relation to filmic conventions. As Cooper notes, '[t]he Dardenne brothers' quest for novelty through their filmmaking lies in breaking key cinematic codes in an attempt to start from scratch, but they couple this with recognition that this is impossible. Their resultant, compromised aim is not to buy wholesale into cinematic convention.'[31] Hence this tension between what the viewer knows – recognisable cinematic forms – and what the film does to undercut these.

There is, for example, a tension – but also, therefore, an unavoidable link – between the film's traditional three-act narrative structure and Francis's interruptions. Every time Olivier tries to control the rhythm, the pace, of the association with Francis, the latter does something (unwittingly) to disrupt it. From the film's first camera shot, the character of Olivier is conveyed through these interruptions. Wilson says that in the literature of Marguerite Duras and Marcel Proust, 'so much emphasis is laid in both their texts on the viewing arena, on the scene of reading'[32] that the reader has the theme of reading in mind – it is part of the texts' self-reflexivity. There is no emphasis laid in *Le Fils* on the film viewing process, but there is an emphasis on looking, lines of sight, listening, and the contemplation of off-screen space. As Francis interrupts Olivier's mastery of his environment, so the film interrupts the viewer's mastery of their own viewing pleasure – so that substitution, the-one-for-the-other, can be felt.

As an example of this, I want to consider the night-time sequence in the car park. This sequence comes shortly after the half-hour mark; it follows Olivier's visit to the gas station, in which he tells his ex-partner Magali (Isabella Soupart) that Francis has been released. Magali, immediately distressed, asks Olivier if he has seen the boy, and Olivier lies to her, saying he has not seen him. When Olivier mentions that he has been considering taking the boy into his class, Magali blurts out the horrible revelation (to us – Olivier already knows it) that Francis killed their son; she is shocked that Olivier can be thinking of teaching him. As that sequence includes the moment in which we discover the reason for Olivier's interest in Francis, the night-time car-park sequence affords us our first look at Olivier with our new knowledge. The sequence begins with him in the café, waiting for his baguette and very possibly reflecting on his conversation with Magali. After he has received his baguette, he comes out of the take-away and runs into Francis, who says to him, 'Hello sir. You hungry, too?' (Figure 2.2) Olivier answers with a simple, 'Yes.' As Francis carries on into the take-away, Olivier pauses, watching him, and then continues on his way.

Figure 2.2 Olivier turns as he hears Francis's question; Francis pauses as he walks past

What ensues is an example of what Cooper terms 'the disarticulation of a conventional filmic vocabulary'. The film cuts to a shot inside Olivier's car. The camera is behind Olivier and to the side, in a close over-the-shoulder shot. This is the paradigmatic shot in *Le Fils*: close enough to Olivier that it seems to extend an invitation to the viewer to step into Olivier's shoes but just about far enough away that Olivier can be scrutinised objectively. He turns round (towards the camera) to look off-screen, and then turns back. What he has looked at off-screen, we can surmise, is Francis at the take-away. The off-screen space is not off-screen for him, of course – for Olivier is not in a film in *his* world, only in *our* world.³³ This time, he interrupts himself: with a sigh, he gets out of the car. At the start of the next shot (which will last approximately four minutes), Olivier is leaning against his car, eating his baguette, and his eyes throw quick occasional glances away to the distance. Although spatially the film is not conventional – no master shot has provided an overview of the layout of take-away and car park – it is possible to piece together, from Olivier's eyeline, the relative positions of car and take-away. What happens – Francis's arrival and the halting conversation that ensues – feels as if it emerges out of Olivier's engagement with otherness, his interruption of his own selfhood. Secure (and presumably hidden) in his car, Olivier was in theory under no obligation to confront the Other. And yet, something motivated Olivier to get out of his car and initiate the meeting. Is this the inescapable ethical pull of the Other? Olivier's sigh in deciding to exit his car is a particularly notable detail: it may be a concession to guilt in being about to initiate the encounter, a small enactment of his sense that the encounter must be played out or a more primal expression of how he is hostage to the Other, unwittingly drawn to Francis. However we interpret the sigh, it can be understood to signal the exertion required by the hostage to the Other. It is a moment in which the *dénucléation* of the ego manifests itself in the day-to-day, a moment in which Olivier opens himself to the possibility (indeed, the probability) of challenge, hurt and obligation. For Levinas, '[r]esponsibility goes beyond being':³⁴

> Vulnerability, exposure to outrage, to wounding, passivity more passive than all patience, passivity of the accusative form, trauma of accusation suffered by a hostage to the point of persecution, implicating the identity of the hostage who substitutes himself for the others: all this is the self, a defecting or defeat of the ego's identity. And this, pushed to the limit, is sensibility, sensibility as the subjectivity of the subject. It is a substitution for another, one in the place of another, expiation.³⁵

The wrenching difficulty of what Olivier is doing – stepping out of his car, instigating the conversation/confrontation with Francis – is akin to the enormity of the Levinasian ethical demand. And the viewer has been invited to feel this, by virtue of having been placed in an active participatory role in imagining both the spatial and the motivational aspects of the sequence. Our experience of what Olivier is going through is inextricably linked with our navigation through the unfamiliar style in which the sequence is filmed. This coupling of 'raw' experience and reflective viewing ensures the film's originary performativity, its play on convention to create the unpredictable.

The World as it Is, the World as it Could Be

The test of this is measured most acutely in relation to the film's climax and resolution. Having stayed late in the workshop on a Friday to help Francis finish making his toolbox, Olivier gives the boy a lift home, and asks him if he would like to accompany him on a trip to the wood yard the next day to fetch wood for the centre. Francis accepts, and the film enters its final stretch – the road trip to the wood yard, including tense conversations between Olivier and Francis in the car. In these scenes – which consist, as before, of singular, long takes – Olivier and Francis are captured more and more in close proximity to each other, which conveys a growing association between them. When they have a snack in a café on the way, they look as if they could be father and son. This scene refers back to the night-time car-park scene: there they were framed in two-shots at times, but mostly the camera was shifting so as to concentrate exclusively on one or other of them as Francis measured the distance between their feet with his carpenter's ruler on the ground. They came together awkwardly, but their food – Olivier's baguette, Francis's chips – illustrated their relationship at this point: man and boy each had only half a meal, an illustration of how they needed something from each other. But in the café scene on the road trip, the camera keeps them together virtually all the time – notably for the duration of their chat at the cafe's counter, where Francis asks Olivier if he would consider being his guardian. Here, man and boy each have an apple turnover – not half a meal each but matching sustenance – and while Olivier has a very adult cup of tea or coffee and Francis has a very adolescent glass of coke, the way they are framed, and the way Francis – subconsciously or otherwise – mimics Olivier when he drinks, asserts a more harmonious pairing than has been hitherto presented (Figure 2.3).

But there is considerable and rising tension. During a game of table football that they play in the café, Olivier quizzes Francis about the incident that led to his incarceration, while immediately after this there is a short, quiet scene in the bathroom where Olivier washes his glasses, dries his hands, and regards himself grimly in the mirror. He knows that a moment of reckoning is near, and getting nearer. Outside, Francis asks him for a cigarette, saying he will pay him back on Monday. There is something chilling about Olivier's giving of the cigarette to Francis, as if he is bestowing it on a Death Row prisoner on the morning of his execution. Will Francis be alive on the Monday to pay Olivier back?

The rising tension of the film's final act has come about partly through the increase in signs that Olivier wants to control the situation; he is seen mending his back brace the night before the trip, a meditative gesture

Figure 2.3 Olivier and Francis: from half a meal each to matching sustenance

that is also preparation for a physical challenge, and he is seen assembling equipment useful for the trip but also ominous in its implication: rope, tarpaulin. The length of the car journey, too, feels different in rhythm from what the film has shown us before. The duration of the shots has not notably changed, but the sense of the journey through rural landscapes (trees outside the car windows, long stretches of fast road, the quiet car park by the roadside diner, more stretches of road) introduces the extended traversing of geographical distance such as has not been featured hitherto in the film. Furthermore, the journey into the woods feels more dramatic than what has come before because, in taking the characters into such a seemingly isolated location, it takes them away from distractions, outside interventions, and, crucially, referents. Now more than ever in the film, we as viewers are denied help on two levels: the consoling filmic tropes (emotive music, declared suspense, voiced motivations) that tell us how to understand the events that are coming to a head and the consoling devices of societal contexts with which to assess the human behaviours we are witness to. The isolated settings of first the car journey and then the wood yard deny both Olivier and Francis, as well as viewers, the societal context that enables structures of communication (locutionary effects), motives (illocutionary effects), and reactions (perlocutionary effects) to be identified and judged in terms of their conventional social readability. This lack of consolation is entirely in keeping with the story of ethical suspense that the film is telling.

The tension between the conventionality of a climactic third act and the unconventionality of how this particular film uses it is an instance of Derrida's originary performativity. Stylistically, the film is using convention to overturn convention. The car drive to the wood yard and the scenes set within it represent both a physical movement away from society and a filmic representation of the Saying. This emphasises every action that Olivier performs. And, in the performative sense in which the viewing encounter is, to invoke Wilson, 'volatile, affective, unknowable, distorting, and transformative', the onus begins to fall more squarely on the viewer to assess, by proxy, what to do with regard to Francis. Whatever is about to happen – whatever Olivier is about to do – will play out shorn of the context that would more usually render it readable, and perhaps predictable. Instead, Olivier's actions – whatever they will be – will be readable primarily for themselves. The setting is a return to the primal, the pre-original – where ethics can potentially come first. At the same time – as an example of how the film seeks to overturn convention through convention – the filmmaking is not too radical. When the film crosses its threshold and arrives at the location of the final reckoning, the car is seen in long shot as it moves through the gated entrance and parks, in the distance, in the yard. This moment in the film represents the most distanced view of Olivier – the film is providing maximum spatial perspective on Olivier's position and actions and on the setting to which he has brought Francis. It is a moment in which the viewer is cued to contemplate the implications of all that Olivier has done (in the film) and all that he might be about to do.

Up to this point, *Le Fils* has contained many moments in which it has appeared as if Olivier were having to suppress his animosity towards

Francis (for example, in letting Francis measure the distance between their feet in the car park, in being encouraging to him after he falls off the ladder, in enduring defeat by Francis at table football – and, before that, in being asked to consider being his guardian), and the film is now moving towards its climax in which Olivier will finally be able to express himself the way he wants to most of all. In fact, all of these moments have been showing Olivier the real him. He really is that ethical, generous, loving person. No sooner has he told Francis that the boy he murdered was his son, he is seeking to moderate his meaning. But Francis fights back, and there is a chase, at the climax of which Olivier overpowers Francis. Given the perfect chance to enact his murderous, vengeful impulse, he begins to strangle the struggling Francis on the forest floor – but finds he cannot go through with it. Levinas says that 'the other absolutely other – the Other – does not limit the freedom of the same; calling it to responsibility, it founds it and justifies it'.[36] Olivier is defined by the ethical response that emerges from him in his encounter with Francis.

In *Le Fils*, Olivier is not part of the world if he is not connected with others. His apartment, which has figured in two earlier scenes, is a place but not a world. This is why the film does not show the apartment much – the film does not want to patronise the audience; the film expects that the audience will understand. To show the apartment would be to make too much of the production design and set decoration; we would be encouraged to admire the clarity with which Olivier's lonely home life is depicted. As it is, it is there in the background: Olivier knows it and we are aligned with Olivier, so we do not need to be reminded of it any more than he does. Olivier's home life is empty not because he lives alone but because he does not have what he wants. He has lost his family (son murdered, ex newly pregnant by a new partner) and not yet found a replacement.

Francis is that replacement. If Olivier kills him, Olivier is alone, with no hope of connection. When he has his hands around Francis's throat, the shot frames them separately. Murder is disconnection between self and Other. When Olivier relents, the camera takes in him and Francis together as they sit next to each other, recovering. The liberation of Francis, the chance that Olivier gives him for a future, illustrates the result of Olivier's ethical response. The story of *Le Fils* is chiefly Olivier's but it is also the story of the trajectory the two of them follow, from intertwined tension to mutual freedom. As they share a further, final scene, loading planks of wood onto the car's trailer, it is not reconciliation that the film wishes to express; survival, the chance to live on, is what counts. Luc Dardenne has said, 'Olivier, in not killing Francis, is the father who perhaps allows Francis to reconnect with life.'[37] The wood yard thus represents both the profession in which Olivier is training Francis and an abstract place in which a new type of society – confoundingly ethical – has been inaugurated.

The final gesture towards this is the silence with which the film ends. Films ending in silence can often have a quality of 'speechlessness', as if they have been rendered mute by the shattering nature of the tragic events. In *Le Fils*, the silence takes on a Levinasian dimension. The film is not a tragedy, and so the cut to black and the slow crawl of the end credits do not provide dramatic closure and finality on a tragic outcome. Rather, the silence that accompanies the credits is a further, and resounding, act of Levinasian ethics, the literal and positive pre-ontological ethical encounter, a silence outside the meaning of the conventional film soundtrack. It is not only tragedy that has been averted, it is also predictability. In the lives of Olivier and Francis, everything is still to play for.

We have seen how originary performativity – and specifically a document such as the United States Declaration of Independence – works the seemingly impossible act of inaugurating a people it claims already to be representing, by enacting a rupture at the root of convention. We can read the Dardennes' work in *Le Fils* as drawing on cinematic antecedents to construct a film that operates in conventional ways and at the same time manages to perform a Levinasian break with convention. The viewer's participation in Olivier's dilemma, as performed by the film's unconventional use of style, *is* the viewer enacting Levinasian responsibility, and after the film has ended, the achievement will resonate, if at all, as the viewer's. It is in this way that *Le Fils*, enacting the duality at the heart of Derrida's originary performativity, shows us the world as it is – that is, conventional – and the world as it could be – that is, ethical in its anarchic relation to conventionality.

CHAPTER 3

The Kid with a Bike and the Reframing of Ethics

So far I have considered the evolution of the Dardennes' style from their second feature *Je Pense à Vous* through to the achievements of *La Promesse* and *Le Fils* and suggested how the refinements to their filmmaking invite the viewer into a more intensely ethical experience. In this chapter, and with particular regard to *The Kid with a Bike*, I shall explore how their filmmaking style has shifted again in their more recent work and what this means for the treatment of their subject matter, in particular the self's responsibility for the Other.

Since *Le Fils*, the Dardennes have written and directed several more feature films, including *L'Enfant*, *The Silence of Lorna*, *The Kid with a Bike*, *Deux jours, une nuit* (*Two Days, One Night*, dirs Jean-Pierre and Luc Dardenne, 2014), *La Fille inconnue* (*The Unknown Girl*, dirs Jean-Pierre and Luc Dardenne, 2016) and *Le Jeune Ahmed* (*Young Ahmed*, dirs Jean-Pierre and Luc Dardenne, 2019). They also contributed a short work, 'Dans l'obscurité', to the anthology film *Chacun son cinéma* (*To Each His Own Cinema*, various directors, 2007).[1] *L'Enfant* consolidated the filmmakers' reputations, winning them a second Palme d'Or, their first having been for *Rosetta* six years earlier, and with this success the Dardennes were undoubtedly established as among the most acclaimed filmmakers in the world. Their easily recognised style, with its restless camera, its dearth of music, its long scenes often shot in single takes and frequently featuring very little dialogue, and its blunt editing that often cuts between scenes abruptly, achieved greater exposure. But although it may initially seem as if their style, from *La Promesse* onwards, is consistent from film to film, it is not the case. *La Promesse*, *Rosetta* and *Le Fils* are closest to what I would argue people think of when they talk about the Dardennes' style. From *L'Enfant* onwards, there has been a subtle move away from the style of *Le Fils*. We can read this shift as Levinasian in its implications both for the directors' body of work and for the viewing experience.

A Recognisable but Ever-changing Style

Luc Dardenne has commented on how they felt the need to push their filmmaking in a new direction after *L'Enfant*. In a diary entry dated 27 January 2006, he writes: 'One hesitates. Must we make this film with the boy [an early incarnation of what was to become *The Kid with a Bike*]? Are we not taken by a form we won't succeed in leaving, which we don't dare to leave? I no longer know. We'll see.'² And in an entry from 22 September 2008 (therefore, a few weeks after the release of *The Silence of Lorna*), he writes: '[S]omething must change in our cinema. I sense that the year to come won't be restful. If our cinema becomes more narrative-based, if we film more a plot (and its subplots) than a character, how do we not lose the vibration of the shot?'³ Here, then, are conscious efforts on the part of the Dardennes to expand their craft and to refuse to rest with what has worked before. It is important, therefore, to note that their work has stayed recognisably theirs while subtly developing and changing: they modified and revised their style from film to film even within the cycle from *La Promesse* to *L'Enfant* and they continue to do so within their more recent films. Mosley, discussing *The Silence of Lorna*, says that '[t]he brothers choose less to innovate than to vary slightly their artistic approach'.⁴ For Benoît Dillet and Tara Puri, '[t]his repetition is actually an expanding resonance, a practised style that creates the oeuvre of the Dardennes'.⁵

One of the most striking aspects of this 'expanding resonance' is the gradual reintroduction into the Dardennes' films of some of the more conventional tools of narrative cinema that had been absent since *Je Pense à Vous*. For example, *L'Enfant* features a small number of edits within scenes, and *The Silence of Lorna* is shot on 35mm, which, after the Super 16mm format of their immediately preceding films, adds a slightly more detached, traditionally cinematic air. Luc Dardenne says with regard to shooting *The Silence of Lorna*,

> We will shoot on Kodak 35mm. There will of course be less restlessness than in our movements with the Super 16mm camera. A larger inertia that would have to contribute to the meaning of what we want to film: the observation of Lorna, the recording of her behaviour, of her presence, which is difficult to identify, to feel. To see this, it is not necessary to get caught up in her movements, to mime her energy; it is necessary that we keep a distance and therefore move with her less.⁶

We can also see a new foregrounding of plot and story structure, especially in *The Silence of Lorna*, *Two Days, One Night* and *The Unknown Girl*. If we consider the Dardennes' typical style to be rather unconventional, and this unconventionality to be a key factor in how the films seek to perform their ethics, it would be possible to see the recent reintroduction of the more conventional elements as a dissolution of this effect, a violation of the Levinasian Saying that the films had been performing. But, as Seán Hand notes,

> an obvious problem with this extreme presentation of saying, of course, is that it so absolutely tries to counteract the power and repressiveness of the said, or the violence of ontology itself, that it starts to exert its own violence. The being-for-the-other testified to by this extreme ethical saying can come to sound like a masochistic scenario that confers humiliation and real pain on the subject.[7]

I do not mean to suggest that the style of a film such as *Le Fils* is in itself presenting a 'masochistic scenario'; rather, it is simply that we may feel that the Dardennes' style had, precisely because of its effectiveness, become so established that, if they had continued with it without much variation, it could have begun to run the risk of being counterproductive, diluting its ethical effects through predictability. My view, therefore, is that the changes in style, including the reintroduction of conventional filmic tropes, do not short-circuit the notion of Levinasian ethics in the Dardennes' work but instead reframe it. Robert Pippin notes how the Dardennes' use of style ensures that their modes of expression are placed to the fore:

> The Dardenne brothers obviously must realize that the unconventionality of their framing, camera position from the rear and instability, de-emphasis on dialogue and exposition, indifference to conventional plot, and so forth are immediately and starkly noticeable to the viewer. This means in effect that each of their films, whatever else it is about, is about itself; each film is a kind of allegory of film, instructing us about what cinematic representability is, can be (and cannot be), must be now.[8]

It is as if this foregrounding signals their desire not to let their style congeal into the fixed ontologies of the Said and rather allows it to maintain its vibrant performance of the self's inescapable responsibility for the Other.

Accordingly, we can read these examples in relation to a different aspect of performativity, one that enacts what Butler has termed the '*re*signification' of language.[9] Derrida, in 'Signature Event Context', complicated Austin's already complex notion of language's conventionality by arguing for its iterability, that is, its repeatability and citationality. For Derrida, every instance of language is made up of 'marks' that, while fixed in one sense, are also endlessly reappropriated and reused in new contexts. This means that the performativity of language has a split at its heart, between its recognisability (through its iterability) and its essential difference from itself (as each iteration shows that there are two signs and that therefore they cannot be the same).[10] So, just as 'I bet you sixpence' is both a recognition of the existing, standard terms of bet-making and a new bet, so language can draw on the recognisability of a pre-existing form or format in order to bring something new into being – as we saw with originary performativity in the previous chapter. Butler picks up on this in her discussion of racist hate speech. She notes that, while certain racist terms are understood initially to carry an unshakeable power to offend and hurt, the ability to re-state them in different contexts – even a context as simple as a discussion of the word itself – creates the possibility that the hurtful connotations of such terms can be opened to erosion.[11] For Butler, with this resignification '[t]he possibility of decontextualizing and recontextualizing such terms through radical acts of public misappropriation constitutes the basis of an ironic hopefulness that the conventional relation between word and wound might become tenuous and even broken in time'.[12] I would argue that the Dardennes' reintroduction of overtly conventional stylistic tropes into their films operates in a similar sense of resignification. That is not to say that the filmic tropes they resignify previously did the damage of racism, or that they constituted a form of hate speech, or that they necessarily served to offend and hurt. I mean only to point to the potential for a standard, conventionally performative, and overused filmic trope to be refreshed and reused given certain filmic conditions.

The Return of Music in *The Silence of Lorna* and *The Kid with a Bike*

One of the most striking examples, since *La Promesse*, of this sense of resignification in the Dardennes' film style occurs in the final moments of *The Silence of Lorna*. Lorna (Arta Dobroshi), the complicit but increasingly desperate pawn in a gangsters' game of illegal citizenship deals, has fled from the menace of Fabio (Fabrizio Rongione) and his sidekick Spirou (Morgan Marinne) and has taken refuge in a forest area. As she settles down for the night in an abandoned cabin, steadying herself for whatever awaits her in the morning, we hear music come in. It can only be extra-diegetic: the isolation of the location and the paucity of resources in the cabin mean that this music cannot be occurring within the diegesis. This is the first instance of extra-diegetic music in a Dardenne film since Wim Mertens' score in *Je Pense à Vous* five films earlier. As such, the extra-diegetic music in *The Silence of Lorna* intrudes into the style the Dardennes had developed from *La Promesse* onwards. The music that closes *The Silence of Lorna* is Beethoven's Piano Sonata No. 32 in C minor, Op. 111, and with its mood of compassion and contemplation coming at the end of what has been a drama of hardship and harshness for Lorna it is certainly a fitting piece with which to close the film, but it is a departure from *La Promesse*,

Rosetta, *Le Fils* and *L'Enfant*, none of which include extra-diegetic music in their endings or elsewhere. What is especially intriguing, however, is that *The Silence of Lorna* has already established this mood in its preceding minutes, when the camera observes Lorna in the forest with an objectivity that nevertheless, in its gentle charting of her movements, communicates a sense of compassion; whatever we have felt about Lorna's dubious actions through the course of the story, it is hard not to feel for her at this moment. As it is, the extra-diegetic music, arriving in the closing moments of the film, is both in keeping with the mood that has been set and a slightly jarring 'surprise'. Due to the nature of the music, however – the gentle piano, the lilting melody – the surprise gives way quite rapidly to a continuation, even an enhancement, of the tender and compassionate mood. We may say, therefore, that the use of music should not work but does. This is an example of what I am reading as the development of the Dardennes' style. Having forsaken extra-diegetic music after *Je Pense à Vous*, they have now found a fresh use for it, one that somehow manages to work within their carefully evolved style.

This achievement is repeated and expanded in *The Kid with a Bike*, in which they use extra-diegetic music several times. The same piece of music is used each time, a short passage – approximately twenty seconds – of emotive chords from the second movement (the adagio) of Beethoven's Piano Concerto No. 5 in E-flat major, Op. 73, otherwise known as the *Emperor Concerto*. It occurs four times: first, approximately three minutes into the film, when Cyril (Thomas Doret) is trying to escape from the children's home his father has placed him in, and is being restrained by two men; second, almost thirty-eight minutes into the film, when Cyril and his weekend guardian, Samantha (Cécile de France), are both crying in the car after Cyril has found out that his father, Guy (Jérémie Renier), does not want him in his life; third, just over one hour and eight minutes into the film, during Cyril's bike ride after he has tried to give his father the money he has stolen in a bungled robbery and his father has reiterated that Cyril is not to come visiting anymore (Figure 3.1); and, lastly, in the film's final shot, as Cyril rides away on his bike and the film cuts to black and the end credits roll, the music continuing into the credits. Luc Dardenne's reasoning for their use of the music touches on what he considers to be the film's fairytale quality: 'It's very rare in our films and we hesitated for a long time. In a fairytale there has to be a development, with emotions and new beginnings. It seemed to us that music, at certain points, could act like a calming caress for Cyril.'[13] Of all the pieces of music available to them, the filmmakers have selected twenty seconds of melody that convey two clear emotions: hope (through the rising major-key

Figure 3.1 Cyril rides his bike away, having been rejected by his father again.

melodic line) and concern (through the answering phrase in the relative minor chord). The music's affect is thus indeed a 'calming caress', but to touch on the other aspect of Luc Dardenne's comment – the fairytale quality – it is important to note the schematic way in which the music is used. Each instance occurs at a moment of particular stress or hardship for Cyril. And the brevity of these uses of extra-diegetic music renders them more prominent than perhaps would have been the case had the film used more extensive scoring. These brief bursts of music therefore mark out key moments of development within the story and thus help to give the film its fairytale quality, in which good and bad forces are competing influences on an impressionable character.

These brief uses of music in *The Silence of Lorna* and *The Kid with a Bike* are clear breaks with the directors' past practice, from *La Promesse* to *L'Enfant*, of not drawing on extra-diegetic music to prompt emotional reactions in the audience. And that past practice has worked superbly as an invitation to engage with the characters' ethical struggles; one has only to imagine *La Promesse* or *Le Fils*, for example, *with* extra-diegetic music to recognise how much greater the field of reaction is when it is *not* stalked by musical accompaniment. One could therefore see these brief uses of music in *The Silence of Lorna* and *The Kid with a Bike* as lapses in style or focus; to evoke my earlier discussion of *Le Fils*, they may be examples of the player touching the wire with the loop before reaching the end of the game. But the resignification reading asserts that the inclusion of music in *The Silence of Lorna* and *The Kid with a Bike* points to a sense that the stylistic properties shared by the four films from *La Promesse* to *L'Enfant* had become an expectation and that the more recent Dardenne films would set themselves up as performative in a different way. Although the music in *The Kid with a Bike*, for example, offers a calming caress for Cyril, Igor in *La Promesse*, Rosetta in *Rosetta*, Francis (and perhaps Olivier) in *Le Fils* and Bruno (and perhaps Sonia) in *L'Enfant* could have used a similar calming caress, but they did not receive one. This suggests either that there is something about Cyril specifically that prompts this care or that it is a question of the evolution of style, that it is this new period of the Dardennes' work that is enabling of the presence of a calming caress in musical form. We can read it as an example of the Dardennes' commitment to sustaining a performance of the Levinasian Saying on film, the directors searching for ways to keep their style fresh, to save it from falling into the trap of becoming predictable, thematisable, congealed – the Said.

Two further aspects of *The Kid with a Bike* are especially illustrative of this avoidance of congealment: its use of two central characters rather than one and the way in which its less rampantly expressive style can be read as making greater demands on viewers than the earlier films.

A Widening Point of View: Cyril and Samantha

Of all the Dardennes' feature films since *La Promesse*, *The Kid with a Bike* contains perhaps their most intriguing distribution of point of view with regard to main characters. *Rosetta* and *Le Fils* both offer, at least at first glance, singular points of view – those of, respectively, Rosetta and Olivier. We should note, however, that the question of point of view in film is never straightforward: even a film that is pledged to a single character's point of view for its duration cannot help but present its own, alternative point of view. In *Le Fils*, for example, the camerawork and mise en scène, as we have seen, evoke the character of Olivier but they also comment on that character; we are observing with Olivier but we are also observing Olivier himself. *L'Enfant* has two central characters, the young parents Bruno (Jérémie Renier) and Sonia (Déborah François), and *The Silence of Lorna* is centred on Lorna, who is caught in a trap and whose story is illuminated by a relatively larger number of characters with whom she is required to interact. When it comes to *The Kid with a Bike*, the questions as to what and who the film is about can be posed differently, and I argue that this difference can, in its own way, be read as Levinasian.

Cyril is, of course, the title character; furthermore, everything in the film turns around him. It is fair to say in general, however, that even when he is clearly the focus of a scene or sequence, the film's presentation of him differs stylistically to some considerable degree from, for example, the presentation of Olivier in *Le Fils*. *The Kid with a Bike*, with its different stylistic properties – smoother camerawork, less reliance on close-ups, more conventionally coherent presentation of diegetic space – does not align itself as closely with Cyril's physical presence as *Le Fils* does with Olivier's. Furthermore, although Cyril is in the film throughout, he is not in every scene: there are two intriguing absences. The first comes in the sequence in which he and Samantha first find his father, Guy: there is a moment in which Guy asks to speak with Samantha alone, instructs Cyril to wait at the bottom of the stairs, and then takes Samantha up the stairs to a room and closes two doors between them and Cyril, so that the boy will not hear what Guy has to say (namely, that he cannot handle having Cyril in his life). The second time in which Cyril is not in a scene is slightly different. It comes very near the end of the film: Cyril has been chased by a teenage boy (Valentin Jacob) whom he had hurt in the botched robbery attempt; Cyril climbs a tree to escape, and the boy flings stones at him. One stone strikes Cyril, and he falls out of the tree to the ground. He lies motionless; the teenager worries that he is dead, and runs to his father (Fabrizio Rongione) for help. During these moments, Cyril is unconscious on the ground. While father and son debate what to do, Cyril begins to stir: he picks himself up, rubs his head, refuses their offer of help, and walks away. Technically, he is in the scene throughout, but as he was knocked out when he hit the ground, he could not have been party to the debate between father and son. And so *The Kid with a Bike* intriguingly deviates from its focus on Cyril in these two moments.

That said, these moments are nevertheless readable as being about Cyril, in that the characters' conversations relate directly to what they are going to do with regard to Cyril. In this respect, *The Kid with a Bike* features a second principal character – Samantha. It is Samantha's kindly patronage of Cyril that begins to make a difference in his life, as he finally has an adult from outside the confines of the children's home wanting to look after him. I believe that Samantha's function as a character in this film serves as a touchstone for the viewer, an almost hypothetical 'goodness', a *stylised* goodness that infuses the naturalism of the presentation of the fictional world and nourishes Cyril in the face of the opposing forces in that world. I consider this goodness to be Levinasian in the way in which it is introduced into and then sustains the narrative.

Levinas says that '[t]he passivity of the "for-another" expresses a sense in it in which no reference, positive or negative, to a prior will enters'.[14] In *The Kid with a Bike*, Samantha arrives as, before anything else, a force of good who exists 'for' Cyril. For example, the scene in which we first meet Samantha works as a moment in which the character is 'founded' by

THE KID WITH A BIKE AND THE REFRAMING OF ETHICS 77

coming into contact with an Other. We have not seen her in the film until she comes into contact with Cyril – or, more precisely, until he comes into contact with her, when he runs right into her in the doctor's waiting room, knocking her off her chair, and then grabs onto her and refuses to let go (Figure 3.2). From that moment of contact, Samantha, whom we can read as having been waiting there, passively 'for-another', is hooked into Cyril's plight, and soon after this, she has found his missing bike for him and agreed to his staying with her at weekends. Her reasons for this generosity are not made clear. Luc Dardenne has said how some of the people who read the screenplay have asked about Samantha's motivation in looking after Cyril. His view is,

> There is no answer (certainly not the fashionable psychological response: she has lost a child in the past or she cannot have a child) and that's precisely how the film works: to prevent the formulation of an answer that would relieve the spectator of this question: 'Why does she accept this child?' . . . In delivering the spectator to Samantha's mysterious behaviour, we hope to drive him to what he will accept for himself, like for Samantha, that there is no other motivation than to have been faced with Cyril's suffering.[15]

Luc Dardenne's hope that the film 'drive [the spectator] to what he will accept for himself' suggests the effect they want their film to have on viewers.

I should like to suggest how the film aims for this effect: before Samantha comes into contact with Cyril, *she does not exist*. What I am drawing on is our awareness that Samantha is a film character and not a real person. In introducing Samantha into the film at the exact moment that Cyril knocks

Figure 3.2 Cyril clings to Samantha in the doctor's surgery.

her off her chair and holds onto her tightly, the Dardennes create, for the viewer, the possibility of seeing Samantha as first and foremost linked with the boy. After that scene, the next time we see her is when she comes to the children's home to visit Cyril and return his bike to him. That visit ends with Cyril asking her if he can stay with her at weekends and her agreement, seemingly without hesitation, to speak to the director of the children's home. Her subsequent goodness towards Cyril – allowing him to stay with her at weekends, enduring his angry temperament, helping him to see good things in the world, and even sacrificing her relationship with her boyfriend in order to take care of the boy – characterises her, in this film, as wholly decent. And the casting of Cécile de France in the role enhances this effect. De France has a naturally warm, benevolent presence; Jean-Pierre Dardenne has explained how '[f]ilming a character who has someone else's best interests at heart hasn't often happened to us. Shooting in the summer helped us give the film a certain brightness and softness. And Cécile de France conveys these qualities naturally.'[16] And Luc Dardenne has noted, 'We never write with a specific actor in mind. As soon as we finished the screenplay we started to think about actresses and about Cécile first. With her we knew we'd avoid all psychology . . . that her body and her face were enough.'[17] The effect of this is that the presence of de France combined with the film's structurally effective use of her character conveys a precise sense of Samantha's goodness.

One scene in particular demonstrates this. After Cyril has been out late into the evening with young neighbourhood tough guy Wes (Egon Di Mateo), without letting Samantha know where he is, she and her boyfriend Gilles (Laurent Caron) eventually track him down. On the drive home, Gilles berates Cyril for having hung up when Samantha called. He does not believe Cyril's excuse and calls him a liar, to which Cyril replies, 'Liar yourself!' Gilles demands that Cyril apologise, and says that Cyril will otherwise not be allowed to live with Samantha anymore. Samantha asks Gilles not to say that, and when Gilles repeats his demand, she says he has no right to say it. Gilles says, 'It's him or me', thus demanding that Samantha make a choice between them. Samantha says, 'It's him', and Gilles gets out of the car and walks off. The moment is remarkable for the way in which Samantha delivers her answer to Gilles. It is almost a reflex action. She says it without changing her expression – she hesitates slightly, but her unchanging expression and her simple enunciation of the words 'C'est lui' ('It's him') articulate her feeling that Cyril simply needs looking after. As with Olivier in *Le Fils*, it is almost as if there is no choice for Samantha – this is not about her, it is about the kid. It is notable that we will never see Gilles again in the film: one might expect that Samantha would have lingering feelings for him, but in this film they would only divert attention from the point of her character's inclusion, which is her devotion to Cyril.

Thus, in *The Kid with a Bike* there are two approaches to narrative and character, and they run concurrently. The first approach is observational – the Dardennes, with their camera often set at a fair distance from the characters and the action, and with their deployment of edits within scenes and (occasional) extra-diegetic music, offer a film in which the style 'observes' the events without 'intruding' on them as they unfold or purporting to enact the feelings of Cyril within the frame. Rather, Cyril is there to be observed, commented upon – he is a kid, and is offered up for the fascination of the viewer: what will this kid do, and what will happen to him? But with the addition of Samantha, the film takes on more overtly performative elements: Samantha is *a device*, and is being used in illocutionary ways to invite the viewer's ethical engagement with her sacrifice.

Accordingly, we can consider the style of *The Kid with a Bike* to be both more conventional (noting, of course, as we know, that conventionality is itself a product of performativity) than that of the earlier cycle and nevertheless performative in how it brings into being a depiction of unwavering goodness – Samantha's – when brought into contact with an Other – Cyril – who has presented a demand. What this means for viewers is that, rather than being invited into an experience of proximity to one character, there is an invitation to engage with two characters – Cyril, redolent of the child protagonists of such Italian neorealist dramas as *Sciuscià* (*Shoeshine*, dir. Vittorio De Sica, 1946) and *Ladri di biciclette* (*Bicycle Thieves*, dir. Vittorio De Sica, 1948), and Samantha, who is ready to sacrifice herself for the boy, to perform the-one-for-the-other, the Levinasian movement towards substitution and sacrifice – responsibility for an Other. This double focus on Cyril and Samantha is a new challenge in the Dardennes' filmography, a newly demanding way to invite the viewer into an engagement with the enormity of Levinasian responsibility. It is this sense of greater demands that I shall now examine.

Greater Demands on the Viewer

Much has been made in discussions of the Dardennes' films of the stylistic aspects that are perhaps unexpected – the lack of overt exposition, the narrative ellipses, the details that are kept outside the frame, the absence of consoling, easily readable, conventional filmic elements – and how these unexpected aspects can encourage attentiveness. The implication is that the demands placed on the viewer are higher than for a film in a more mainstream style (whether it be a classical or post-classical Hollywood style or even a more evidently 'arty' aesthetic), for which the viewer can afford to sit back and receive everything the film provides – which is, so the implication goes, everything the viewer needs in order to understand the film. In contrast, films such as *La Promesse* and *Le Fils* are more demanding, and, therefore, potentially more rewarding.

But I believe that, in one sense, the style of *The Kid with a Bike* places an even greater emphasis on the viewer's attentiveness than did those earlier films: the style is less overtly aligned with a sole protagonist than before and therefore is not as easily read as performing a Levinasian ethics. If we consider *La Promesse* and *Le Fils* as being constructed for audiences to experience what Igor and Olivier, respectively, are going through, so as to recognise how they respond to the Other's ethical demand, then that constructedness – so cleverly thought through, and so demanding of its audience – is also, by dint of its being so constructed, doing a lot of the work for the viewer. If we are receptive to the films, we are held in the grip of their powerfully performative styles; in one sense, we do not really have to do much more than turn up and watch and listen to the films. All those facets of the style that make it strangely lacking in overt manipulation are, in another sense, evidence of *covert* manipulation. For example, we could consider the absence of music in the films to be as powerful an effect – even if subliminally registered – as the most emotive Hollywood film score by, for example, Max Steiner or John Williams. The handheld camerawork arrests attention, and we could say that it virtually takes the viewer by the scruff of the neck, demanding that they look left, right, wherever the camera wants them to. The lack of editing within scenes, while a gesture towards avoidance of dogma, and the near-absence of subplots, while evading many of the trappings of clichéd storytelling, are also signs of a type of single-mindedness, a tunnel vision that the films engender. In the face of this effective manipulation, the viewer is both an active participant and a passive receptor – and Levinas says that '[o]utside of any mysticism, in this respiration, the possibility of every sacrifice for the other, activity and passivity coincide'.[18] In a sense, *La Promesse* and, especially, *Le Fils* gave the viewer everything they needed for the ethical engagement in question. Films such as *The Silence of Lorna* and *The Kid with a Bike*, however, reward something different. We might say that, being less urgent in their styles, they are more dependent than *La Promesse* or *Le Fils* on the viewer's willingness to keep watching. The Dardennes' narrative manoeuvres – ellipses, withholding exposition, obscuring motivation – are more unusual when allied to films that have more sedate styles. The more sedate style gives us more time to contemplate the events in the film. If we say that, on a first viewing, *La Promesse*, *Rosetta*, *Le Fils* and *L'Enfant* are so compelling that we view first and think later – as per Frampton's point, which we have seen, that 'we should feel meanings directly without undue reflection (until the film is over)' – then the likes of *The Silence of Lorna* and *The Kid with a Bike* are not as overtly gripping in their performances of their themes of ethics – which is perhaps why, in ethical terms, the viewing experience is more demanding.

This chimes with Rushton's reading of the Dardennes' films. Drawing on work on the Dardennes by a number of scholars, Rushton considers various notions of 'doubling' in the Dardennes' films, and in particular the conjunction of realism and modernism:

> [R]ealism gives us detail, while modernism delivers a certain abstraction. At the level of narrative, realism gives us something that seems realistic – the handheld camera, its shakiness that appears to place us 'on the scene of reality', the chronicling of the details of everyday life and the struggle to stay alive – while the generic elements also make the narrative mannered, as though we were being exposed to morality tales or fables rather than to realist narratives.[19]

For Rushton, these supposedly contradictory stylistic approaches work together fruitfully to create an 'imaginative act . . . that is, not *being* in someone else's shoes, but imagining what it *might be like*; to try to think what another person is thinking, to feel what another is feeling'.[20] This sense of an 'imaginative act' suggests a conscious engagement with the film's processes rather than simply an unconscious experience. Similarly, O'Shaughnessy considers that the films prompt 'an engaged yet resistant spectatorship, one that refuses to see from an objectifying distance but one that also avoids emotional or political absorption into that which is shown'.[21] With regard to Rushton's and O'Shaughnessy's views, it is my contention that in the Dardennes' most recent work, the onus is on the viewer more than was the case before, because the performative energy of the films does not overpower the viewer to the extent that it did in the earlier cycle. A film such as *The Kid with a Bike* offers easy pleasures – but it also invites us in its own way to experience Levinasian responsibility for the Other, partly through its performative creation of a character who did not exist prior to her goodness and partly through its benign challenge to us not to rely on the film's own performative force but to work harder to recognise the film's aims and achievements.

Through the stylistic shifts we have considered in *The Kid with a Bike* and other recent Dardenne films, we can see how the filmmakers have reframed their film style and how we can read this in terms of an evolving approach to ethics and film. Whereas in earlier films such as *La Promesse* and *Le Fils* the style is relentlessly focused on a protagonist's struggle to be ethical and involves abundant use of close-ups and fast movement so as to convey the character's motivations largely through physical action, more recent Dardenne films have exhibited a somewhat less frantic style, as well as deploying a number of more conventional cinematic tropes such as establishing shots, soundtrack music, and a focus on a larger number of characters. The result is a literal and figurative reframing, but not a reduction in ethical concerns. Rather, the Dardennes' style has evolved to emphasise narrative structure, décor, and dialogue. In some ways, this makes their newer films feel more overtly constructed; in other ways, it makes them feel more naturalistic, the camera observing the characters' interactions rather than participating as closely as it did before. This more conventionally classical use of film style is close to Butler's notion of 'resignification', the reusing of terms for new socio-political ends. The Dardennes use style to explore their Levinasian concerns in ever new ways, deploying classical cinematic tools so as to 'resignify' them as ethical in relation to the films' fictional worlds. The resignification of filmic tropes brilliantly enables the Dardennes to maintain the 'shock' of Levinas's ethics.

PART II

Barbet Schroeder: Devoted to the Other

Part II Introduction

The link between the work of the director Barbet Schroeder and Levinas's ethics is perhaps not immediately apparent. Unlike the Dardennes, Schroeder has disclosed no explicit debt to Levinas's philosophy, and so there is not an obvious invitation to consider Schroeder's films in Levinasian terms. Furthermore, while we have seen how the Dardennes, from *La Promesse* onwards, use a style in their films that is relatively consistent from film to film – even as it maintains a freshness and non-fixity through subtle modifications to that style – in Schroeder's work there is no instantly recognisable style. His films are therefore harder to discuss as a unified body of work – it is difficult to say what 'a Barbet Schroeder film' might be. Nevertheless, I believe that there is much to say about Schroeder's films in terms of both Levinasian ethics and performativity – and that it is important to articulate it.

Such a discussion is important partly because it enables appreciation of Levinas and film to be expanded, so as to take in films in which the Levinasian dimension is less immediately apparent, and thus in which the force of the films in ethical terms is easier to miss. This has value from the perspective of the performative, for if performativity theory helps us see how all films are connected to the societies in which they exist, it is important to allow that films can have ethical power that is *not* immediately apparent, given that it is just as present as the more obvious examples. Schroeder's work, in contrast to that of the Dardennes, cannot be said to be explicitly Levinasian in its approach but it can be said to have qualities that produce Levinasian ethical effects.

My discussion of Schroeder's work is also important because his films have received surprisingly little scholarly attention across the half-century of his career. A Schroeder retrospective held in the north-eastern Parisian suburb of Bobigny in 2012 produced a substantial catalogue that collected together a range of French-language articles and pieces about his films, and 2017 saw the publication of a monograph on the filmmaker by

Jérôme d'Estais[1] – the same year that another retrospective on Schroeder's work was held, at the Pompidou Centre in Paris – but there is very little English-language criticism on Schroeder and his films. One likely reason for this is that his body of work does not offer itself up to straightforward digestion or interpretation. David Thomson has said that 'Schroeder has the air of a stranger who is always at ease',[2] and this touches on the issue in question: one could say that, more than many directors, Schroeder has a very diverse background, international but without a clear identity, and that this has made it difficult for writers to assess his work. Schroeder was born in Tehran, Iran, in 1941, to a Swiss father and a German mother. He spent much of his childhood in Colombia, coming to live in France at the age of eleven. In his early twenties, he formed a production company, Les Films du Losange, with filmmaker Éric Rohmer and began producing films, principally some of Rohmer's early works. Schroeder added acting to his producing efforts, appearing in Rohmer's *La Boulangère de Monceau* (*The Bakery Girl of Monceau*, a.k.a. *The Girl at the Monceau Bakery*, 1963), the Jean Rouch segment 'Gare du Nord' of the anthology film *Paris vu par...* (dirs Claude Chabrol, Jean Douchet, Jean-Luc Godard, Jean-Daniel Pollet, Éric Rohmer, and Jean Rouch, 1965) and Jacques Rivette's *Out 1* (1971) and *Céline et Julie vont en bateau* (*Céline and Julie Go Boating*, 1974). Schroeder's first feature film as a director was *More* (1969), a drama about drug addiction set largely on Ibiza, since which he has directed many other feature films. These range from French-language dramas set in Papua New Guinea (*La Vallée* [*The Valley (Obscured by Clouds)*, 1972]), Paris (*Maîtresse*) and Portugal (*Tricheurs* [1984]) to American dramas (*Barfly* [1987], *Reversal of Fortune*, *Before and After* [1996]), Hollywood thrillers (*Single White Female* [1992], *Kiss of Death* [1995], *Desperate Measures* [1998], *Murder by Numbers* [2002]), documentaries from Uganda, the US, Europe and the Middle East, and Myanmar (respectively, *Général Idi Amin Dada: autoportrait* [*General Idi Amin Dada: A Self Portrait*, 1974], *Koko, le gorille qui parle* [*Koko: A Talking Gorilla*, 1978], *The Charles Bukowski Tapes* [1987], *Terror's Advocate*, *Le Vénérable W.* (*The Venerable W.*, 2017), the French-produced, Colombian-shot, Spanish-language *Our Lady of the Assassins*, a multilanguage Japanese thriller, *Inju, la bête dans l'ombre* (*Inju: The Beast in the Shadow*, 2008), and a return to the island of Ibiza that featured in *More* for a story of German identity and regret, the drama *Amnesia* (2015). These, along with a handful of shorts and even an episode of the hit US television series *Mad Men* (Season 3, Episode 12: 'The Grown-Ups' [2009]), suggest how it is not immediately possible to see what, if anything, ties his directorial work together, either thematically or stylistically.

Published quotations from Schroeder himself suggest further why he has not been the subject of much attention, academic or otherwise: he has a desire to efface his own identity as a director so that the subject matter of his films can come through unhindered. Schroeder has said, for example: 'My film career doesn't have an orientation, a single direction. I like to change with each film, to take a path that is absolutely different from that which preceded it. My objective is to surprise. I don't like being labelled.'[3] The above quotation from Schroeder is consistent with pronouncements he has made in various interviews over the years on his approach to film-making, and it raises the question of how – or even if – one can discuss his work without damaging the very spirit in which he approaches it and, by implication, would like it to be received. I believe that, when the subject matter of each film is considered alongside the sheer number of stylistic approaches across his work, this can lead us to view his films collectively as demonstrating a consistently flexible openness to alterity. D'Estais asserts as much when he makes the following poetically abrupt claim about Schroeder's work: 'Leave what one knows so as to go towards the unknown ... Always change. Country, style, genre. Start again at zero.'[4] The lack of an immediately recognisable directorial style therefore opens this filmmaker's body of work to a Levinasian interpretation, as the stylistically unassuming becomes the filmically ethical.

Furthermore, the absence of a consistent and readily identifiable directorial signature in Schroeder's work raises productive questions about what it might mean to think of Schroeder himself as a Levinasian figure devoted to the alterity of the Other. This is something I am reading as an aspect of the Levinasian in his work: the idea of Schroeder himself practising Levinasian responsibility through his selfless devotion to the lives of his characters. Levinas talks about how the giving of oneself to the Other, in substitution for the Other, divests the self of identity: 'The passivity of the exposure responds to an assignation that identifies me as the unique one, not by reducing me to myself, but by stripping me of every identical quiddity, and thus of all form, all investiture, which would still slip into the assignation.'[5] For Levinas, to be ethical is to be turned away from oneself, and I posit the notion that we can see a similar process at work in Schroeder's approach to his career. In the following readings, I shall reconfigure the varied styles of the films in terms constitutive of an exceptionally open and accepting attitude towards the sexually and/or socially marginalised lives of his protagonists.

I have elected to discuss four films in detail: *Maîtresse*, *Reversal of Fortune*, *Terror's Advocate* and *Our Lady of the Assassins*. In *Maîtresse*, Schroeder enters the world of a particular couple – a young drifter and a dominatrix – and does so by way of a film style that is both relaxed and alert to the possibilities inherent in this encounter between two individuals. My discussion of *Maîtresse* therefore serves as an introduction to the way in which I am reading Schroeder's self-effacing style as Levinasian. *Reversal of Fortune* is one of the most richly layered of Schroeder's films, in both its story structure and its filmmaking style, and I argue that these aesthetic components are a perfect match for its subject, the complex legal case surrounding the von Bülow affair. I have also chosen to discuss *Terror's Advocate*, for two main reasons: first, thematically it concentrates on a figure – the lawyer Jacques Vergès – who can himself be fruitfully discussed in terms of Levinasian ethics, and, second, stylistically it raises relevant questions regarding the performativity of its documentary form. And my reading of *Our Lady of the Assassins* turns on how its application of classical film style and modern technology to the story of a homosexual love affair can be read as constituting an enactment of a Levinasian pre-originary goodness. The pre-originary self is that which exists anterior to the formation of the ego: it is the goodness of the foundational ethical encounter with the Other, and it relates to why Levinas claims ethics as first philosophy.

We have seen in the Dardennes' work that style can be deployed so as to support the ethical issues of a story such that style and content become inseparable – for example, that the way in which the films are lit, filmed and edited is so crucial that to change any of those stylistic decisions would be to change the 'content' of the stories. Although Schroeder is, by contrast, deploying a range of styles in his films, in each case the achievement is readable in terms similar to those in which I read the films of the Dardennes: we will see in Schroeder's work a desire to strip away many of the standard or predictable tropes of film narrative through directorial decisions that show a disinclination to make judgements on characters or to assist the viewer in doing so. Thus, we can discuss his films, just as much as those of the Dardennes, in performative terms to reveal Levinasian ethics through film.

CHAPTER 4

Maîtresse: Direction without Domination

Maîtresse, Schroeder's fourth feature film as a director, dates from 1975, and it is important to my discussion of Levinas and performativity in this film to begin by considering the film as a product of the era in which it was released, partly because it helps to contextualise the permissiveness of the film's images but also because central to my reading of *Maîtresse* is the way it treats its potentially sensational subject matter.

There have always been films that push at the boundaries of acceptability, not just in terms of their themes and ideas but also in terms of what they show on-screen. The 1960s and the first half of the 1970s were one of the most significant periods in this regard. A combination of events – among them the breaking down, in Hollywood, of the studio system and the dismantling of the antiquated Production Code, the rise of the young American 'Movie Brat' directors as well as the 'New Waves' in France, Japan, Czechoslovakia and other countries, and the individual artistic efforts of a range of international filmmakers whose works were beginning to achieve wider distribution[1] – resulted in a succession of groundbreaking films that presented sex, violence, sexual violence, drug use and strong language with a new and bracing frankness.[2] The story in *Maîtresse* of the love affair between a drifter and a dominatrix was not, in itself, controversial, but the level of detail shown with regard to the dominatrix's practices would have been unimaginable on-screen only a few years earlier. Consequently, the film's release created some controversy. In an interview in 2011, Bulle Ogier, who plays Ariane, the dominatrix who is the Maîtresse of the title, recalls that 'Gérard [Depardieu, her co-star in the film] had said: "It's important that we get out our waterproofs and our umbrellas as we are truly going to receive a deluge." And that proved to be the case. People were very shocked . . .'[3] Each of Schroeder's first three films had dealt with a form of 'extremity': drug addiction in *More*, a search into territory 'off the map' in *La Vallée* and a disarming but unflinching look at the Ugandan dictator Idi Amin in the documentary *General*

Idi Amin Dada. Jean-Louis Bory, writing not long after the initial French release of *Maîtresse*, notes elements of continuity between the films but also suggests that Schroeder's work goes beyond the obvious:

> As with *La Vallée*, as with *Général Idi Amin Dada*, *Maîtresse* recapitulates *More*. A gallery of monsters? A descent into hell? On the surface, yes, for those who are content with surfaces. This is not the case with Schroeder. He persists in burrowing under the surface to dig up the human roots.[4]

By the time of *Maîtresse*, therefore, one would be able to say of Schroeder's work that it is unafraid of 'shocking' subjects and dedicated to depicting those subjects in their truthful details. *Maîtresse*, written by Schroeder and Paul Voujargol, presents a world of BDSM and does not avoid the most extreme examples of this pleasure-in-pain. The film includes explicit imagery of practices such as a man having his anus and testicles prodded with knitting needles, a woman having her genitalia probed with a belt and then being whipped on her buttocks until red welts appear, and a man having his penis nailed to a block of wood and then having his nipples pierced with pins. And yet what is particularly striking about *Maîtresse* is that, alongside the above episodes, the film manages to reveal itself to be interested in mundane, everyday details; for example, Patricia MacCormack notes that it is 'a very domestic, very almost naïve, subtle little film about two people who are quite unsure of each other because they have different sexual politics'.[5] *Maîtresse* is therefore a prime example of a film that plays very differently in practice from how it initially sounds.

Into the Den of the *Maîtresse*

The opening sequence of *Maîtresse* and the sequences immediately following it establish the style of the film and therefore the terms in which it will be telling its story. The film begins with a shot outside a train carriage window, looking through it to a sleeping man (Olivier, played by Depardieu) as the credits begin. A hand on our side taps on the window – a guard is shouting 'Austerlitz', the name of a railway terminus on Paris's Left Bank – and Olivier wakes up. In the next shot, he exits the train and gets on a motorbike. As he rides off from the train station and along the street, the camera is filming him from in front, and as the shot continues the camera frames him riding along as the credits continue. As the credits come to an end, so does Olivier's ride: he parks the bike by the pavement, and the shot widens slightly to accommodate him and the setting he is arriving at – a Parisian street. The shot continues as he walks along the pavement, enters a bar and finds his contact, Mario (André Rouyer); he joins him and the two of them chat.

What is notable about the entire three-minute, single-take moving shot of Olivier from the station to the bar is how unnotable it is. The shot gives us very little information – Olivier is on a bike; it is Paris he is riding through; Mario is a friend or an acquaintance. We have time to read the credits without being too distracted. And the mechanics of the shot are nothing spectacular or exceptional – this is not a lengthy shot notable for its evident cleverness or complexity, such as the Dunkirk beach scene in *Atonement* (dir. Joe Wright, 2007) or the sweeping forward momentum of the arrival of Henry and Karen at the Copacabana in *GoodFellas* (dir. Martin Scorsese, 1990). Schroeder's shot in *Maîtresse* is conceived simply and executed straightforwardly. And yet this shot sets the tone for Schroeder's style throughout the film. The shot is subtly training us not to look to camera movement, framing or editing to be particularly pointed or telling in this film. This is not to say that those things do not matter in *Maîtresse* – their selection is a vital aspect of the film's performative presentation of its world – but it is part of the film's significance that they should not hit us directly. Olivier moves at a steady but unhurried pace, and concomitantly the shot unfolds without recourse to the shaping tools of edits, emphatic camera movement or pronounced framing. The shot also suggests to us, through its natural lighting and straightforward texture, that this is a film in which the image is not going to be worked especially pointedly. (Schroeder's Paris in *Maîtresse*, shot with a team headed by renowned cinematographer Néstor Almendros, will be presented with none of the gliding movements and sensual lighting of Bertolucci and *his* renowned cinematographer Vittorio Storaro's camera in *Last Tango in Paris*, for example.) With nothing obviously eye-catching, therefore, the shot discourages judgement, opinion, and even, perhaps, conventional enjoyment.

The film is therefore proceeding with a dual sense of observation and evocation in respect of Olivier. This has something in common with how the Dardennes film their protagonists: the camera both observes the action and conditions it through its own movements. We may feel that *Maîtresse* is not as closely aligned with its protagonist as, for example, *La Promesse* and *Le Fils* are with theirs, or that the alignment is similar but that what it is evoking is simply different: Olivier's situation in *Maîtresse*, at least in these early stages of the film, affords him a relaxed air; he has not yet become entangled in the sorts of stressful encounters that Igor in *La Promesse* and Olivier in *Le Fils* are experiencing early in those films. Nevertheless, Olivier in *Maîtresse* is just as present and yet as unknowable to us at this early point in Schroeder's film: in all three cases, we are denied an easy context for why these characters are doing what they are doing. This lack of context puts us in a position akin to what Levinas calls the 'anarchy of responsibility'.[6] Denied straightforward exposition or explanation, we are discouraged from deciding how we feel about the person and actions we are seeing. Olivier is, at this early stage of the film, our protagonist – but he is also an Other to us, unknowable and yet present before us. And it is the very plainness of Schroeder's storytelling here that has initiated my reading of the film. Thus, style does not just depict the film's fictional world; it performs it, by dint of conditioning our view of it so comprehensively. The style that Schroeder has chosen to deploy prompts us to regard the film's fictional world in a somewhat detached way that will avoid easy judgements. As we saw in Chapter 3, Pippin has said of the Dardennes that 'each of their films, whatever else it is about, is about itself; each film is a kind of allegory of film, instructing us about what cinematic representability is'.[7] We may say that Schroeder's style in *Maîtresse* is similarly 'about itself', 'instructing us' in how to watch the film.

This stylistic strategy continues into the next scenes, which take Olivier into unexpected territory. Olivier has arrived in Paris with a job lined up as a gardener, but not starting until September, in several weeks' time. He therefore has the quality of a drifter, a casual labourer who has arrived in the big city with nothing immediate to do. His friend Mario sells books door to door but is also something of a petty thief. He takes Olivier with him on his rounds, and after the two of them startle a resident (Ariane, played by Ogier) whose bath is overflowing, they break into the apartment below, thinking it empty. As they begin to search the apartment in the darkness, we are primarily with Olivier, whose torch picks out some bizarre details, such as a tray of torture implements, a hangman's noose, and a man tied up in a cage. As the men prepare to leave, certain that they have stumbled upon something they have not bargained for, the lights come on and some metal steps descend from the ceiling. Ariane comes down, now dressed very differently and accompanied by a ferocious-looking Dobermann called Texas. Ariane handcuffs Olivier and Mario to a radiator. She then frees Olivier, requiring him to assist her in her trick: she asks him to urinate into the face of a client waiting for her in her den.

It may be, then, that we are now into something we had not bargained for either. It may be, too, that the opening of *Maîtresse* has been designed to mislead us, the plainness of the opening scenes contrasting with the darker space of the den that has been awaiting discovery. We might think, for comparison, of *Ôdishon* (*Audition*, dir. Takashi Miike, 1999), in which the plainness and gently wry sobriety of the first half give way to the Grand Guignol gorefest of the film's unforgettable final act. But it is worth noting that during the break-in sequence in *Maîtresse* the only source of light as we follow Olivier around the otherwise dark rooms under Ariane's apartment comes from Olivier's torch. This means that when he sees the items in the den, the dramatic lighting is provided not 'by the film' but by Olivier himself, such as in the moment when he is holding the torch beneath his face, shining it on the noose and casting his face in a ghostly, haunting – or haunted – light (Figure 4.1).[8] As such, Olivier is the only obvious source of interpretation, a kind of Levinasian self reacting to the unfamiliar world of the Other (while remaining an Other to us himself). Thus, the sequence, along with the opening scenes, draws us in without the film itself offering overt judgements.

Nevertheless, it would be wrong to claim that the film is without design or precision. We can look, for example, to the scene on the stairs outside Ariane's apartment following the break-in. The strange episode has left Mario clearly feeling they have had a lucky escape, while Olivier, who is beginning to feel interested in Ariane and has surreptitiously asked her to join him for dinner, wants to get rid of his accomplice so that he can wait for Ariane. Mario does not take the hint, and Olivier gives him money to get him to leave. Mario trundles off down the stairs, and Olivier sits down on a step. The camera frames him with the stairs continuing downwards on one side and upwards on the other. As Olivier looks first downwards and then up (Figure 4.2), he is poised between the worlds of the familiar (the downward look after the departing Mario) and the unfamiliar (the look up towards the off-screen Ariane's apartment). The significance of this is

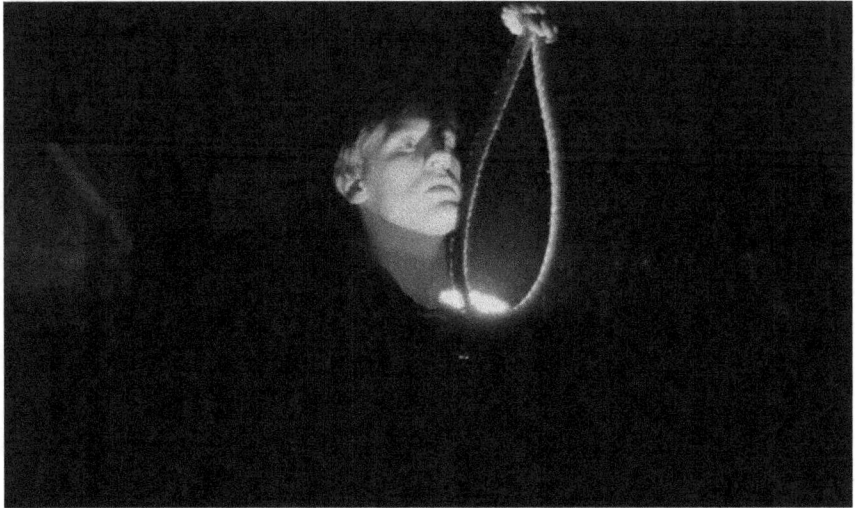

Figure 4.1 Olivier discovers the noose in Ariane's den.

Figure 4.2 Olivier looks down in the direction of Mario's departure ... and looks up towards Ariane's apartment.

clear – Olivier has a choice to make – but crucially, the moment's lack of emphasis is in itself significant: the options for Olivier are offered neutrally, partly through the simple camera angle and partly through Depardieu's relative lack of facial expression, and if the film risks disinterest in its efforts to present the Ariane option as unexcitingly as possible, it thereby avoids making Ariane out to be any more strange than Mario or Olivier. It is training us in how it wants us to regard Ariane and her unfamiliar world.

Olivier, Ariane and the Film: A Levinasian Triangulation

With the first den sequence having introduced us to Ariane, we find in the ensuing scenes that she is the film's second major character and that she is in many ways the controlling force, the director, in the situation between her and Olivier. The film's two most-used settings – the apartment and the den beneath it – are hers, and it is largely her actions that guide us around them. Russell Campbell has noted of the film that

> what drives the drama is the [female] protagonist's insistence on her personal agency ('I am a whore, I like it, I chose it, it's my life, do you understand?') and the pleasure that she takes in fulfilling her clients' perverted fantasies ('It's wonderful to be able to enter people's madness in such an intimate way').[9]

Accordingly, as *Maîtresse* develops its story, Ariane becomes a figure equal to Olivier. When we first meet Olivier, the film is presenting him not just as the protagonist but as the audience surrogate – most notably in his entering of, and reacting to, the unfamiliarity of Ariane's den. At the same time, the film does not offer or encourage much closeness to Olivier: we find out very little about him beyond what we can read in his face and his physical form from the perspective of the film's medium shots. As for Ariane, even though her entry down the stairs to the den is perhaps a shock, we also realise that Olivier and Mario have broken into what is *her* apartment; as such, it quickly becomes clear that her space has been violated. Therefore, while Olivier has been our guide into Ariane's world, even in these early scenes we can make a distinction, as I have suggested, between Olivier's perspective and that of the film. And as *Maîtresse* progresses it becomes clearer how much the film has an independent viewpoint encompassing the strangeness and the familiarity of both Ariane *and* Olivier. Crano, writing about the Dardennes, has noted a triangulated structure provided by the camera and the characters in front of it: 'Rather than cut back and forth between two speaking subjects, the Dardennes' camera – always already there – affectively triangulates a given scene and, along the way, reveals a spatial alterity *between* those subjects concealed by the classical shot-reverse shot form.'[10] Although *Maîtresse* does sometimes cut back and forth between Olivier and Ariane, the preponderance of shots framing them together, along with the general triangulating addition of the camera's presence, brings to mind Levinas's introduction, in *Totality and Infinity*, of the third party into the self–Other relationship. Levinas describes the third party as 'the whole of humanity which looks at us',[11] and it is through this third party that the self has access to the multitude of others beyond the Other that has immediately captured the self's attention. For Peperzak, the third party represents the Other because it represents all those others whom I cannot possibly hope to know personally, whose names I cannot know, but for whom I am nevertheless responsible:

> The third is one who, *with* and already *in* the primary Other, concerns me *like* the Other. The fact that I cannot get to know everyone and that most other people stay nameless for me cannot degrade them into a secondary species of human beings . . . All concern and obligate me, for exactly the same reasons as does this Other whose face and words reach me here and now.[12]

Factoring Levinas's third party into an analysis of film heightens the sense of the triangulation of viewer and characters. The question then is which sides of the triangle are represented by whom/what. If the image provided by the camera initiates the presence of the viewer as third party, it heightens the sense of the ethics contained within the drama, the subject's treatment of the Other placed under extra ethical scrutiny by the viewer's observing position. But if the camera's provision of the image enables the film to appeal, as Other, to the viewer, the viewer is then unable to escape the ethical demand, and the viewer's response is placed under ethical scrutiny by the presence of not one fictional character but two or more characters. Thus, in *Maîtresse* the slow incorporation of Olivier into Ariane's plane – as he goes from being an 'innocent' self to being a willing participant, and even at times a threat, within Ariane's world – places the responsibility back on the viewer, the self caught in the presence of both Olivier and Ariane and obligated to both of them.

An illustration of this comes in the sequence in which Olivier and Ariane take a car drive out of the city for the day. The sequence begins at the parked car in the Parisian street outside Ariane's apartment: there is a brief humorous tussle between them over who will drive (an expression, perhaps, of the confusion over who is 'driving' the film's narrative), and then Ariane lets Olivier take the driver's seat. Next, Olivier and Ariane are at an outdoor restaurant, and here we find out that Ariane has a son. In contrast to earlier moments in which Ariane has put up an inscrutable front to Olivier – such as when she says to him, 'Questions are wasted on me. Either I lie or I don't answer' – here the two of them are getting to know each other, and their relationship begins to be established on a more even footing. An effect of this is that Olivier is no longer the surrogate self for the viewer; instead, Olivier and Ariane become 'The Other and the Others' (to borrow the title of a section in *Totality and Infinity* in which Levinas discusses the third party).[13] As if to instil this in us, there follows a moment that initially feels unremarkable but that, on closer inspection, speaks volumes about the film's presentation of its characters. Back in the car after lunch, Ariane sits in the driver's seat and exclaims to Olivier, 'I'm in control!' She then explains how there is a friend of hers who lives nearby, and asks Olivier if he would like to visit. Olivier is not especially enthusiastic; we sense that he wants her all to himself. But Ariane quietly persists, saying that the friend is expecting her. Olivier realises Ariane has organised the trip to enable them to visit her friend. He is not pleased. But there is nothing he can do about it – Ariane has taken the wheel. She starts up the engine, and just before the car begins to move, the film cuts to the driveway of her friend's house as she and Olivier drive in.

It is the cut, with its elision of the journey from the woods to Ariane's friend's house, that is of particular significance here. By cutting as soon as the car's engine starts, the film conveys a strong sense of Olivier's displeasure at having been conned into the visit to Ariane's friend: the elision of the journey by the cut suggests how far Olivier's thoughts are eaten up with annoyance. In this respect, the film's style performs a kind of sympathy with Olivier. But the cut is *also* a performance of Ariane's domination over Olivier – namely, that no sooner has she started the car than they are arriving at her friend's house, almost as if she has snapped her fingers and they are there. This cut is therefore a moment in which the film is performatively enabling of a developing engagement with *both* characters. The initial concentration on Olivier as he led us into the strange world of the Maîtresse has been superseded by his sharing the narrative with Ariane. Because of this, there is a *third* level of performativity in this moment: a performativity in respect of 'the couple'. The cut therefore offers a triangulation between the viewer, Olivier and Ariane such that Ariane cannot be relegated to the background – cannot become, in Peperzak's words, 'a secondary species'. Schroeder's skill is that the use of style is so subtle that it initiates this engagement without drawing attention to any ethical achievement in itself. Thus, viewers are encouraged to inhabit this viewing position but are not patronised.

Sexuality without Morality: Explicitness and the 'Distance of Love'

The subtlety of Schroeder's stylistic approach in *Maîtresse* leaves space for various interpretations. I have already suggested that the film's style may risk being unenjoyable, and, indeed, some reviewers have felt that Schroeder's directorial approach in *Maîtresse* is ineffective. It is as if his attempt at balance and impartiality sits uneasily with the expectations some reviewers place on the film, and this reveals something about what we may mean when we discuss film direction in a work such as *Maîtresse*.

For example, in a review of the film upon its initial New York release in November 1976, John Simon writes that 'the "sadomasochist documentary" part of the film is told in copious detail yet without any sort of directorial inventiveness or moral or intellectual passion' and that 'there is a signal lack of curiosity about getting beyond the sensational surfaces, so that the accumulation of scabrous details emerges, whether intentionally or not, as a piece of wan sensationalism'.[14] Simon's comments reveal, in a way, the difficulty of arguing for the value of Schroeder's directorial approach in the face of a film such as *Maîtresse* that does not clearly signpost its strategies to the viewer. Terms such as 'directorial inventiveness' and 'moral or intellectual passion' suggest a standard against which the film is being measured. But passion can be expressed in many ways – for example, as a commitment to an idea. And *Maîtresse* can be seen as an instance of a director's inventiveness in managing to avoid the pitfalls a project such as this film could have fallen into. For example, when Ariane first descends the steps into her den, startling Olivier and Mario, the absence of music on the soundtrack and the coolness of Ogier's responses, as Ariane, to the intrusion, along with the bizarre and humorous detail of the steps that ascend back into the ceiling, work with the more threatening aspects of the scene, such as the barking dog and the handcuffs Ariane uses to attach the two men to a radiator, to give the moment a mixture of shock and matter-of-factness. From this style, we may recognise the lengths to which many conventional filmic approaches would serve to condition our response as *either* matter-of-factness *or* shock. A shock cut, a moment of emotive music, an emphatic camera movement or angle all aid a film's performative transcription of drama into reaction, which we, as viewers, are expected helplessly to follow. And these devices count as totalising elements in our absorption and understanding of the film's unfamiliar world. Schroeder's decisions in *Maîtresse*, by contrast, serve to undermine any sense that the film is doing much of our work for us and that we can therefore relax and turn away from ethics, as suggested by Levinas's concerns about artworks in 'Reality and its Shadow'. *Maîtresse* is performing the open-minded, open-ended take on characters that some other films seek to close down. If we see how a Levinasian reading draws out the film's ethics as performed through its style, then both ethically and intellectually this is a film of great directorial openness.

Key to this is the film's frequent use of medium and three-quarter shots. Medium shots avoid the overt editorialising that comes with close-ups: they show us more of the actor's body along with spatial relations between the actors within the frame, allowing for greater contemplation of the positions of the characters in relation to one another (Figure 4.3).

Figure 4.3 'The distance of love': Ariane interacts with clients in her den.

For Elliott Stein, the film's sexual scenes 'are presented in a sober, unsensational style, with Schroeder's use of real-life devotees of sadomasochism contributing to a frank portrait of a subculture rather than a freak show'.[15] In the scene in which one of Ariane's clients has his penis and scrotum nailed to a plank of wood and his nipples pierced, for example, the camera is essentially stationary; it moves only to accommodate subtle pieces of behaviour or movement within the frame.[16] Stein has quoted Schroeder saying that

> [i]t's important to me all the way through to avoid any moral approach to the subject ... It seemed a question of having the right distance, always, even in terms of the camera: the proper distance for someone just contemplating these scenes. If you're too far – and this is true especially of the scenes downstairs – if you're too far, you're avoiding the subject. If you're too close, you're trying to manipulate the audience; it has no choices to make. The right distance – it's strange for me – I call the distance of love.[17]

This 'distance of love' finds a counterpart in Lisa Downing's theorisation of a Levinasian mode of spectatorship as 'looking with love'. Drawing on comments made by filmmaker Catherine Breillat, Downing discusses Levinas's equation of the image with the violence done through dominant patriarchal representations of sexuality and asks, 'Does the ethical "looking with love" formulated by Breillat and fleshed out through, with and sometimes *despite* Levinas help us to move beyond the traditional model of gaze as possessive?'[18] She suggests that '[i]n following Levinas's exhortation to abandon the desire to possess (knowledge, meaning, the other) in favour of the caress, the ethical viewer might radically disturb established ways of watching'.[19] Thus, in both Downing's 'looking with love' and Schroeder's 'distance of love', there is a resistance to possession, and instead an invitation: to the caress in Downing's work and, in Schroeder's work, to something like contemplation or openness. And both Downing's and Schroeder's invitations have the potential to arrive at a 'queering' of dominant discourse. In the case of *Maîtresse*, this queering is particularly pronounced because it is in respect of sexual practices that are, to mainstream eyes, already set outside the norm of sexual representation. And so, to look with love, from a distance of love, at the BDSM on display in *Maîtresse* is to give further space and liberty to something that some viewers may feel has already had more than enough space and attention devoted to it.

Furthermore, we can consider Schroeder's 'distance of love', the plainness with which he films *Maîtresse*, in relation to Levinas's conceptualisation of the face in *Totality and Infinity*. There, Levinas insists on the ethical demand of the Other being received by the self in a totally unmediated fashion. As Hand reminds us, 'our response to what the face exposes as an ethical demand cannot be mediated or interpreted by us prior to accepting the message'.[20] If, to take an obvious view, the world of BDSM in the film imposes itself on us like a Levinasian Other, then it is apt that this be presented in as unfettered a way as possible, so as to preserve its otherness and resist totalisation. In the penis-nailing and nipple-piercing scene, as the camera, the soundtrack and the acting are not overtly directing the viewer as to how to respond, the level of detail in the scene – the penis-nailing and nipple-piercing are carried out for real – may provoke a sense of outrage in the viewer, that such things are being shown and in such a relaxed fashion. But this presentation diverts attention away from preconceived attitudes and towards the specifics of the moment, with the sound of the whimpers of pain from the dominated man drawing attention towards him as an individual, a figure who, despite his mask, has a real, human face. Thus, rather than seeing moments like this, as Simon in his review does, as offering 'the accumulation of scabrous details', I suggest that the more the BDSM world is broken down into its constituent parts – the dominatrix, her dominated clients, the implements involved in their transaction (whips, chains and even the amusing hi-tech ladder) – the harder it is for it to be viewed as a singularly abhorrent 'other' world. In *Otherwise than Being*, Levinas says that '[a] breakdown of essence is needed, so that it not be repelled by violence'.[21] It may be too simplistic to say that essence is the enemy of ethics, but Levinas certainly posits it as a barrier to ethics. Essence encourages a blanket response, an obliteration. Accordingly, to see Ariane's world as a single, abhorrent thing might be to wish for its annihilation. Breaking it down into constituent parts, however, and then showing how these parts each contribute to Ariane's engagement with the needs of the others in her den, renders it harder to reconstruct her world as a whole. The source of Olivier's jealousy of Ariane is not, as it may at first appear, his lack of understanding of what she does; it is the opposite: it is that, to him, he understands all too well what she does, and he feels threatened by the attention she gives her clients. Coming closer to her is, for him, a process of deconstructing his understanding, going beyond essence, as in the full title of *Otherwise than Being*, so as to embrace devotion to the Other from a position of *unknowability*. Schroeder's film, in showing us Ariane's world in so much detail, but with that detail broken down, performs a similar process of moving from the ontology of the film's world to a psychological realm beyond essence. Philippe Azoury writes that

> *Maîtresse* is an absolutely vertiginous film. We are a thousand miles from a neat little bourgeois performance, from a cinema that would like to shock. The film seeks something else: an intimate understanding of the mechanics of masochism. The result comes about through the intelligence of a performance that places itself beyond morality.[22]

Everything about the film's style feels designed to perform this, by negating any sense of an obvious judgement on the events in the film.

Schroeder has commented on his attitude to filmmaking, and his comments would seem to support such a reading of *Maîtresse*: '[T]he one thing I hate is the power of the director. I'm trying to make movies where I minimize my power in every aspect because I hate power itself . . . It's obscene and power corrupts and the more you have the more it corrupts you. So I try to have as little as possible.'[23] It is impossible for a director to put something on film without a degree of power and control, simply by dint of there being options available and choices that must be made, but Schroeder's point about power is that he is seeking to exercise it to the minimum degree. His approach is reminiscent of Cooper's observation about the Dardennes' work that '[their] quest for novelty through their filmmaking lies in breaking key cinematic codes in an attempt to start from scratch, but they couple this with recognition that this is impossible. Their resultant, compromised aim is not to buy wholesale into cinematic convention.'[24] Schroeder is inescapably the director of *Maîtresse*, but that does not have to mean that the film's guiding hand is domineering. In a film such as this, the notion of film 'direction' indicates more a sense of 'direction of travel' than 'directedness'.

This striving for a lack of power surely marks Schroeder out as the opposite of an auteur, in that it is extremely difficult to see his films as representative of a consistent directorial identity in any obvious sense. Schroeder has criticised what he has called 'the pose of the auteur' and has said of himself, 'I consider myself as . . . an adventurer and an explorer and I like to explore things to try to find out more about reality.'[25] His varied output can therefore be seen as a conscious effort on his part to extend his working practices and explore different projects and territories, with scant regard for a consistency in style or directorial signature. Let us consider Levinas's notion that 'in everyday language we approach our fellow-man instead of forgetting him in the "enthusiasm" of eloquence'.[26] Here, Levinas hints at the egoism that can overtake a person, such that they get caught up in the thrill of their own self-expression, denying themselves the opportunity to respond to their 'fellow-man'. And Levinas's thoughts on identity in *Otherwise than Being* prove instructive in how we might recognise Schroeder's achievements: 'The uniqueness of the chosen or required one . . . is without identity. Not an identity, it is beyond consciousness, which is in itself and for itself. For it is already a substitution for the other.'[27] Levinas thus asserts the notion that to claim an identity for oneself is to obscure one's pre-existing ethical tendency – namely, to assume responsibility for the Other. In line with this, we could argue that for a filmmaker to enable the significance of the material to come across most strongly, they must get out of the film's way, so that the material can flourish without being affected by questions of directorial style.[28]

In this regard, we come back to Schroeder's claim that he considers himself 'an adventurer and an explorer'. Levinas asserts that '[n]othing is more grave, more august, than responsibility for the other, and saying, in which there is no play, has a gravity more grave than its own being or not being'.[29] If we feel that Schroeder strives, in a variety of ways, to occupy the dual position of a participant immersed in the culture being explored and a detached observer keen to let the characters speak for themselves, an achievement of *Maîtresse* is the way in which, through a use of style that is often notable for its basic anonymity, it has the ability to return the viewer to something approximating that Levinasian 'nothing'. Thus, Levinas's ethics has a counterpart in what Gary Indiana has termed Schroeder's 'fastidious neutrality'.[30] We can see in the apparent 'neutrality' of Schroeder's style an absence of directorial identity, reflecting, in the filmic realm, Levinas's notion of the pre-original – the identity-free, the 'otherwise than being' – that is a necessary aspect of the selflessness of responsibility for the Other. Schroeder uses style in such a way as to attempt to avoid any suggestion that it serves as a personal imprint. Instead, he uses it to create a form that offers an experience of Levinasian responsibility with regard to his characters.

A Happy Ending for the Transgressive Lovers

It is the ending of *Maîtresse* that provides the clearest commentary on the film's ethical stance with regard to its protagonists and its subject matter. Many films entertain us with stories of amoral or even immoral characters – the gangster genre being an obvious example – but in many cases, the amorality or immorality has to be paid for, if not by us as viewers then certainly by the principal character. The famous Hollywood gangster films of the 1930s, for example, made stars out of such actors as James Cagney (*The Public Enemy* [dir. William A. Wellman, 1931], *Angels with Dirty Faces* [dir. Michael Curtiz, 1938]), Paul Muni (*Scarface* [dir. Howard Hawks, 1932]) and Edward G. Robinson (*Little Caesar* [dir. Mervyn LeRoy, 1931]), but in each case, the protagonist meets a violent end, as if the film has (sometimes for censorship reasons) tempered its implicit – and sometimes explicit – desire to celebrate the gangster figure with an insistence that he die.[31] And in the era in which *Maîtresse* was first released, many of the other sexually 'transgressive' films of the 1970s also included this sense of payment or retribution: the love affair in *L'Empire des sens*, based on a true story, ends tragically, with the woman killing the man by cutting off his penis, a desperate act of love, while *Last Tango in Paris* culminates in an act of violence that results in the demise of one character and the survival of another (a resolution that is one of Bertolucci's many cineliterate nods in that film to the legacy of French cinema, in this case the ending of *À Bout de souffle* [*Breathless*, dir. Jean-Luc Godard, 1960]). So when, in the final sequence of *Maîtresse*, Olivier and Ariane are making love while driving (Figure 4.4), and the car crashes, we may feel that this has been inevitable: the lovers have had their fun, and now they must die – as if the film is suggesting that we cannot have such people running around on the loose and that audiences must be sent away from the film with a proper sense of justice and morality. We may think of the ending of the story of *The Postman Always Rings Twice* in which the female partner in the illicit love affair dies at the end in a car crash.[32] But in *Maîtresse*, the lovers survive, 'cheating death' to walk free from the wrecked car, laughing together as they stagger off into the distance. The lovers are not required to pay for their transgressive acts.

Figure 4.4 Ariane and Olivier drive along at the film's climax.

Schroeder describes his reasons for the ending as follows:

> Unlike what happens with the drugs in *More*, proselytising is practically impossible when it comes to masochism if one doesn't already have it in one; and, while drugs can perhaps be shown as a symbol of destruction, in *Maîtresse* it would have been dishonest to adopt this role in respect of masochism. As such, it's for this reason that I brought myself to modify a first version of the *dénouement* where the couple's suicidal accident ended with their certain destruction, as it had the effect of introducing a moral aspect when this dimension was absolutely nowhere else, and it was important for me to make a film in which morality did not enter into it in any way . . .[33]

Thus, Schroeder mounts a Levinasian challenge to morality: not only will the style refuse to pass judgement on the characters but the narrative, too, lets the lovers live, to continue their pleasure. The 'distance of love' practised by the style heightens the viewer's awareness of their response to the alterity on display; we might find elements of the film difficult to experience but this challenge can be seen as fundamental to a Levinasian encounter with alterity. In its disciplined dedication to its characters above and beyond any overt assertion of its own filmic identity, *Maîtresse* offers to the viewer a subtly performative example of a life without focus on the self.

CHAPTER 5

The Ethical and the Juridical in *Reversal of Fortune* and *Terror's Advocate*

Following on from my discussion of *Maîtresse*, we can begin to see how a subtle use of film style such as Schroeder exhibits in that film can be read as Levinasian in its feeling and its effects just as much as the more 'explicitly' ethical styles and subject matter of the Dardennes' work. In *Maîtresse*, it is precisely the unassertiveness of Schroeder's direction that enables the film to bring into being the world it is describing. But Schroeder deploys a variety of styles across his films, and in this chapter I want to discuss two films – *Reversal of Fortune* and *Terror's Advocate* – that use very different styles, both from *Maîtresse* and from each other. In doing so, I wish to draw out something they have in common – namely, what I consider to be a Levinasian approach to the subject of justice and the law.

Any sophisticated justice system seeks to strike an effective balance between an individual situation and a broader consistency and transparency across different cases. Levinas makes brief references to justice and law in *Totality and Infinity*, to be found primarily in Section I.C, 'Truth and Justice',[1] while *Otherwise than Being* develops Levinas's important conception of the third party, introduced in the earlier text, as a presence that founds justice. But typically for Levinas, and despite numerous other references to justice and law throughout his work, practical applications are not easily discerned or developed. Consider, for example, an essay such as 'The Rights of Man and the Rights of the Other', which is one of Levinas's most self-contained discussions of law in relation to ethics.[2] Levinas begins by discussing 'The Original Right', describing the rights of man as existing 'prior to all entitlement: to all tradition, all jurisprudence, all granting of privileges, awards or titles, all consecration by a will abusively claiming the name of reason',[3] suggesting, therefore, that legal rights are *founded by* this preexisting 'irrevocable and inalienable' right.[4] Therefore, the legal system is not something that creates ethics; ethics exists first, and the legal system follows on from it. 'The Broad Notion of the Rights of Man' is discussed next, after which Levinas pits those rights against 'The Rights of the Other Man'.

But the conclusion Levinas reaches – that each self has '[a]n inexhaustible responsibility'[5] towards the Other – is more a matter of abstract ethics than a philosophy readily applicable to real-world examples. He articulates a set of ideals it would be difficult to refute, but he does not attempt to tell us how we might go about creating a real-world system analogous to them.

Commentators have identified problems this poses for discussing Levinas in relation to law. In his introduction to the edited collection *Essays on Levinas and Law: A Mosaic*, Desmond Manderson suggests four reasons as to why Levinas has not been discussed much in relation to law: first, Levinas's prose is difficult (Manderson says it can be 'blisteringly obscure');[6] second, Levinas's work is part of Continental philosophy (although one might dispute this claim of Manderson's), which in itself has not been used much in relation to law; third, many of Levinas's own references to law can be considered to be slightly simplistic, and, fourth, Levinas's writing on law indicates 'a deep and irreparable schism between the ethical relation, intimate, personal, absolute, and singular; and the legal relation, which is none of these things'.[7] This fourth point relates to my primary concern here, the usefulness of Levinas's ethics for lawmakers and for those who practise law. The point is picked up in the same collection by Nick Smith, in an essay entitled 'Questions for a Reluctant Jurisprudence of Alterity'.[8] Here, Smith discusses the work of both Levinas and Theodor W. Adorno and questions the degree to which they can be of help in a practical application of ethical philosophy to the world of law. One of Smith's key points is that Levinas and Adorno both distrust the kinds of practical solutions that can result in authoritarian, totalising systems. For Smith, while it is understandable that Levinas and Adorno wish to avoid a concrete suggestion as to how justice might work or be applied in practice, 'their outright refusal to be drawn into applied theory has caused innumerable difficulties for progressive theorists compelled by their critiques of instrumental reason but handcuffed by their skepticism toward practical reform'.[9] The difficulty, says Smith, is that '[r]egardless of their content, theories of justice appear inextricable from totalizing viewpoints that categorize, organize, and codify alterity'.[10] It is a point that tallies with Séan Hand's observation that, in Levinas's work,

> [t]his justice, of course, is precisely not law, and is even the opposite of it, at the level of ethical saying as opposed to the juridical said. The problem here is that, inevitably, the promotion of justice for all must involve the introduction of thematization, and the imposition of a said onto a pure anarchic saying.[11]

All of these writers, therefore, pinpoint a fundamental challenge to lawmakers who hope to find a practicable approach to the law in Levinas's writing.

But their comments also indicate ways in which Levinas's work can provide vital perspectives on the practical business of justice. Matthew Stone observes how 'instead of using his work to think about how we inject ethics into law or unveil law's ethical foundation, his philosophy provides resources to understand how the ethical structure of the encounter with the other arises as a persistent challenge to the law's ontological fixity'.[12] The lawyers in *Reversal of Fortune* and *Terror's Advocate* encounter others who will severely challenge the expectations of the legal system. I shall first discuss *Reversal of Fortune* and in particular how we can relate questions of the film's stylistic and structural properties to an idea of the performativity of the law.

Reversal of Fortune: Performing Justice through Style

Adapted for the screen by Nicholas Kazan from a book by Alan M. Dershowitz, *Reversal of Fortune* centres on the true-life von Bülow case.[13] In December 1979, the wealthy socialite Sunny von Bülow inexplicably fell into a coma. She recovered, but a year later she fell into a second coma, from which she would never awake. Her husband, Claus von Bülow, was arrested, tried, and found guilty on two counts of attempted murder. Claus hired Dershowitz, a Harvard law professor and lawyer, to help him appeal against the ruling. In narrative terms, then, this is a story about the workings of the legal system, and therefore about justice. Thomas Leitch, writing on *Reversal of Fortune* and other films about the law, notes that 'a founding convention of these films is that any system that puts citizens on trial, holding their actions up to the measure of the law, is open to question itself, particularly in those films that present an innocent defendant or some other miscarriage of justice'.[14] What I will argue with regard to *Reversal of Fortune* is that it questions the institution of the law and the uncertainty that surrounds the evidence in the von Bülow case not just through dramatised scenes in which characters wrestle with these issues but also through its own film style. David Thomson has said of the film that it 'has many problems of construction, and far too many loose ends'.[15] Thomson's comment implies a criticism of the film – namely, that its narrative fails to 'work' in a traditional sense. Thomson does not say what he believes the 'loose ends' to be, but I would like to suggest some and then to look at how they contribute to the film's Levinasian take on its subject.

The film differs a fair amount from the book on which it is based, first of all structurally: whereas the book covers the whole case of the von Bülows – the first trial; the appeal that led to the reversal of the guilty verdicts and the right to a second trial; the second trial itself, and the aftermath – the film concentrates on the central portion of the book, the appeal that gave the book and film their titles. A greater difference between the book and the film concerns point of view. The book places its author, Dershowitz, at the centre of the narrative, recounting the details of the case through his own perspective, having been intricately involved with it for so many months. In the film, however, the story is told through multiple points of view, dividing its perspectives between three principal characters: Alan (Ron Silver), Sunny (Glenn Close) and Claus (Jeremy Irons). This in itself creates a number of loose ends. Alan is in a sense the film's central character, occupying as he does the position of the audience's surrogate, the 'ordinary' person who takes us into a strange world. That world has been first shown to us in the film's opening credits sequence, in which, in a shot taken from a helicopter, we are given a privileged view of the affluent mansions along the coast of Newport, Rhode Island, where the von Bülow residence, Clarendon Court, is located; by contrast, we are introduced to Alan in his more modest home from a ground-level angle of his yard as he plays basketball, followed by a scene in his homely kitchen. And yet Claus, too, acts as a guide into a strange world, as his conversations with Alan provide insights into his life with Sunny in their mansion, the film recreating these incidents to accompany (although not necessarily to match) his narration of them. Fracturing point of view yet further, the entire film is framed and presided over by Sunny's narration, emanating from her comatose state in her hospital bed. Hers is the first voice we hear on the soundtrack, and it guides us through the film's story with a sardonic air. It is as if, unable to participate in the world any longer, she has earned the right to cast a jaded and sceptical eye over her situation.

Schroeder distinguishes these three strands of the narration from one another by filming them in subtly different styles. We encounter Sunny first, the camera entering her hospital bedroom and observing her as she lies in her coma (Figure 5.1). Schroeder describes this style as '"fantastical", where the camera floats, flies, and represents something like the soul of Sunny'.[16] And in other shots of Sunny from her second coma onwards, be it in the 'present day' of the film's voiceover scenes or in moments that speculate as to her actions on the fateful day, she is frequently filmed from a slightly hovering angle, as if she has already semi-departed from the ordinary world. The second style is for Claus; Schroeder says that this style 'applied itself to different versions of events. Like the fictions of cinema: it was for me something from Douglas Sirk, an idea of luxury and of beauty. And it was necessary that it be accompanied by symphonic music...'[17] This style alludes to the melodramatic and perhaps fictive quality of Claus's recollections. In these scenes, such as when he is on a yacht with his mistress Alexandra (Julie Hagerty) (Figure 5.2) or exercising at

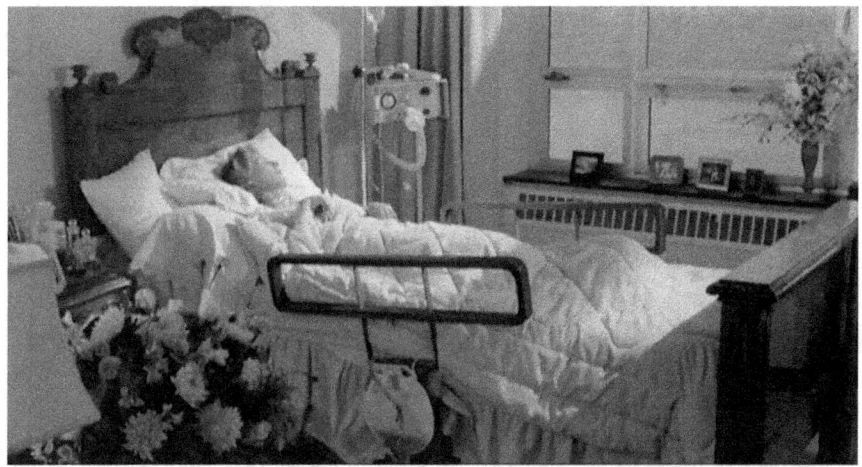

Figure 5.1 Sunny in her hospital bed is shown from above.

Figure 5.2 Claus romances Alexandra on a spacious yacht.

home, Claus is often shown with a lot of space around him, and via camera movements that are smooth and languid; this creates an understated irony in that one of the things Claus stands to lose if Alan and his team do not manage to reverse the first jury's verdict is the spaciousness of freedom. The third style – depicting Alan – contrasts with this again; for Schroeder, 'in the reality of Dershowitz, no extra-diegetic music, just the vague echoes of radio. We had to be more "documentary-like" in these sequences . . .'[18]

In Alan's world there is often clutter – be it piles of books and papers, people crowding him in the frame, tables and chairs in between him and us (Figure 5.3). Alan's world does not have the spaciousness of Claus's – but Alan has freedom where Claus does not.

As well as these three points of view, there is a fourth, that of the film itself, which, in presenting such a triangulated take on the events, establishes its overarching narrative as omniscient. We have already discussed, in relation to *Maîtresse*, the notion of the third party and of the triangulation that can happen, in film, between the viewer, the camera, and the actors within the diegesis. The third party is perhaps the key indicator in Levinas's philosophy in relation to justice. For Levinas, it is the existence, or addition, of the third party that is the founding of justice, for the third party interrupts the self–Other dynamic, announcing its presence and in effect startling the self into an acknowledgement that there is more to ethical responsibility than just a responsibility for a single Other.[19] As Peperzak explains, the third party expands the self's view of the world and of the Other and can lead to a sense that justice must be sought:

> [T]he multiplication of persons to whom I am close blurs their faces and makes them more or less anonymous. As instances of a sort of genus called 'other persons,' they urge me to perceive and treat them as equally entitled to my devotion. This way of coming to the fore identifies them as competing subjects of right and care. As such, they demand that justice be done to everyone.[20]

Thus, the third party represents all those others whom I cannot possibly hope to know personally, whose names I cannot know, but for whom I am

Figure 5.3 Alan is surrounded by his students at Harvard.

nevertheless responsible. In this way, my awareness, through the third party, of my responsibility puts me within a world in which justice must be sought. In *Reversal of Fortune*, the film deepens the portrait of the von Bülow case by bringing into being a world in which no one point of view dominates; unable to align ourselves easily with any one of these characters, we see that each of them deserves a fair hearing. Our inability to align with any particular character ensures that their otherness is preserved and that, through the film's stylistic performance of this uncertainty, we feel the burden of Levinasian responsibility not just for one Other but for all others.

This performance of uncertainty extends into other areas of the film that could also be considered 'loose ends' by dint of their incompleteness or unclear relation to the film's main narrative. For example, when we first meet Alan, he receives a phone call giving him an update on the plight of two of his current clients, the Johnson brothers (whom we never see in the film), two young men on death row for a crime Alan believes they did not commit. They are mentioned a few other times in the film, but it is unclear as to why it was felt necessary to include them at all. Another point of confusion is the film's use of Alan's law student Minnie (Felicity Huffman): she is introduced strikingly, raising an objection to Alan's taking on the case, in response to which Alan delivers a mini-lecture to her (and for the benefit of viewers) on the importance of defence lawyers, but after this, Minnie becomes only a minor character, one of Alan's team, whereas we might have expected her to become a key supporting figure. Also, Alan's relationship with Sarah (Annabella Sciorra) is unclear: the film never explains whether she is an estranged wife, an ex-wife, or what their history is. Their relationship throughout the film is rather vague: in their first scene together, when he asks her to work with him on the case, she says she hopes it will be strictly professional; later on, when he criticises her interpretation of one aspect of the case, she says that the idea that their relationship is strictly professional is 'bullshit'; finally, towards the end of the film, she is resigned to living with him and loving him again. Perhaps most intriguingly unclear is the film's use of the character of David Marriott: in the book he features heavily, a man who begins by seemingly wanting to help Claus and Alan, by providing information and affidavits, but who then seems to go out of his way to disrupt the case and to milk the controversy for his own self-aggrandising ends. Dershowitz in the book offers a lawyer's maxim as justification for having dealt with Marriott at all: '"When you're trying to prosecute the Devil, you have to go to hell for the witnesses".'[21] In the film, Marriott, played vividly by Fisher Stevens, creates a strong impression, but there are simply not nearly enough scenes devoted to him to explore exactly what he is up to.

And yet this refusal to deliver on these aspects of the film helps it to perform its themes of ethical and legal uncertainty. If the film were to handle its various narrative strands in a neater or more organically connected fashion, it would risk achieving an overdetermined take on the events involved in the case. What the film offers instead – deliberately or unwittingly – is a sense that it is better to remain unsure as to how best to fit all the strands together because this seems fairer to the idea of 'the truth' in legal terms being very difficult to know or to define. We can read the film's handling of the narrative strands as a filmic version of the Levinasian Saying in its refusal to settle into a determined clarity. Schroeder explains that he approached the making of *Reversal of Fortune* as if it were Claus von Bülow directing the film, the reason being that '[b]ecause you don't give answers, you cultivate ambiguity, you find a perverse pleasure in always leaving open all kinds of possibilities'.[22] He says he could not approach the film as if it were Dershowitz making it because

> he is a lawyer, he would try to prove something, he would just plead for something . . . For me, if you have characters they have to have their own life and their own complexities. If you're trying to prove something you of course try to force the characters into something, you make them lose some of their life because you want to prove a point.[23]

Where the book does what a good defence lawyer should do – creates a persuasive defence from the evidence and from legal argument – the film is more interested in obfuscating notions of 'truth' and instead creating and sustaining a mood of uncertainty. Manderson notes that 'the legal code itself comes to resemble a mosaic, whose broken and irregular surface can only be properly seen by the continual exercise of imagination'.[24] Similarly, the labyrinthine structure of the narrative in *Reversal of Fortune* becomes an essential component of the film's performance of the disorientation required to dislodge the viewer's expectations. For Thierry Jousse: '[i]t is the idea of all these contradictory voiceovers, of these testimonies within testimonies, of these scrolled-through flashbacks, of this reversibility of fictional time as enunciated by the mouth of the very same Sunny von Bülow, that permanently destabilises the belief of the spectator'.[25] Through this structure, the film evokes a sense of the Levinasian triangulation of self, Other and third party. The pairs of characters on-screen (either Alan and Claus or Claus and Sunny, although never Alan and Sunny) form two-thirds of the triangulation with viewers at the third corner. This puts viewers in the position of not being able to enact a relationship, or engagement, with just one of the main characters but instead being invited to engage with multiple characters. For Levinas, '[c]onsciousness is born as the presence of a third party . . . It is the entry of the third party, a permanent entry, into the intimacy of the face to face.'²⁶ The 'contradictory' nature, as noted by Jousse, of the film of *Reversal of Fortune* initiates an ethical engagement on the part of the viewer. Thus, Thomson's observation of loose ends becomes less troubling, more triumphant.

Memory Enhancement

The idea of a performance that undermines any sense of certainty also has significance for the film's depiction of what Dershowitz calls 'memory enhancement', which is key to understanding how evidence in trials can work. In his book, Dershowitz explains it thus:

> I knew from experience how witnesses' trial memories worked – exactly the opposite from the way one might expect. In a legal case, the memories of witnesses – particularly those with a stake in the outcome – tend to get better as time passes. Often their initial recollection of an event is hazy, because it's not part of any coherent pattern of events or theory. While the theory begins to emerge, the memory begins to fit into it, losing some of the haze. As the trial approaches and the witnesses are coached and rehearsed, they tend to 'remember' the event with even more clarity and less ambiguity. And eventually, what began as a hazy recollection becomes frozen into crystalline clarity. In the end, what is remembered is not even the event. It is the *memory* of repeating and clarifying the event through a process of enhanced certainty.²⁷

The justice system is revealed to be a stage on which narratives are created, generic expectations followed, 'truths' arrived at. One example of this in the film concerns Sunny's maid, Maria (Uta Hagen). During the first trial, Maria testifies in court that she discovered a black bag of Claus's that contained an insulin-encrusted needle. She asks, 'For what, insulin? My lady's not diabetic.' At one point in the construction of the appeal, Alan realises that while the conviction of Claus was aided in part by Maria's damning evidence that she found insulin in a black bag belonging to Claus, it may have been that Maria had originally thought the black bag was *Sunny's*. Alan determines to show that it was only *later*, through the prosecution's legal strategy, that she came to believe it was Claus's: the idea that it belonged to Claus fitted the prosecution's theory so snugly that Maria came to believe it herself. In these terms, the process of giving evidence is performative, bringing into being 'facts' that it purports to be explaining. As with Levinas's prose style in *Otherwise than Being*, witnesses construct descriptions in reverse: what they are describing does not exist until they begin to describe it.

In handling this theme, *Reversal of Fortune* adopts a sceptical position with regard to storytelling and refuses to take the satisfying tropes of narrative for granted. A comparison of the film with other legal/

courtroom thrillers contemporaneous with it, such as *Jagged Edge* (dir. Richard Marquand, 1985), *Suspect* (dir. Peter Yates, 1987) and *Presumed Innocent* (dir. Alan J. Pakula, 1990), shows just how far *Reversal of Fortune* evades easy categorisation as a 'legal thriller'. Those other films all contain standard – and often very pleasurable – generic tropes surrounding an accused, a mystery, a legalistic procedure and an ultimate revelation that gives us the real 'truth'. By contrast, *Reversal of Fortune* does not contain a shock revelation; Leitch notes how the film is 'remarkable for its refusal of the melodrama *Presumed Innocent* handles so resourcefully and expertly'.[28] *Reversal of Fortune* is, of course, based on a true story, and the 'facts' of the case are known;[29] even so, it makes efforts to disavow many of the key generic tropes of the courtroom drama and the suspense thriller, and these disavowals are key aspects of the film's Levinasian sense of non-fixity. Levinas says that '[t]he pre-original, anarchic saying is proximity, contact, duty without end, a saying still indifferent to the said and saying itself without giving the said, the-one-for-the-other, a substitution'.[30] *Reversal of Fortune*, in denying viewers the easy comforts of straightforward generic satisfaction, is able to create an ethical 'shock' through its 'pre-original' approach to the topic of the ethical and the juridical, thereby allowing a more demanding, Levinasian ethics to emerge. It establishes this from its opening credits sequence, in which the travelling shot over the Newport mansions is accompanied by a music score (by Mark Isham) that shifts repeatedly between melodic phrases suggestive of a conventionally exciting murder-mystery film and less tonally distinct phrases of quiet but insistent menace. The music itself is not just introducing but performing the film's desire to undercut its generic trappings even as it pays homage to them. This scepticism enables the film to come closer to the events at Clarendon Court and to the legal process than any of the more clarified and verifiable evidence. Sarah says, after the appeal hearing, 'Face it: all we had to do was prove that the state made a lousy case. We didn't prove that Claus was innocent. We couldn't, we didn't have to, and he probably isn't.' When you cannot know for sure what happened, any argument you put forward is part of the legal game. This suggests that the legal process is constructed from a set of speech acts, each performing what they describe – namely, a piece of evidence. Austin touches on this in his first lecture as published in *How to Do Things with Words*, when he is discussing the descriptive fallacy, the tendency to take statements as facts when they may not be so. In a footnote, he offers the following: 'Of all people, jurists should be best aware of the true state of affairs. Perhaps some now are. Yet they will succumb to their own timorous fiction, that a statement of "the law" is a statement of fact.'[31] Thinking about Austin's thoughts in relation to *Reversal of Fortune*, we can see how juries do not necessarily have facts presented to them – they only have evidence to go on. Nothing in the legal argument can reveal the truth that the followers of the case really want to know – in the von Bülow case, how did Sunny get to be in an irreversible coma? And so, the only truth available is the truth of logical argument.

Solidity and the Performance of Uncertainty

Truth in this case, therefore, is something that is constructed, brought into being. As if to hint at this, the film subtly contrasts the uncertainty of the legal process, and of testimony, with the solidity of the settings in which the events in question took place. Schroeder and his crew have assembled a very plausible presentation of the affluent world of Newport, Rhode Island; Peter Travers says that '[y]ou don't just see wealth in this picture; you hear it purr',[32] and Thomson says that Schroeder 'has a connoisseur's eye for decadence'.[33] The surfaces – the luxurious furnishings of Clarendon Court, but also the legal documents that will enable Alan and his team to construct Claus's appeal, and even the film's distancing 'surface' of structural complexity – take on a Levinasian flavour in teasing the viewer with the impossibility, despite all the evidence on display, of ever having an answer, a totality. In tandem with this, the film in various moments – especially in scenes set in and around Clarendon Court but also, for example, the scenes at the boating club – exhibits symmetrical framing (Figure 5.4). It is as if the symmetry gives to these locations a

Figure 5.4 Symmetry: Christmas at Clarendon Court; Sunny walking towards her bathroom; Claus and Alan at the club; Clarendon Court in the snow. (*continued*)

Figure 5.4 (*continued*) Symmetry: Christmas at Clarendon Court; Sunny walking towards her bathroom; Claus and Alan at the club; Clarendon Court in the snow.

THE ETHICAL AND THE JURIDICAL   117

sense of stability and certainty, in contrast with the overarching instability and uncertainty of the various testimonies and 'memory enhancements' in the case and the chaotic, cramped interiors in which Alan and his team try to get to the bottom of it.

It is, in particular, the faces of the characters that contrast with the solidity of the surfaces and the reassuring certainty of the symmetrical framing. This is a film that, unassertively and unostentatiously, contains a large number of close-ups and medium close-ups that chart the fugitive feelings of the characters – their stress, their bewilderment, their possible duplicity. Jeremy Irons's acclaimed performance as Claus is crucial to this.[34] His presence in the film represents different levels of performance, those of Irons the actor as Claus, the performance of Claus as himself, and the performances Claus gives to different people – Alan and his team, Sunny, the rest of the household, and the other women he is involved with. This is Performativity$_1$ and Performativity$_2$ simultaneously: it is the bringing into being of a character through bodily and vocal gestures on a macro level (Performativity$_1$) to reveal aspects of performativity within the film's own world (Performativity$_2$). Irons's is a difficult performance to realise, not just psychologically but physically. The real Claus was in his late fifties at the time of the appeal, while Irons was in his early forties when filming *Reversal of Fortune*; as such, he is made up to look older – his hair appears thinned, he has been given jowls, and he is often lit in a way that makes his skin appear somewhat sallow (Figure 5.5). This look, combined with the

Figure 5.5 Jeremy Irons made up to play Claus von Bülow.

mid-European drawl Irons uses, gives the actor a lot to concentrate on. The resulting performance, in all its intricacy, helps create a mood of complicity in the film's theme of the unreliability of evidence, the unknowability of the defendant, the awareness that the law is a game, and therefore the need to avoid making snap judgements. There are numerous moments in which other characters are seen to be looking at Claus, scrutinising him, trying to puzzle him out; in this light, one of Irons's many achievements is to make Claus so compelling precisely as a surface that it has the effect of frustrating the viewer's desire to comprehend him – a reminder that the Levinasian face of the Other is something neither tangible nor otherwise readily graspable. The film thus encourages a Levinasian viewing mode, working with the surfaces to look beyond them into a sort of contemplative middle distance that gives us access to the unknowability of the Other and therefore to our ethical responsibility for the Other.

Reversal of Fortune is a film that does not only tell a story about uncertainty but also *performs* uncertainty, and this is a fundamental part of its effect. It performs it on at least two levels – through its characters and, perhaps more fundamentally for my topic here, through its style and structure. The style and structure are constitutive of an analytical air; by contrast, Dershowitz's book, which is in a way more overtly analytical in tone, is also, oddly, more emotional, more moving. The relatively subdued emotional impact of the film is a key part of its project: it does not want to deliver catharsis – and neither does Levinas, for catharsis breeds satisfaction and risks complacency, the opposite of *dénucléation*. Justice systems strive to deliver verdicts, and accordingly, in *Reversal of Fortune*, Alan is striving to achieve a verdict of 'not guilty' for Claus. At the same time, however, the film performatively brings into being an uncertainty that can draw us towards the ethical within the juridical, the individuals within the due process of law.

Terror's Advocate: Documenting a Life of Ethics and Style

The central figure of *Terror's Advocate*, real-life lawyer Jacques Vergès, could be considered a cross between Alan Dershowitz and Claus von Bülow. He has the brilliant crusading lawyer's bravado and he has the *bon vivant*'s expensive tastes, as well as Claus's way of teasing us with the truth. And Vergès can be said to share a quality with both Alan and Claus: an interest in fame and notoriety.

Terror's Advocate intersects with four strands of Schroeder's work: it is a return to French-language cinema (his most recent French film prior to this being *Tricheurs* in 1984), it is his third documentary feature (after *General Idi Amin Dada: A Self Portrait* and *Koko: A Talking Gorilla*), it is his third film about lawyers and justice (after *Reversal of Fortune* and *Before and After*) and it is the middle film in what has come to be called Schroeder's Trilogy of Evil, three documentaries looking at controversial figures, the first being *General Idi Amin Dada* and the most recent being *Le Vénérable W.*, on the Burmese Buddhist monk Ashin Wirathu. *Terror's Advocate* is also a signal demonstration of the scope of Schroeder's work, in that its narrative landscape encompasses a number of international political events of the latter half of the twentieth century. My reading of the film concentrates on how its style creates a portrait of Vergès that could be said to present him as a Levinasian figure.

In common with *Reversal of Fortune* and *Before and After*, *Terror's Advocate* has an interest in the legal process itself, over and above any question of whether the defendants in each case committed the crimes of which they are accused. In this respect, all three of these films turn away from the potential for conventional generic suspense. The films therefore contribute to the characterisation of Schroeder the director, in revealing a consistent socio-political intent in his work that places a greater importance on questioning the structures in which we live than on scrutinising the preferences we express or the personal choices we make. But it is also important to consider ways in which the films are distinct from one another. Strictly speaking, *Reversal of Fortune* and *Before and After* are both 'fictional' features: *Before and After*, which stars Meryl Streep and Liam Neeson as parents whose son, played by Edward Furlong, has been accused of murdering his girlfriend, is based on a novel by Rosellen Brown, and while *Reversal of Fortune* is based on real-life events – even to the extent that it features as one of its principal characters the man (Alan Dershowitz) who wrote the book that inspired the film, which was co-executive produced by one of his sons (Elon Dershowitz) – audiences are nevertheless paying to see a mainstream Hollywood film with big stars acting for the purposes of dramatic entertainment. By contrast, *Terror's Advocate* is a documentary, in that it centres on real-life figures discussing real events. I do not want to categorise the films too easily; *Reversal of Fortune*, after all, is based on real-life events. But it is important, in this discussion of *Terror's Advocate*, to begin from the position of contrast with the earlier films, that this is a not a 'fiction' film but a documentary. A documentary creates different expectations for the viewer from a fiction film, and so *Terror's Advocate* is a film we might reasonably expect to come away from with an increased understanding of the period in history with which it deals, and feeling we have been presented with if not 'facts' then certainly information about facts. But the ways in which the film undercuts expectations as a documentary is central to how it conveys its subject matter.

Terror's Advocate concentrates primarily on the life and career of Vergès, who made his name defending some of the most contentious public figures of the last few decades, among them a renowned nationalist in the Algerian War of Independence, Djamila Bouhired, the notorious terrorist Carlos the Jackal, and Klaus Barbie, the Nazi war criminal nicknamed the Butcher of Lyon. The film is composed of interviews with Vergès and other real-life figures of the times, as well as archive footage of the events being discussed. There is virtually no concentration on the interviewer, be it Schroeder or one of his collaborators, and so the documentary does not take on a self-reflexive sense of the documentarist's role; nor is there a narrator to provide an overt commentary on the events depicted. And yet the film treats its subject from a very pointed angle. Schroeder opens the film with an on-screen disclaimer: 'This film is the director's point of view on Jacques Vergès, which may differ from the opinions of people interviewed in it.' This foregrounds the partiality of this documentary. But a paradox arises in that, in making such an overt statement of individual filmmaking point of view, Schroeder also makes apparent the possibility of other points of view. This statement therefore situates the film very much as a documentary that is not pretending to offer an impartial view of the legal system. This is reminiscent of Leitch's observation with regard to *Reversal of Fortune* and the conventions of the lawyer film that 'any system that puts citizens on trial, holding their actions up to the measure of the law, is open to question itself'.[35] With the disclaimer in place, the film is then able to present Vergès's life and work in a multi-dimensional cinematic way, using various elements that are designed to draw out not just the political implications of what Vergès is telling us but the emotional implications as well. These are in contrast to the much more detached and observational styles Schroeder deployed in his previous two documentaries. For Michel Marie,

> the achronological construction of the film, the use of archive documents, the mosaic of witnesses transform the portrait of the driven lawyer into a veritable political-espionage film, as thrilling as an inquiry from political fiction. Admittedly, Vergès is a fascinating witness, of an almost diabolical intelligence, but it's the editing of the film that gives to him this density of historical reflection, above and beyond his provocative counterarguments.[36]

Again there is the idea of a mosaic, as suggested in the title of Manderson's edited collection on Levinas and the law, and with regard to *Terror's Advocate*, it provides a context in which we can understand some of Vergès's more contentious or unfamiliar strategies. For example, around the time of the Bouhired trial, as the film tells us, Vergès began to use the 'rupture defence'. This is a defence based on attacking the authority of the court and, by implication or in fact, blaming the legal system, and even the government, for crimes that have gone on to cause the crimes of which the defendant is accused – or perhaps for crimes far worse than the ones of which the defendant is accused. From here, the film proceeds to portray Vergès – and, it is fair to say, Vergès proceeds to portray himself – as a lawyer who has dynamically sought some of the most difficult cases to take on, cases that carry a political dimension reaching wider than the implications for any of the individuals who stand accused. *Terror's Advocate* is therefore a film that highlights distinctions between the workings of the legal system and a sense of ethics.

The Mystery of Vergès: Bravado and Detachment

With such an emphasis on Vergès's motivations for taking on these supremely difficult cases, one of the central topics of this documentary is his strength of character. Vergès appears to have a strong sense of style – he is the film's primary interviewee but he is also a raconteur: he is very aware of the image he is projecting and comes across as if he believes himself to be the star of the show. There are many occasions in the film where, having made a controversial or provocative statement, he smiles – and sometimes even puffs on his cigar – and the film stays with him for a brief moment before cutting to the next scene (Figure 5.6). These smiles – such as when he mentions Pol Pot or when he discusses his declaration in Israel – condition this documentary, leading it away somewhat from socio-political history and towards a portrait of a man who seeks to provoke and yet also to impress (and many of Vergès's achievements are breathtaking in their audacity). Vergès conducts himself with figurative, and sometimes almost literal, sly winks to the camera, enjoying his displays of insinuation and the ways in which he both reveals and conceals information. Vergès's presence perhaps pushes the film towards being a performative documentary in the sense theorised by Bruzzi:

> [T]he performative documentary uses performance within a non-fiction context to draw attention to the impossibilities of authentic documentary representation. The performative element within the framework of non-fiction is thereby an alienating, distancing device, not one which actively promotes identification and a straightforward response to a film's content.[37]

Accordingly, Vergès's presence is in some senses a performance that, unwittingly or otherwise, distracts attention from the wider topic of the legal and political context in which he has worked; Libby Saxton, for example, in a chapter that looks in part at the film's use of montage to juxtapose events from different historical time periods, notes that '[t]he subject of

Figure 5.6 Jacques Vergès brandishes his cigar.

L'Avocat de la terreur, we discover, is *mise-en-scène* as much as history and role-playing as much as bearing witness'.[38] That said, it is precisely this quality in Vergès's presence that aids the film's shape and content, for we are perhaps able to understand better some of the events Vergès is discussing if we observe his own 'performance' of his recollections and the part he has played in the events recounted. Further to the notion of a performative documentary, we could say that Schroeder's direction – and in particular some of the timing of the editing in these moments – creates this impression, but we might feel rather that the film simply expresses something already there in abundance. As with his documentary on Idi Amin, Schroeder does not have to do much to expose the particularities of a powerful, self-aggrandising personality.

With regard to Vergès, however, this method does something else, too. It reveals something of his poise, his self-confidence, his self-possession, and these might very well be attributes he has needed to see him through some of the difficult times he has faced in his career. In the film, Vergès says that '[o]n my first case as a public defender, as I sat facing my small-time hoodlum client, I said to myself: "That guy is me. I could've done what he did, if I'd been in his shoes." Then I knew it was my calling.' Vergès's words are suggestive of Levinasian substitution, the-one-for-the-other: he has been able to take on the burdens of the Other, to claim responsibility for the Other, by choosing to represent the Other in court, no matter the odds stacked against them. It is fair to say that this reaches its apex in his defence of Klaus Barbie. The film uses archive footage of the courtroom and of Vergès, Barbie and other figures at the trial. Vergès defends Barbie against a team of thirty-nine prosecuting lawyers. And he says that this means they are each worth only one fortieth of him. This sardonic detachment – and in particular the *performance* of detachment – might contain the seeds for a Levinasian approach to the juridical.

But if in order to remove yourself from the Said and return to the Saying you have to exude a strong sense of self-confidence and self-worth, of individuality independent from the totalising Said of the juridical, does this not risk enhancing the self's self-regard to the point of prioritising the self over the obligation to the Other? In *Terror's Advocate*, the legal system is shown to be a system that can be appropriated for personal – egocentric – ends, and therefore a system in which the commitment to pursuing the rights of man is not invulnerable to exploitation and corruption. There is also in the film a sense that Vergès's actions are often even anti-social, such as his mysterious and unsolved eight-year disappearance from family and friends in the 1970s. The journalist and historian Lionel Duroy, discussing this episode in the film, says that Vergès, during his disappearance, 'rethought the world', that 'he did his revolution all alone', and that '[h]is strength is to have never turned his struggle into something official'. Duroy observes that '[o]nce he got back, it was like he'd lost faith in political models. He expected nothing from politics. So he settled in France, became a lawyer, and a multi-purpose lawyer, as has been said.' This adds to the complexity and intrigue surrounding Vergès and raises the question as to whom he is dedicated. This relates to whether the self in *Otherwise than Being* doesn't somehow *enjoy* the process of substitution, despite the book's assertions to the contrary. Certainly there is a sense of the duality of the pleasure in the pain of being a hostage, that the hostage status is preferable to the self-indulgent pursuit of the ego, that it is a 'restlessness' that is 'better than rest'.[39] Peperzak reads a link between Levinasian ethics and law in the notion of the self acknowledging to himself that he has the ability to see himself as an Other for an Other – and therefore to be deserving of the rights he might ethically attempt to assign to an Other:

> I am myself an Other for the Other: an Other whom both the Other and myself should look after . . . Then I am also *for me, but* in a radically *other* sense than that of economic delight. I must prepare myself for a *disinterested* love for myself. Despite all the hidden snares along this path, it is possible and necessary to love oneself as a being who needs justice and mercy.[40]

For Peperzak, then, there is an element of loving oneself as a condition that can lead to the recognition of justice. This would appear analogous to the Levinasian stance regarding the Other and others, and it may be what gave Vergès the ability to become the effective lawyer he became.

Repetition in Film Style and in Levinas's Prose

Vergès's achievement is conveyed, I believe, in large part through the film's style. To see the film as performative is to see how its style brings into being a sense of *Vergès's* style as a key aspect of how he approached the events in which he was involved and which the film recounts. Levinas's ethics, as we have seen, hinges, by the time of *Otherwise than Being*, on his choice of prose style to perform what he wants to convey. Similarly, in *Terror's Advocate*, there is no finite sense of truth – there is only the conflation of points of view (Schroeder's as director, Vergès's as principal participant, and the other interviewees' in support or contradiction of him) as expressed through the film's own particular use of style.

A key element of the film is its music (composed by Jorge Arriagada). The opening credits music, with its minor-key melody, sumptuous harmonic structure, and rich strings pounding out a driving rhythm, gives the film the feel of a thriller – helped by the dramatic cut that takes us from Vergès in the pre-credits sequence into the credits themselves. At this point, the music is giving the film an ominousness – in articulating a concern about the state of the world – and a provocative air that will suit its subject. There are also places in which the music is in a lower register. When Vergès and Bouhired go to China, for example, their visit is covered by actuality footage, but the music underscoring the sequence expresses sorrow, tension, and the momentousness (both at the time and in hindsight) of the events. It is as if, even though the interviewees are speaking in an understated way, the film is being pulled taut with feeling.

This tautness is reflected in the mise en scène, which comprises a steady, stately succession of medium close-ups of interviewees (with the occasional long shot), along with actuality footage, newspaper headlines, and subtle graphics (names, places, occupations, years, dates). The energy and repetitiveness of this information onslaught (Figure 5.7) give to the film a kinship with Levinas's textual performance in many of his works. A passage in 'The Rights of Man and the Rights of the Other', for example, encapsulates Levinas's prose style: the paragraph runs on, and Levinas's words become quite fervent and repetitive. For example, he uses the expression 'tearing loose' twice, he uses 'unique' or 'uniqueness' six times, and he begins five sentences in the paragraph in very similar ways: 'A tearing loose', 'A uniqueness', 'A uniqueness', 'A unity', 'A uniqueness'. He also uses many words that look similar on the page: 'irrevocable', 'inalienable',

THE ETHICAL AND THE JURIDICAL 125

Figure 5.7 The film's information onslaught. (*continued*)

126 PERFORMING ETHICS THROUGH FILM STYLE

Figure 5.7 (*continued*) The film's information onslaught.

'incomparable', 'non-interchangeable', 'individuality', 'individuals', 'individuating', 'indiscernible'.[41] This language, as well as carrying ideas, puts us in a contemplative mood, as we absorb the rhythms of the words, being slowly persuaded by them. Something similar can be seen at work in *Terror's Advocate*, in which the same points – such as Vergès's inscrutability, his egotism, and the repeated exploitation of terrorists/freedom fighters by the state and, to a degree, by Vergès himself – are made over and over again. This gives the film a quality akin to Levinas's prose, such that we feel massaged by the movie. I use this term because in massage, of course, the massage therapist goes over a portion of the body – the shoulders, the back, the thighs – again and again, massaging the area, the body gaining from the repetition. We can also recall Derrida's description of Levinas's prose as being like 'the infinite insistence of waves on a beach: return and repetition, always, of the same wave against the same shore, in which, however, as each return recapitulates itself, it also infinitely renews and enriches itself'.[42] This is why, far from having a purely abstract style with scant concern for real-world applicability, Levinas's prose is able to be read in real-world terms. Levinas's prose – above all, I would suggest, in *Otherwise than Being* – reflects the brain's process of steeling itself for a task, and allows for the implementation time necessary for the philosophy to seep into the psyche. In reading Levinas, patience and discipline begin to reside in the body in place of self-indulgence, converting desire into responsibility for the Other. In this respect, *Terror's Advocate* is, stylistically, a Levinasian film. The film trains us in a kind of stoicism of the body: as we become more aware of our bodies, they become paradoxically less important to us as sources of self-centred pleasure and more instruments and purveyors of ethical responsibility towards the Other. If the film is a thriller, it is, in a sense, a thriller that delves into the heart of moral enquiry. The subject of the film's enquiry is the legal system, and it is, of course, Vergès himself – but it is also its own subtle yet robust stance, its refusal to present its case in an easily digestible way. If the viewer responds favourably to the film's performative encapsulation of the irreducibility of ethics and law to either a simple distinction or a pleasing harmony, the subject matter can offer an immersive experience in style in tandem with ethical food for thought.

This chapter has sought to describe the ethico-performative similarities between Levinas's philosophy, with its rhythmic insistence on and encouragement of the self's responsibility for the Other, and the two Schroeder films in question, with their textual performances of the dissipation, through multiple viewpoints, of certainty, accompanied by the quietly assertive performative qualities of their own insistence and encouragement. *Reversal of Fortune* and *Terror's Advocate* articulate a difficulty with pursuing a purely juridical angle with regard to people's rights in that they show the legal system to be a game, with brave and imaginative lawyers able to twist its structures to their own ends. Concerns over the difficulties of applying Levinas's philosophy to a practical enactment of law, such as those expressed by Smith, are not assuaged by the subject matter of these two films, but their textual performances – their uses of style not just to articulate their themes but to embody, create and in a sense *be* those themes – can in themselves school us in the mettle necessary to withstand the vagaries of what the legal system might otherwise lead us to believe is 'the truth'. The ways in which the structure and style of *Reversal of Fortune* expose the game-like qualities of the legal system in which Claus von Bülow is enmeshed and Vergès' performance of himself in, for and as articulated by *Terror's Advocate* have the effect of turning these protagonists' experiences into forms through which we might feel more able to reckon with the compromises and 'sly winks' of life in the justice system.

CHAPTER 6

Our Lady of the Assassins and Levinas's Ethics as First Philosophy

Although the Schroeder films we have considered so far are in many ways very different from one another – principally in terms of both subject matter and film style – if there is one thing they certainly share it is an interest in overturning the perceived wisdom surrounding appearances, actions and roles in society. In *Maîtresse*, *Reversal of Fortune*, and *Terror's Advocate*, the unemphasised illocutionary acts of the film styles coupled with the subject matter posit a searching openness, questioning the categories society uses to define people and their relations to one another.

For Levinas, too, such categories stand in the way of the ethical relation. Levinas notes powerfully that 'it is said . . . that nothing is more *conditioned* than the allegedly originary consciousness and the ego. The illusion that human subjectivity is capable of falling into is said to be particularly insidious.'[1] This is expressive of Levinas's position, fundamental to his work, that ethics is first philosophy: consciousness and the ego are only 'allegedly' originary, and it is rather the ethical encounter that forms our relation to the world, *prior to* Being, knowledge and ontology. In Levinas's work, therefore, the ethical relationship between the self and the Other exists anterior to the categorisation that makes such relationships easy to prejudge.

I shall consider Schroeder's violent and romantic Colombian drama *Our Lady of the Assassins* from this angle. The film, adapted by Fernando Vallejo from his 1994 novel, tells the story of the love affair between a disillusioned middle-aged writer and a teenage gang member. Their relationship plays out against a backdrop of violence and tension in Medellín, Colombia. Schroeder treats this material matter-of-factly, stressing the ordinariness of the relationship. The result is a film that embraces a non-judgemental take on a type of relationship that movies are not accustomed to portraying. This film occupies yet another corner of Schroeder's work – a drama set in Colombia, in Spanish, and shot on early High Definition (HD) cameras. Due to the limited distribution it has received since its first release, it is one of the least-seen and least-known of Schroeder's films, but Schroeder has said: 'To me it's one of the best movies I've ever made.'[2] There are a number of elements in *Our Lady of the Assassins* that deserve much attention, but I want to discuss the film in terms of its treatment of the sexuality of its main characters and the notion of categorisation, as this will draw out some of the ethical implications of what the film achieves, particularly in relation to Levinas's assertion of ethics as first philosophy.

Constructed and Normalised Sexualities

Categorisations of sexuality are socially constructed, with heterosexuality the dominant category and homosexuality, bisexuality and other sexualities, including those that refuse to define themselves, slowly achieving more recognition over the years. Richard Dyer has suggested that

> [h]eterosexuality as a social reality seems to be invisible to those who benefit from it. In part, this is because of the remorseless construction of heterosexuality as natural. If things are natural, they cannot really be questioned or scrutinized and so they fade from view. Such naturalization often characterizes how we see, and don't see, the powerful; how they see, and don't see, themselves.[3]

For Dyer, therefore, we need 'to try to see it', in order 'to make heterosexuality strange ... Then we might be able to start considering how heterosexuality, like homosexuality, has been socially constructed.'[4] Luc Dardenne, coming from a more generalised philosophical perspective, observes: 'The majority ignores the minority. The majority lives in the evidence of being everything. How could it be otherwise, given that all institutions and all customs are its mirror? Rare and precious are the individuals from the majority who bore a hole through the mirror.'[5] If, in our society, heterosexuality is the 'norm' from which all other sexualities deviate, then one way in which a film might assert that gay relationships are (or should be) equal to heterosexual relationships is by portraying the inequality so as to work up the indignation of the audience. But if a film makes explicit its desire to overturn society's heteronormativity, then although the result is often a sincere and emotional film, a potentially counterproductive consequence of this is that the film ends up being more about the struggle than about the desired outcome. In this approach, viewers are reminded of the struggle but perhaps not necessarily told anything they did not already know.

An alternative approach, then, would be for a film to start from a position that people are essentially good and that it is *inequality* that society creates, not equality. *Our Lady of the Assassins* takes this approach – to remove the strangeness from homosexuality, to make it 'invisible'. Although Levinas's work does not address homosexuality, his ethics can be engaged with from a generalised queer perspective in the ways in which it speaks for the primacy of the Saying as against the categorisations of the Said and in how it promotes all others as worthy of ethical engagement. *Otherwise than Being*, in particular, uses style to convey the idea that there is something primal about goodness, that goodness comes first, has always been there, *will* always be there, and that therefore we *are* good, even (or especially) in spite of ourselves. This belief can be adopted in a queer fashion to slay pessimistic takes on the possibilities of integration and acceptance for minorities. Similarly, therefore, a film might enable viewers to experience the goodness that comes before choice and discrimination and thus to reconnect with the pre-originary ethics that Levinas posits so powerfully. To take an example from literature: the novelist Alan Hollinghurst has said in interview that he tries to write 'from a presumption of the gayness of the narrative position . . . To write about gay life from a gay perspective unapologetically and as naturally as most novels are written from a heterosexual position.'[6] Hollinghurst's principal gay characters – William Beckwith in *The Swimming-Pool Library*, Edward Manners in *The Folding Star*, the quartet of male protagonists in *The Spell*, Nick Guest in *The Line of Beauty*, Paul Bryant in *The Stranger's Child*, Johnny Sparsholt in *The Sparsholt Affair*[7] – all already 'know' their (homo)sexuality before we meet them, and so it would distance us from them if we had to be told it, to be 'prepared' for it or to have it 'excused'. Hollinghurst's prose does not flinch in the face of a gay protagonist's sexuality; rather, in his fiction, the homosexuality of the protagonists is a given. The approach seeks to give readers what they get from normalised heterosexual narratives – namely, a performance of normalised sexuality, the only difference being that this time it is homosexuality that is normalised. The powerful illocutionary effect of this is to tackle the issue not through an appeal to readers to engage with a problem but rather through an illustration of the solution.

In discussing his approach to the making of *Our Lady of the Assassins*, Schroeder has explained that 'the decision I made was to make it as a given, as if there was no discussion, no problem'.[8] My analysis of the film will explore ways in which it can be said to normalise homosexuality through its use of a style that makes the normality of homosexuality a mere given.

Falling in Love in Medellín

Schroeder has explained that for a long time he had wanted to make a film set in Colombia, a country he had lived in for several years as a child.[9] He decided to film Fernando Vallejo's 1994 novel *La Virgen de los Sicarios*.[10] The main character, of both the novel and the film, is a middle-aged writer, also called Fernando Vallejo – which adds perhaps an element of autobiography to the story's portrait of the time and the place. When we first see Fernando (Germán Jaramillo) in the film, he is returning to his home city of Medellín after a thirty-year absence. At a party thrown by his old friend Alfonso (Manuel Busquets), Fernando is introduced to Alexis (Anderson Ballesteros), a teenager who, as we soon find out, is a member of a gang and a *sicario* (assassin). Fernando is immediately attracted to Alexis, and Alexis returns his feelings. The two therefore begin to spend their time together. But Alexis is being hunted by a rival gang. And so everywhere he and Fernando go, they are followed by the possibility of assassination attempts.

Early on in the film comes a sequence indicative both of Fernando and Alexis's relationship and of the film's technique. On their first excursion, the day after they have met and first slept with each other, the two of them take a taxi ride out to the smaller city of Sabaneta. Fernando argues with the taxi driver as he does not like the music being played in the taxi; when they are dropped off, the taxi driver leaves them with a shouted homophobic insult. Fernando and Alexis, walking along, come to a bar Fernando used to know. They go inside, order drinks, and Fernando engages the jukebox. The song he selects is 'Senderito de Amor', sung by the Mexican superstar Pedro Infante. As the song starts up, the film cuts from a close-up of Alexis watching the mechanism of the jukebox to a shot of Fernando, seen at first only from below the waist as he walks to a chair, and then, as the camera angles up, sitting down at a table and turning his head away. He puts his hand to his head, his head on the table. Alexis sits down diagonally across the table from him. The barman brings their drinks; Alexis slides a glass towards Fernando, gently nudging him to take it. Fernando looks up with tears in his eyes (Figure 6.1). He explains that the song is a childhood memory, and that all he can think about is all the people he used to know who are no longer around. The style is 'invisible', in a sense, the camerawork designed to give us a window onto the scene rather than to show itself off, the editing slowly cutting back and forth between Alexis and Fernando in a classical style. The moment between the new friends and lovers is tender: Alexis's nudge, Fernando's tear-stained smile at him. But also, the style, in its simple, unforced, classical shot/reverse shot pattern, makes nothing special out of the nature of their relationship. What is notable about this scene is its presentation of the bond between Fernando and Alexis as something worthy of the most ordinary, conventional cinematic moment. The film style here is classical in an understated way, comprising a master shot, shot/reverse shots, matches on action, and close-ups to show reactions in more detail. And story-wise, there is nothing in the scene that

Figure 6.1 Fernando cries at the table in the bar; Alexis attends to him. (*continued*)

Figure 6.1 (*continued*) Fernando cries at the table in the bar; Alexis attends to him.

should cause Fernando and Alexis to feel self-conscious: the barman's reaction (whatever it may be) to their tenderness is not presented as significant, and they are not shown looking round to protect themselves or each other; Alexis is not fazed by Fernando's tears (or by the age gap between them, which has of course become pronounced by Fernando's reminiscing about long ago); Fernando is not embarrassed to have cried when he might have wanted to show himself as being 'in control'. The scene is shorn of any categorisation of the lovers. At that moment, they are not a gay man and a gay teenager. Indeed, in one sense, they are not even shown here as lovers. Rather, the moment shows the closeness of two people who do not know each other but who are nevertheless responding to each other. When Alexis proffers the drink to Fernando, Alexis's facial expression is impassive, and yet it is possible to read on his face a mixture of feelings: bewilderment but also an instinct for what Fernando needs – support and a drink. The taxi driver's earlier insult feels far away. The result of these combined elements is a filmic moment of unremarkable, unexceptional tenderness that, in its avoidance of defining Fernando and Alexis's relationship in opposition to an established 'norm', normalises the desire between them. For that reason, the scene, in its understated way, is remarkable and exceptional.

To understand this moment as a filmic example of ethics as first philosophy, we can turn to the issue of chronology. It is not just as though *before* I meet the totalising categorisations that prejudice my views of people, I am ethical towards all others. Ethics as first philosophy is perhaps best approached as an abstract notion – not because it cannot exist in the everyday world but because it is a paradox, involving a state pre-Being, or rather, outside or 'otherwise than' being. Peperzak suggests that

> the 'pre' of 'pre-original' and the precedence constitutive of transcendent diachrony are differently 'before' than the 'before' with which we are familiar through the ontological understanding of time characteristic of our culture. In some sense, which it remains difficult to make more precise, all the expressions here become metaphorical, and as soon as we try to clarify them, we transform them into elements of a said, which, as said, obeys the temporal commands of ontology.[11]

Peperzak's argument, therefore, is that we should avoid defining this idea of the 'before' in relation to an understanding of time. Rather, it is a 'before' that stands 'otherwise than' linearity – and 'otherwise than' definition; Levinas says that '[t]he movement back to the saying is the phenomenological reduction. In it the indescribable is described.'[12] As Davis explains, 'the logical incoherence of Levinas's prose entails a rejection of logic as the privileged tool of intellectual analysis. Whatever Levinas is getting at cannot be reached within a conventionally coherent discourse.'[13] What Levinas is conveying through this 'logical incoherence' is the Saying as an idea of anteriority that, if it were more clearly defined, would not challenge us to strive for it. The Levinasian pre-original represents a sense of the unformed, an ideal state, the unfettered ethical relation. At the same time, as the idea is referred to as ethics as *first* philosophy, it does invite us to think of something that happens *next*. It acknowledges Levinas's sense that people are naturally good but that they 'lose' this goodness through their egocentric attachment to the fixity of the categorisations through which the world operates. For Levinas, 'Goodness is always older than choice; the Good has always already chosen and required the unique one.'[14] From this, we can say that people would be good if only they were not compromised by the unethical clutter of everyday linguistics – the compromise of the Said.

A key way in which *Our Lady of the Assassins* strives to perform this sense of a pre-originary goodness is to be found in its presentation of its central relationship as occupying spaces typically the domain of a 'normal' cinematic heterosexual couple. In a discussion of the AIDS-themed film *Philadelphia* (dir. Jonathan Demme, 1993), Noël Carroll explains what he calls the film's use of 'recalibration', that is, how it makes the homosexuality of its protagonist Andrew Beckett more acceptable to a general audience by situating him within the context of a loving family – thereby recalibrating more comforting elements of the narrative so as to assimilate the more difficult topic.[15] I believe that, in a similar way, *Our Lady of the Assassins* 'normalises' the relationship between Fernando and Alexis by showing them together in a succession of common everyday scenes: a drink in a bar, reminiscing about the past, having breakfast together at home, eating out, sleeping together, discussing their noisy neighbour, and so on. In each case, the moment serves, to borrow Carroll's term, to 'recalibrate' familiar domesticity, turning Fernando and Alexis's relationship into a mainstream romance. The moment between Fernando and Alexis in the bar can be read in such a way. The lack of any 'issues' of sexuality in the scene constitutes an ethical encounter, not between Fernando and Alexis but between us and the film. Something the bar scene shows is that stylistic conventionality in film can in itself carry an ethical charge, for example, by presenting a radical idea in what it is hoped will be an easily digestible way so as to embed it in the consciousnesses of general filmgoers. Stylistic conventionality allows for a shorthand way of achieving filmic effectiveness: a conversation presented in shot/reverse shot, for example – such as we see in the bar scene – is easily recognisable because of all the other shot/reverse shot conversations we have seen in films over the years. The more conventionally presented certain subject matter is, the more it performs the ethical act of furthering the cause for the subject matter in question. The scene does not overtly invite scrutiny or comment on the issue; in its goodness, it simply accepts Fernando and Alexis's right to be together. Schroeder has noted,

> It's really an impossible love story – they come from very different backgrounds, but they learn from each other. Fernando learns about the new realities of his town – the paradise of his childhood that has been transformed into some kind of hell. And the boy has an admiration for this adult who is an iconoclast and a rebel. It's a learning situation for both of them.[16]

In describing the love story as impossible, however, Schroeder does not give himself credit for its performative effects. The normalisation of the relationship between Fernando and Alexis in filmic terms means that its only impossibility is its imperilled existence within the turbulent world of the film's Medellín.

The Importance of Categorising the Film

In spite of its focusing on Fernando and Alexis's relationship, however, *Our Lady of the Assassins*, like *Maîtresse*, *Reversal of Fortune* and *Terror's Advocate*, refuses easy categorisation in terms of genre. *Our Lady of the Assassins* does join a number of other films about teenagers and crime in the Medellín slums, notably *Rodrigo D: No Futuro* (*Rodrigo D: No Future*, dir. Víctor Gaviria, 1990) and *Jairo El Sicario* (*Sicario*, dir. José Novoa, 1994). And it arrived just in advance of the cycle of Latin American gang-violence movies that achieved success in the 2000s, at the forefront of which was *Cidade de Deus* (*City of God*, dir. Fernando Meirelles, 2002), its TV spin-off series *Cidade dos Homens* (*City of Men*, various directors, 2002–5) and the big-screen version of the same name (dir. Paulo Morelli, 2007), and *Linha de Passe* (dirs Walter Salles and Daniela Thomas, 2008). But Schroeder's film can also be seen in many other ways. Following the cue of the source material, a novel that is both a narrative and a polemic, the film of *Our Lady of the Assassins* is a love story, a portrait of a homosexual relationship across the generation gap and a character study of a writer. It also has the hard edge of a suspense thriller, the vivid location shooting and spectacular vistas of a travelogue and the intimate, slightly dreamy atmosphere of an erotic poem. The film's resistance to genre categorisation importantly aids its Levinasian flavour of non-fixity.

Yet in another sense, a degree of fixity is important in assessing the film's achievements. Without wanting to violate my reading of the film as offering an experience of a type of filmic Levinasian ethics as first philosophy, I want to suggest ways in which the film can also *productively* take its place *within* the conventions of filmic categorisation. Earlier in my discussion of this film, I suggested that one way in which a film could seek to 'normalise' representations of homosexual relationships on-screen is, as Hollinghurst does in his fiction, to start from a presumption of gayness, to enact the flipside of Dyer's argument about making heterosexuality strange, and make homosexuality invisible as a category within the story. But this is where categorisation can be useful in highlighting such an achievement. Gary Needham's work on the film of *Brokeback Mountain* (dir. Ang Lee, 2005) is useful in this regard. Needham has argued how efforts to play down *Brokeback Mountain*'s status as both a Western and a gay romance – in order, so he argues, to stress the 'universality' of the film's themes[17] – work against the film's progressiveness, and how only by discussing the film *as* a Western can the film's radicalism with regard to the portrayal of its central gay relationship be felt. For Needham, '[a] general tendency of film scholars of the Western is to highlight the genre's role in making sense of national and cultural identity; it is clear that viewing *Brokeback Mountain* as a queer Western becomes an important strategy in writing homosexuality in to that history'.[18] Thus, *Brokeback Mountain*, so Needham asserts, must be discussed in terms of the Western genre in order for us to identify both how it subverts that genre and how it inserts homosexuality into the history of that same genre.

It is difficult to discuss *Our Lady of the Assassins* in terms of how it subverts genre, because, as we have seen, it does not readily fit into any one genre. But a fruitful way of anchoring the film's achievement, following Needham's work on *Brokeback Mountain*, is in relation to its appropriation of many tropes of classical film style. For that reason, I want to consider

Schroeder's choice of shooting format. Schroeder has published a short diary covering the making of *Our Lady of the Assassins*. It provides information relating to the shooting of the film, the casting and direction of the non-professional actors, the tense shooting circumstances and the creative decisions that resulted from those tensions. As the diary explains, shooting in Medellín was to prove rather dangerous: Schroeder was at risk of being kidnapped, and the filming equipment was a prize for thieves; therefore, armed guards were deployed to help protect the production and its personnel. Also, younger cast members in the film had involvement with gangs and trouble with the law.[19] The situation therefore called for some considerable bravery, boldness and problem-solving. The difficulty of the film shoot in Medellín brings to mind Lingis's description of *Otherwise than Being* as 'entirely a labor of articulating the inevitably strange, non-objective and non-ontic, but also non-ontological, terms with which the original form of responsible subjectivity has to be described'.[20] The implication in Lingis's remarks is that the successful rendition of Levinas's philosophy comes about only through hard work, through consistent application. Schroeder's efforts in getting the film made could therefore be said to amount to a laborious process akin to Lingis's perception of Levinas's undertaking in writing *Otherwise than Being*. Schroeder decided to shoot the film with HD cameras (in the very early days of HD being used for feature films), partly because HD allowed for a particular type of image quality as well as visual effects that could be achieved relatively easily and partly because the equipment's relative smallness and lightness would help him and his crew achieve a much-needed flexibility in their filmmaking circumstances.[21] This choice proves significant not just for production reasons but also for matters of film style. As we saw in the bar scene, the film deploys a largely classical style – master shots, shot/reverse shots, matches on action, close-ups – and this provides an interesting tension with the 'newness' of this early HD aesthetic.

For example, the film begins with an opening sequence of white credits on a black background, accompanied by the plaintive strings of Jorge Arriagada's touching score, which conveys the sense of downbeat drama that will underpin the film's actions and characters. It is a beginning that works in classical, conventional terms, reminiscent, with the Mahler-like emotion of the music, of the opening credits sequence of the film adaptation of *Death in Venice* (dir. Luchino Visconti, 1971), another story about a middle-aged artist and the youth he idolises. And yet when the credits fade into a travelling shot as Fernando approaches the entrance to the apartment block where he will meet Alexis for the first time, the traffic noise on the soundtrack has a surprising, unfiltered quality rather akin to a home movie, while the image has a clean, grain-free appearance that, in the early days of HD, departs from the richly textured appearance of images that have been shot on film.²² But when Fernando arrives at the apartment, and his old friend Alfonso opens the door to greet him, the film frames the moment in a pair of tight over-the-shoulder shots, the first over Fernando's shoulder, and so revealing Alfonso's face, and then the reverse shot over Alfonso's shoulder, thus affording us our first emphatic close-up view of Fernando's face (Figure 6.2). It feels like an absolutely classic way for a film to introduce its main character.

Figure 6.2 The two old friends hug and Fernando is shown in a classic first close-up. (*continued*)

Figure 6.2 (*continued*) The two old friends hug and Fernando is shown in a classic first close-up.

Schroeder is using classical techniques in order to make the strangeness of the world and its characters more palatable; by introducing setting, situation and character in a way that we can easily recognise, the film style serves both to break us in to the (then unfamiliar) shooting format and to locate us securely within this strange world, to show us, perhaps, that there is nothing 'strange' about it. Any tension between the style and the format only enhances the film's achievement: in presenting such a chaotically made film with such organisation, Schroeder's direction is able to provide an easy way in for the viewer, such that the potentially off-putting subject matter is made palatable through its conventional recognisability. Through its practical usage, therefore, the HD format not only facilitates the making of the film, it also gives to it a performative dimension, for rather than just being a decision taken once the film has already been envisaged, the technology helps *make* the film, not just literally but also figuratively. Thus, the tensions between conventionality and the technological aspects of the film become crucial elements of its performative power as a work that can transcend prejudices, in both filmic and ideological terms.

This also allows for the film's emotionalism, which is somewhat uncharacteristic of Schroeder's work. In *Maîtresse* and many of his other films, Schroeder practises what we have seen Gary Indiana describe as a 'fastidious neutrality'; it is hard, however, to describe *Our Lady of the Assassins* as neutral. The film's use of music is an example of this. If we think back to Butler's notion of resignification in language, which I considered in relation to the development of the Dardennes' style, we can see how a facet of 'normalising' conventionality can be made to twist round to breathe new, ethical life into a text. In *Our Lady of the Assassins*, we have already seen how the opening credits set a classical tone, with the simple credits and the plaintive music. The use of the music has a comforting conventionality that puts the viewer at ease. There is not a great deal of extra-diegetic music in *Our Lady of the Assassins* – but what there is has a pointed emotional impact. Schroeder has said that the music is a sign 'that we are entering in a zone outside of the normal naturalistic reality. And . . . what I like very much in that music is that it helps us to feel the pain of the main character.'[23] Does this shift towards conventional tropes in the film represent a diminution of radicalism in Schroeder's work, and in his use of style? In his *Notes on Cinematography*, Bresson includes this note: 'Music. It isolates your film from the life of your film (musical delectation). It is a powerful modifier and even destroyer of the real, like alcohol or dope.'[24] And it relates to a Levinasian sense of how meaning works against ethical engagement: Levinas says in *Otherwise than Being* that '[i]n the said, to have a meaning is for an element to be in such a way as to turn into references to other elements, and for the others to be evoked by it'.[25] I am reading this as suggestive of elements of film style that can become overused to the point of offering easy responses and a dulling of individuality and ethical freshness. But taking our cue from Needham's work on *Brokeback Mountain*, we can see how, with *Our Lady of the Assassins*, Schroeder has found a way to justify the inclusion of a conventional filmic trope, in that the music, precisely by virtue of its normalising effect within the filmic style, helps to situate the portrayal of the central relationship within terms that benefit from such normalisation. If normalisation breeds invisibility, allowing identities to 'fade from view', to quote Dyer again, then Fernando and Alexis's relationship, presented as 'normal', achieves a productive invisibility, one that removes the notion of categorisation that so often limits and even menaces the status of homosexual relationships.

It is therefore this very adoption of standard classical tropes that helps cement *Our Lady of the Assassins* as such a progressive film in terms of representations of gay characters, and it is precisely through discussing the film in terms of its classicism that we can see what a revolutionary film it is. It is worth noting that Schroeder made this film after his succession of Hollywood dramas and thrillers in the 1990s – *Single White Female*, *Kiss of Death*, *Before and After* and *Desperate Measures*; as such, he may have acquired a taste for an easygoing use of recognisable tropes such that we see in conventional Hollywood product. (Similarly, we may note that *Terror's Advocate*, with its generic thriller trappings, came after another Hollywood thriller, *Murder by Numbers*.) Rather than seeing this as a *relaxation* of

Schroeder's 'fastidious neutrality', however, I would like to suggest that it can be taken as an *evolution* in his approach to his subject matter – not a simple surrender to classical forms but a reworking of them for his own ethical ends. Audiences of all sexualities tend to see heterosexual love stories not as heterosexual love stories but simply as 'love stories' – hence Dyer's assertion that heterosexuality is so normalised that it has become invisible. The achievement of *Our Lady of the Assassins* in placing its gay protagonists *within* the tradition of conventional film style is that it begins to mix things up such that notions of a cultural Said, pre-ordered and pre-ordained, fixed and dictatorial, controlling and complacent, begin to dissipate. We saw in the films of the Dardennes that there was a progression in their use of style from the stripping away of conventional tropes of filmic expression so as to render the filmic language more primitive, more in touch with the unaffected ethical encounter, to a gradual reintroduction of conventionality to reframe and refresh their ethically presented worlds. And it is the conventionality, the classicism, of Hollinghurst's prose style that marks out his novels as normalisations of a gay sensibility in English-language fiction, because his novels have so much in common with the traditions of that fiction. Similarly, in *Our Lady of the Assassins* it is the classicism of the style that initiates the presentation of Fernando and Alexis's relationship as 'normal', performatively conditioning our reading of the film. If a homosexual love story looks much like a heterosexual love story on-screen, it achieves a normalising effect without needing to draw attention to its radicalism. That said, its radicalism seems not to have escaped attention: Michel Ciment, in an interview with Schroeder, puts it to the director that *Our Lady of the Assassins* is one of the few films that depict homosexuality with naturalness, and Schroeder replies,

> It's that which is troubling in the film: that the homosexuality be filmed as if taken for granted. The same as the violence. This combination, and if one adds the age difference of the lovers, makes for a wholly innocent film at first, but which reveals itself to be very subversive, to such an extent that many festivals were frightened by this film.[26]

Such reactions are evidence of the difficulty of performing the Levinasian one-for-the-other. In response, *Our Lady of the Assassins* requires no effort on the part of viewers to recognise the sexuality of its characters; the film serves to render its viewers passive on this point. Thus, a Levinasian passivity is invoked: 'Substitution is not an act; it is a passivity inconvertible into an act . . .'[27] Just as Fernando is awoken from his self-obsession by the ethical call of Alexis, so the film's viewers are invited to feel the passivity of substitution. If felt, this would be a perlocutionary act in concert with the film's illocutionary effects.

Performativity and Ethics as First Philosophy

The result of this is a style that says not that this is the way we would like things to be or the way they could or should be but that this is the way they *are*. The style thereby hopes to convince viewers of this, and of its rightness. A hallmark of this style is that it aims to leave the viewer no choice – just as Levinas says that, prior to being able to choose, we are already ethical.

This returns us to the paradox that I identified in the Introduction in the use of theories of performativity to explain the effects of film style. We have already seen how a reading informed by performativity theory helps to locate the Saying of a film text, such that the viewer's preconceived notions of otherness are disrupted or undone by the process of viewing the film. And yet I am also suggesting that theories of performativity, when applied to film, lead us to identify something in those films that in effect is taking choice away from us. Schroeder's deployment of conventional classical film grammar in *Our Lady of the Assassins* joins the Dardennes' more singular style, Hollinghurst's fiction, the identification of an American people in the Declaration of Independence and Levinas's textual performance in *Otherwise than Being* as instances of performativity that bring into being a new way of thinking, through a resignification of existing, conventional tropes. In doing this, it is as though, in each case, a fait accompli has been carried out. In this regard, the question is, what makes these achievements, which are ostensibly those of the Saying, so very different from the thematised, ontological arena of the Said?

The Saying is nothing if it is not understood in the service of the ethical project to which it is devoted. The very act of writing *Otherwise than Being* was an action designed to posit an ethical stance. The ethical success of that action lies in the way in which Levinas formulates his position. We need not be squeamish about recognising what Levinas's labours have set out to achieve. Peperzak remarks powerfully on the stakes involved:

> The originary Good does not lie in good will or obedience, and this might explain why all moralistic admonitions ring so false. Just like obedience, crimes are preceded, borne and supported by a goodness older than all human initiative – a goodness not destroyed by any evil, and thus more futural than the historical battle between good and evil . . . In admitting that hatred is not strong enough to conquer this anachronic good, we celebrate the creative origin. Even the most pointless suffering cannot kill hope, because hope is stronger than the alternation between life and death.[28]

In describing it thus, Peperzak draws out the utopian implications of Levinas's ethics as first philosophy, indicating ways in which it transcends morality to become a sort of permanent background to everything we do, a background always within our reach if only we could recognise it. Levinas says that 'the signification of saying goes beyond the said. It is not ontology that raises up the speaking subject; it is the signifyingness of saying going beyond essence that can justify the exposedness of being, ontology.'[29] That is why an awareness of the project of the Saying, and a definition of it as such, need not violate its effectiveness as a purveyor of ethics as first philosophy. The Saying is too anarchic to capitulate to the complacency of the Said.

Our Lady of the Assassins is a heartbreakingly beautiful romance within Schroeder's filmography. The lack of explanation for Fernando and Alexis's love serves to emphasise how instinctive it is for them both. Alexis is loyal to Fernando; he loves Fernando and is happy when he is with him. Fernando is equally loyal and loving to Alexis. Fernando's one fault in respect of Alexis – and it is a decisive one – is that he does not grasp well enough the threats to Alexis's life, the realities of the gang warfare. But despite the tension and violence that surround the characters, the film's depiction of desire, as understood here through the Levinasian pre-original dimension, through ethics as first philosophy, is a positive one both for filmmaking culture and for society more broadly. This is the third type of film performativity that I mentioned in the Introduction, the performativity of film more generally, the ways in which it can impact on the wider world. In this regard, we can consider performativity in terms of dissemination: the more widely seen, the wider the effects. *Our Lady of the Assassins* is little-known outside of retrospectives, and yet Schroeder's filmmaking here, as so often, performs a pre-originary goodness that can undo notions of categorisation and prejudice. If we are good prior to anything else, if we have no identity except through our obligation and response to the Other, which founds our identity, then this film can be considered Levinasian for its openness towards the otherness of its central relationship and thus, by extension, to others in the wider world. And if, as Wilson intimates with regard to the reading encounter, we enter into a performative relationship with a text such that the text helps to re-form our identity while we help to re-form reality, then *Our Lady of the Assassins* has the potential to re-form the views of those who believe that homosexual romance on film can never achieve equal status with heterosexual romance. In this way, the film returns us to what Peperzak calls 'a yesteryear without evil, where all good began'.[30]

PART III

Paul Schrader: An Unexpected Ethics

Part III Introduction

In my discussions of the Dardennes and Schroeder, it is important to note that although many of the characters in the films have struggled to take what we might call a Levinasian course of action, I have not questioned the films' *own* performances of what I am reading as a Levinasian ethics. The Dardennes' films are focused on the ethics intrinsic to their stories and styles, and in respect of Schroeder's films I have argued for a subtler but no less Levinasian reading – namely, that despite the different styles deployed, there is a consistency in terms of films that perform a responsibility towards otherness. It is in relation to these questions of ethics and consistency that I now turn to the work of Paul Schrader.

At first glance, Schrader's cinema appears to be averse to Levinasian concerns. Many of his films concentrate relentlessly on a protagonist who appears to resist social interaction – and social interaction, as we have seen, is a precondition for Levinasian ethical engagement. Schrader has talked about what he calls 'a man and his room' stories,[1] and examples in his directorial work include Julian Kay in *American Gigolo*; Yukio Mishima in *Mishima: A Life in Four Chapters*; the isolated drug dealer John LeTour in *Light Sleeper* (1992); Wade Whitehouse, a cop struggling in the shadow of a violent father in *Affliction* (1997); Father Lankester Merrin, battling Satan in *Dominion: Prequel to the Exorcist*; Carter Page III, a lonely male escort in *The Walker* (2007); Adam Stein in *Adam Resurrected*; and Reverend Ernst Toller, whose crisis of faith pushes him towards desperate acts in *First Reformed* (2017). The protagonists of some of the Schrader screenplays directed by other filmmakers can also be said to be this character type, notably Travis Bickle in *Taxi Driver*, Allie Fox in *The Mosquito Coast* (dir. Peter Weir, 1986), based on the novel by Paul Theroux, and even perhaps Christ in *The Last Temptation of Christ* (dir. Martin Scorsese, 1988), Schrader's adaptation of Nikos Kazantzakis's novel. In each of these characters, there is an unwillingness – or even, sometimes, a psychological inability – to enter into an ethical relation with another person. And the relationships that do happen are often so violent or destructive that ethical concerns seem to be far away.

And yet this frequent focus on isolated individuals sets the scene for powerful explorations of what it means to relate, or not to relate, to the Other. As we saw in the discussion of Jacques Vergès's eight-year disappearance as covered in *Terror's Advocate*, social isolation – self-willed or otherwise – can result in a transformed perspective on society and a concomitant awareness of ethical concerns. George Kouvaros has noted: 'The view of the world presented in Schrader's films is essentially that of an outsider . . . Schrader describes this outside figure as "The Peeper, The Wanderer, The Voyeur, The Loner . . ."'[2] This description is redolent of Levinas's mentioning of 'the stranger, the widow, and the orphan' as three examples of the especially vulnerable in society.[3] And Schrader has said of his protagonists, 'I love to make movies about people who are disapproved of by society because I feel if you can get people to identify with a character they don't think is worthy of identification, then you open them up in some way and who knows what happens once they open up'.[4] If this risks suggesting a desire to assimilate otherness into the same, it can also suggest a process of turning towards the Other, akin to what Levinas calls a 'bending back upon itself' that is 'a turning inside out', as we saw in this book's Introduction.[5] Accordingly, Schrader's work, I will argue, raises importantly problematic Levinasian questions about the tortured status of being hostage to the Other, the desire to retreat into the safety of one's own world and the consequences of stepping outside this safety zone and offering oneself to the Other. The Schrader films I have chosen to discuss highlight these questions and throw a new, Levinasian light on this filmmaker's work.

The predicaments of Schrader's protagonists are reflected in, and complicated by, the styles of the films themselves. Many of Schrader's films feel driven by style, while others wear their styles somewhat more mutedly. As such, while the Dardennes' work, with its consistent, if evolving, approach to style, and Schroeder's work, mercurial and without overt directorial identity, can be readily considered as enacting a filmic Saying of originary performativity, Schrader's approach frustrates any Levinasian reading based on stylistic consistency. Nevertheless, Schrader's uses of style offer their own sense of the performativity of film, of its enactment of existing tropes for new ends. Kouvaros has discussed *Mishima: A Life in Four Chapters* in directly performative terms, seeing 'an explicit exchange between the body of the film and the body it seeks to represent',[6] and throughout Schrader's cinema, we can see that the complexities of the bodies in question – self-regarding but reticent, fit and alert but spiritually conflicted – are reflected in the complexity of the 'bodies' of the film-making styles. This complexity of purpose, I argue, invites audiences to remain alert and involved, and, in doing so, kindles ethical awareness. The complexity is, I would like to suggest, in itself Levinasian.

Schrader's own comments on his films often illuminate this complexity. He has spoken extensively about his own work; Kevin Jackson's edited collection *Schrader on Schrader and Other Writings*, which features a selection of Schrader's own writings as well as an extended interview, is a key text in this regard. And, as is well-known, Schrader has a background in film criticism and theory that predates his career as screenwriter and director and that adds to the sense of his ability to articulate his approach to film. In 2018, he published a new edition of *Transcendental Style in Film: Ozu, Bresson, Dreyer*; it includes an extended introduction entitled 'Rethinking Transcendental Style', in which Schrader traces the legacy of transcendental style across the years since his book first came out, relating it especially to theories of slow cinema. For Schrader, transcendental style and slow cinema share a preoccupation with time as an essential component of how the films present their worlds to us. Time can be used to dislodge the viewer's expectations. One outcome is that '[a] new movie is being created. A simultaneous movie. The spectator's movie . . . The film-maker has forced the viewer to enjoin the narrative process, creating his or her own narrative. The two films overlap: the director's tableau and the spectator's meditations on that tableau.'[7] This perspective on viewer involvement is reflected elsewhere in Schrader's critical work. For example, in a 2006 article entitled 'Canon Fodder' for *Film Comment*, Schrader tells us about a project he was involved in to come up with a canon of world cinema and offers criteria for determining this list of greats. One of the criteria is 'viewer engagement'. Schrader says that films on the whole do not require anything of the viewer, because '[e]verything is done for the audience: the information they receive and the emotions they feel are as pre-planned as a railway schedule . . . The viewer needs [*sic*] only sit and stare.'[8] For Schrader, then,

> [a] great film is one that to some degree frees the viewer from this passive stupor and engages him or her in a creative process of viewing . . . The film, either by withholding expected elements or by positing contradictions, causes the viewer to reach into the screen, as it were, and move the creative furniture around. This . . . is a viewer making identifications he or she had no intention of making, coming to conclusions the film can't control, reassembling the film in a unique personal way.[9]

I want to exercise this acknowledgement of film's perlocutionary effects ('conclusions the film can't control') by reading Schrader's films as

Levinasian in their contradictions and complexities. Because Schrader is so articulate about his work, it is tempting to read his films in line with what he has to say about them, which would not seem to include overtly ethical considerations. But Kouvaros notes that if we restrict ourselves to reading films in line with Schrader's own pronouncements, we limit what we can say about them. At the same time, he suggests, we should not disregard what Schrader has to say: '[T]o ignore these comments runs an even greater risk of failing to recognize the contradictory energies, impulses, and ideas that drive his films.'[10] These contradictions are key to my reading of Schrader's work in relation to Levinas's ethics.

I shall begin with *American Gigolo*, which is Schrader's third film as a director, following on from *Blue Collar* (1978) and *Hardcore* (1979). Schrader has said of *American Gigolo*, 'I felt that I had arrived as a director; I felt confident about moving the camera and placing the camera.'[11] In comparison with the styles of *Blue Collar* and *Hardcore*, *American Gigolo* is stylistically ostentatious, positively exploding with flourishes such as elaborate camera movements, expressive lighting, abundant use of music and vivid use of colour, techniques that reappear periodically in Schrader's subsequent work. I shall show how analysing the film's style from a Levinasian perspective reveals the ethical drive of Julian's relationship with his clients, before reflecting on what he gains ethically and what he loses ethically when he turns away from those clients towards a developing love affair with one particular person. I shall then turn to *Mishima: A Life in Four Chapters*. The four-chapter structure of the film initiates a depiction of a life that was also in many ways a piece of performance art. I shall consider the film's depiction of Mishima's life and the (Levinasian) limits it places on Mishima's knowability. Finally, I shall consider three Schrader films – *The Comfort of Strangers*, *Dominion: Prequel to the Exorcist* and *Adam Resurrected* – that feature protagonists who are passive in their wants, desires, and relationship with life; my readings of them will discuss the Levinasian implications of passivity and its ethical importance to film.

In these readings, I shall draw out ways in which the films tacitly invite viewers to engage with the ethical challenges of Schrader's disaffected, socially marginalised protagonists. I shall show how Schrader's work, like that of the Dardennes and Schroeder, often performs what can be read as a Levinasian ethics.

CHAPTER 7

American Gigolo and the Ethics of Falling in Love

With the exception of *Je Pense à Vous*, which acts as a necessary counterpoint in my reading of the Dardennes' work from *La Promesse* onwards, each of the films I have considered so far in this book presents its story, as we have seen, in such a way as to perform a Levinasian ethics by bringing into being, through film style, a world in which judgement is withheld and human curiosity asserted with a view to greater responsibility for others. The effect of Schrader's *American Gigolo* is somewhat different. The film tells the story of a man ostensibly responsible for others, but it does so such that it is unclear to what extent the character commits to his ethics. It is also unclear to what extent the film itself supports or disregards that same ethical commitment. The main character is a high-class gigolo, Julian Kay (played by Richard Gere), and in the course of the film he goes from servicing a roster of wealthy female clients to devoting himself more and more to just one person, someone whom he has met in the slipstream of his regular work, Michelle Stratton (Lauren Hutton). Schrader has said that *American Gigolo* is about 'the inability to express love'.[1] As the film progresses, it slowly becomes apparent that Julian is finding it within himself to express a degree of love for Michelle, and to accept her attention in return. But although this would suggest that Julian is becoming better at meaningful human interaction, we can also read this development as the antithesis of Levinasian responsibility – as a movement from devotion to others to devotion to the self. The question, therefore, is to what extent Julian is a Levinasian protagonist and to what extent he is just taking care of his own needs. This question will be central to my reading of *American Gigolo*.

A Devoted Gigolo: Julian at Work

Julian is a gigolo working out of Los Angeles. He is a young man hired out to spend time with rich women who need a man to perform the function of companion, lover, or both. When we first meet him, Julian appears to be dedicated to the aesthete's life. He has based his career – and indeed, it appears, his entire lifestyle – around fine clothes (designed by Giorgio Armani), a comfortable apartment, the California sunshine, and a career pleasuring women. But while Julian's stylish comportment may appear, on the surface, to be extravagant, indulgent, or self-regarding, we can also read it as a testament to self-control, concentration, and commitment to the needs of other people. He is a curious mix of self-possession and servitude; he may be a narcissist but he also takes pride in his work – and he sees his work as bringing pleasure to women who otherwise would not have access to it. At one point in the film, Julian explains to Michelle why he does what he does. He talks about a recent client, a woman who, in Julian's words, 'hadn't had an orgasm in maybe ten years'. He explains: 'Took me three hours to get her off. For a while there I didn't think I was going to be able to do it. When it was over, I felt like I'd done something, something worthwhile. Who else would have taken that time, or cared enough to do it right?'[2] Julian's monologue speaks to the care and attention with which he approaches his work, and we can read this as his recognition and enactment of an ethical obligation he feels as a central aspect of it: he articulates a desire to help people who might otherwise be marginalised in this respect. Michael L. Morgan, discussing Levinas, says, 'My life has the meaning it does because I encounter other persons as needing me and calling me to aid and support them; I want to respond to them, and in my wanting and responding, goodness and sanctity enter my life.'[3] With this in mind, we could say that Julian's selfhood is enriched by his work. Although his chosen profession of gigolo raises moral questions regarding the selling of sexual services and the position of middle-aged women in an often consumerist, youth-obsessed and sexist society, his occupation is partly one of Levinasian service that performs a responsibility to his female clients.

Indeed, we could say that everything Julian does, he does for the sake of the service he provides. In Levinas's discussions of the ethical relationship between the self and the Other, one of the hallmarks of this relation, certainly by the time of *Otherwise than Being*, is the self's unending, infinite responsibility for the Other and the sacrifices this entails. This is characterised by a kind of ego-free person, a person who does not pursue their own desires, one who, as we have seen, has had their ego 'cored out' in the process of *dénucléation*. In the early stages of *American Gigolo*, Julian, for all his material comforts, occupies something like this position. For his clients, he lives his life according to a professional commitment to style as a tool of communication. Julian, with his stylish comportment, can be seen as a form through which others – namely, his clients – can experience sexual satisfaction. In this regard, he has a connection with Ariane in *Maîtresse*. Julian is also like Vergès in *Terror's Advocate* in exuding a flamboyance that both defines and masks him. And in Schrader's body of work, Julian prefigures Yukio Mishima, whose performance of identity, as we will see in the next chapter, is a key aspect of his art. Julian's personal sense of style, like that of these other characters, is, I believe, performative in the way it substitutes action for explanation, Levinasian in the way it brings his ethics into being. Julian transforms experience into form so that other people can experience *him*. Like any other creative perfectionist dedicated to a craft, Julian applies himself behind the scenes to get the presentation just right. We see this in, for example, the workout scene in his apartment in which Julian trains with his weights while learning Swedish from a tape recorder, in preparation for an appointment he has with a Swedish woman. The film calmly frames Julian's movements and exertions as he hangs upside down by a pair of metal gravity boots (Figure 7.1), pulls his torso up towards the horizontal with supreme effort while repeating the new words he is learning, and then walks across the room, huffing and puffing, to answer the phone. Bill Nichols has said that Julian

> embraces the ethical principles of the man who seeks to act correctly more than to enjoy himself, who guards against losing self-control (through exploitation, manipulation or 'possession' by another), who values ascetic discipline as a way of life, whose pleasure derives from integrity – from obligations dutifully fulfilled.[4]

Figure 7.1 Julian hangs upside down, exercising and learning Swedish.

154   PERFORMING ETHICS THROUGH FILM STYLE

Thus, Julian's lifestyle, although highly materialistic in its attachment to – and even reliance on – objects that speak of style and self-worth, such as his meticulously ordered ties and shirts in the dressing scene, is also one of Levinasian service and sacrifice that demonstrates a responsibility to his clients (Figure 7.2). His hard-working performance of self is another example, after that of Vergès, of the 'restlessness' that is 'better than rest' that Levinas describes in *Otherwise than Being*.[5] For Julian, a sustained commitment to style enables his ethics.

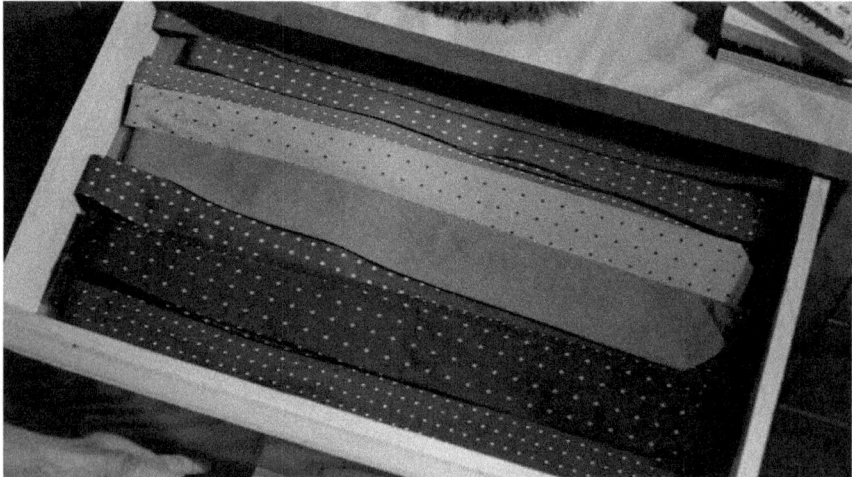

Figure 7.2 Julian's ties and shirts.

We can consider Julian's performance of self to be performativity *in* the film – Performativity$_2$. Related to this, but somewhat distinct from it, the film's style is performativity *of* the film itself – Performativity$_1$. It is important to consider how we can read the film's style as colluding sometimes with Julian's style, as this will suggest how we can read the film in certain parts as bringing Julian's character and situation into being through its own stylistic approach. The opening credits sequence is an example of this.

Performing Julian's Style: The Opening Credits Sequence

The film begins with a small number of names, shown in a slimline, modish white font against a black background. Quiet, slow, minor-key synthesiser music – at once tuneful and faintly ominous – accompanies them, building to a crescendo as the title appears in a 'handwriting' font. Then the title fades out to a drum flourish – the start of the classic Blondie song 'Call Me' (a classic, of course, in retrospect, but in fact written for the film by composer Giorgio Moroder and Blondie's lead singer Debbie Harry). At the same time the film cuts to a shot of a car's wheel in motion on asphalt, then an angle on the tail light, and then a wide overhead shot of Julian, driving along a coastal road in the sun. For the next two and a half minutes as the credits continue we are presented with a range of shots of Julian in his car (a Mercedes), in an upmarket clothing store (Juschi) on the famous shopping street Rodeo Drive, dropping off a female friend at a house, driving down the Pacific Coast Highway, and, as the credits draw to a close, arriving at the home of Anne (Nina van Pallandt), who, as we soon discover, is the procurer of many of Julian's high-class clients.[6] Our first impressions of the world of the American gigolo, then, aided by the song on the soundtrack, are of rapid motion, freedom and a connoisseurial love of fashion.

But another specific and equally important element conveyed by the opening credits sequence is precision. For a start, the images are largely edited in time to the music. The first verse and chorus of the song are traversed by way of three shots: the opening pair on the car (both shots of identical length, in sync with the opening instrumental bars of the song), and then, as Debbie Harry's voice comes in for the first verse, a single shot of Julian driving along, taken from a camera mounted in a vehicle travelling close to him but shifting position, so that we move from a wide angle in front of and above Julian to a closer angle alongside and then slightly behind him. On top of this shot, the film presents the credits of the rest of the main cast members, each one 'written' onto the film in a joined-up handwriting scrawl. As the music cuts to another instrumental passage, the visuals cut to a wide shot angling down onto the Juschi store front as Julian's car pulls up, a doorman greets it, and Julian and a female friend get out and head towards the shop's entrance. The film cuts to the interior of the shop at the exact moment the second verse comes in. From here, the editing pattern changes slightly, with the cuts coming not always on the beat of the musical bar but sometimes just before or just after it. These editing choices save the sequence from slipping into the Levinasian Said of predictability with too many cuts on the beat and instead allow the style to 'breathe'. Nevertheless, throughout the sequence, with the remaining credits presented in the slick handwritten effect as before, the rhythm of the editing remains tightly bound up with the song.

But the effect of precision is not just borne of the film's coordination of camerawork, design, editing and soundtrack; it is also Julian's precision, displayed by him within the frame *and enjoyed by him within the world of the film*. We have an indication of this in the second shot of the sequence, the close-up on the car's tail light, where the background of the roadside shrubbery and railing rises and dips in time with the music; then, as Julian checks his rear-view mirror at the end of the next, lengthier sweeping shot of him in his car, his head movement is perfectly in time to the music at that moment, rounding off the shot with a nice piece of visual rhythm to complement the song. A few shots later, after Julian has delivered his female companion to her front door, he walks back to his car, reaches over and pushes down the convertible's roof just in time for the shot to capture it before needing to cut to the next passage of the music; although this is an effect of the timing of the editing and is not 'intentional' on Julian's part, it gives the impression that his movements are in collusion with the film's own style. Finally, as Julian pulls up at Anne's house, checks his hair, and then gets out and walks in through the entrance, the final credit – 'written and directed by Paul Schrader' – appears just as the song is beginning to fade away, and thus offers a satisfying final flourish, all the more so for being placed self-consciously after a slight pause in the rhythm of the credits, as if announcing Schrader not just as the writer-director but as the principal source of the film's dynamic movement. But with this credit shown over the shot of a rear view of Julian as he enters the house, it is as if the self-consciousness is Julian's as well as the film's. The overall impression from the sequence is of Julian's being at one with the style of the film. He cannot hear the song on the soundtrack; nor is he moving in continuous time with it – almost every cut in the sequence represents a jump in time, and often a change of location – but it is as if he is feeling the rhythm of these edits, or even that he is himself setting the pace, the tone, and the style.[7]

On this note, a comparison of *American Gigolo* with *Maîtresse* is apt. Both Julian and Ariane are sex workers of a sort, but Schrader's filmmaking style differs from Schroeder's in that Schrader deploys a variety of cinematic stylistic effects to depict Julian's corporeal and psychological dilemma whereas Schroeder is more content to use the camera as a relatively dispassionate observer of the action. And while Ariane's costumes in *Maîtresse* were designed by the noted fashion designer Karl Lagerfeld, they are not focused on in the way Julian's Armani wardrobe is in *American Gigolo*. The effect of this is that *Maîtresse* gives the impression of not asserting a particular point of identification; we can observe Ariane at work without the sense that we are being pushed into identifying with her or being invited to feel what it might be like to *be* her. By contrast, in *American Gigolo*, Schrader's style, at certain moments, invites us to join Julian in every hip-shake, every bum-wiggle, every strut and saunter of his stylishly clothed body. We may say that we *observe* Ariane as a dominatrix but that we *feel* what it is like to be Julian the gigolo. Thus, in the early moments of *American Gigolo*, there is a performative quality to the style that can help us experience the protagonist's actions.

Love and Death: Two Interventions in Julian's Life

In this first stretch of the film, two events occur that will come to be especially important for Julian. The first happens when, arriving in an upmarket bar after having attended to business, he sees Michelle for the first time. The scene begins with the camera following Julian as he swaggers through the room and settles himself on a high stool at the bar. The camera moves in on his face as he sees Michelle, seated alone in one of the booths. He goes over to sit with her, and they fall into conversation. There is some initial comedy around their confusion in hearing each other speak French – they are both amused when they realise they both speak English. But then the conversation becomes very intimate, as if, without realising it, they have each stumbled upon a significant person, and Schrader's directing conveys this: the other noises in the bar are reduced on the soundtrack to almost nothing, the red-toned colours of the scene lend it a sense of heat and passion (and also, perhaps, womb-like cosiness), and the camera frames the actors in simple close-ups, while the editing conveys their conversation in a conventionally functional shot/reverse shot pattern (Figure 7.3). After the energy of the opening sequence and the general stylishness and expressiveness of the ensuing scenes, this dialogue

Figure 7.3 Julian and Michelle talk in the bar on their first meeting.

scene – almost abstract in its mise en scène – brings to the film a new and somewhat disquieting intimacy.

Julian walks away from that initial meeting unconvinced that Michelle wants anything other than the 'one fuck' for which she has asked the price. He bids her 'Bonne chance' ('Good luck') and we are shown a rear view of him as he leaves the bar. There is a cut to a different angle, the camera pulling back from Michelle as she watches him go, almost as if Julian were taking the camera with him – and then the film cuts, exhilaratingly, to a very high shot panning along palm trees lining a road, with a pumping rhythmic beat on the soundtrack: once again, it is a driving sequence set to music – in this case, Moroder's re-orchestrated, instrumental version of 'Call Me', slightly slower in tempo than the Blondie version, but still possessed of an exciting momentum, with an electric guitar performing the melody. Even though the shot is not moving especially quickly, the beat of the music gives the scene energy; as the shot continues, Julian's car comes into view from behind the palm trees, its forward movement adding another, exciting and purposeful layer to the sense of motion. A dissolve to a slightly closer shot of the car as it continues on its way subtly conveys the sense of distance being covered. The sequence continues, made up of a small number of shots observing the journey and Julian as he rides along and Moroder's foot-tapping disco-rock music continues on the soundtrack. One close-up of Julian, in particular, is effective in the way it suggests his utter self-containment at being behind the wheel of the car, out in the open, gently smiling from behind his sunglasses as the wind blows his hair (Figure 7.4). He looks off at an angle and we see what he sees – the mountainous land in the distance, the camera then panning back to the car and a shot of Julian from behind, with the open road ahead of him. Unlike in the opening credits sequence, with its precise and ostentatious montage, these shots, with their leisurely editing rhythm, map out a sequence more or less continuous in time and, in doing so, create an impression of a clearly defined, yet relaxed, movement from A to B. Julian can simply enjoy the drive.

This sequence exhibits some of Schrader's most uninhibitedly joyous filmmaking. I attribute this joyousness to the sense of self-esteem that

Figure 7.4 Julian drives along, in his utter self-containment.

comes from personal achievement, performed by the film's style: Julian's status within his profession is inseparable from the pleasures of sound and image. In this sequence, more than anywhere else in the film, we are invited to enjoy his contentment as spectacle, made up of movement, music and rhythm, a simple but exciting melody, the road, the open air, the wind in his hair, the sunglasses adorning his face, and the time to relax on the drive. He has a lot to be proud of: he has a string of clients, he is successful enough to be able to negotiate better terms with his procurer, and he is in great shape. At this point Julian is probably at the pinnacle of his profession, and the film's style conveys a sense of how this achievement feels.

But then there is a cut to a stationary shot of the road snaking round a cliff, and Julian's car driving along it into the far distance. With the transition to this shot, the editing 'breaks' with the harmonious cutting rhythm. The break is reinforced by the introduction of an ominous droning synthesiser rising up on the soundtrack, obliterating the up-tempo rhythm. It is as if the film has decided to step back to convey some foresight into the danger awaiting Julian in Palm Springs, which is the destination of his drive. The effect created is of the film no longer aligning itself with Julian: with the meeting of Michelle having already happened, and with Julian on his way to the Rheiman house to the encounter that will lead to his being framed for the murder of Mrs Rheiman (Patti Carr), details are beginning to amass to suggest that this is a significant transitional period in his life. Julian's profession as gigolo has been set up by the film's structure to be undermined, to be the thing that, in narrative terms, he needs to move away from. It is this shift in the narrative to which I shall now turn.

To 'Forget the World': Julian in Love

Although the early scenes of the film have shown Julian for the most part relaxed and calmly in control, the scene in which he first meets Michelle has provided a notable contrast. Something about this encounter feels different from the others. Michelle is the first woman in the film who is not a client, a business associate or someone with whom he can flirt light-heartedly, such as the young woman he is acquainted with who is working in the cloakroom at the hotel just before he enters the bar. It feels, therefore, as if his encounter with Michelle might be the start of a different set of feelings for Julian – feelings of romantic love for an individual. With this in mind, we can ask what Julian's involvement with Michelle means for his ethical relationship with the others he serves through his work.

This raises questions regarding Levinasian ethics in relation to the film's depiction of Julian's growing feelings for Michelle. There is something of an ambiguous caution in Levinas's ethics on the topic of the self's relationship with a beloved. In a 1954 essay, Levinas writes:

> To love is to exist as though the lover and the beloved were alone in the world. The intersubjective relationship of love is not the beginning, but the negation of society ... Love is the ego satisfied by the you, apprehending in the other the justification of its being. The presence of the other exhausts the content of such a society. The affective warmth of love brings about the consciousness of this satisfaction, contentment, plenitude found outside of, and eccentric to, oneself. The society formed by love is a dual society, a society of solitudes, excluding universality.[8]

And later, in *Totality and Infinity*, Levinas describes 'the self-sufficient "I-Thou" forgetful of the universe'.[9] In both cases, we see Levinas express a caution against a love relationship that operates at the exclusion of engagement with others more generally. The scepticism in *Totality and Infinity* continues with regard to what Levinas calls 'voluptuosity', which hinders access to an ethical relation with the Other:

> The impossibility of reducing voluptuosity to the social, the non-signifyingness upon which it opens, and which is manifested in the indecency of the language that would state voluptuosity, isolates the lovers, as though they were alone in the world. This solitude does not only deny, does not only forget the world; *the common action of the sentient and the sensed* which voluptuosity accomplishes closes, encloses, seals the society of the couple.[10]

Levinas relates this more specifically (and controversially) to a consideration of the relation between masculinity and femininity and its significance for ethics.[11] In my consideration of the central relationship in *American Gigolo*, I do not wish to focus on the issue of romantic love in terms of gender; what is pertinent to my discussion is, rather, the more general point about romantic love in relation to ethics, as this will hopefully enable my comments to be relevant for *any* example of two people loving each other in such a way as to 'forget the world'.

Levinas modifies his position on the couple through the idea of the third party in *Totality and Infinity* and *Otherwise than Being*. I have already looked at the concept of the third party in relation to *Maîtresse* and *Reversal of Fortune* in terms of the triangulation between viewer, camera and characters; in relation to my discussion of *American Gigolo*, the intervention of the third party acts as a sort of guarantee against the exclusivity, the non-universality, of the self–Other dynamic: the third party reminds the self of the existence of other others and, as such, is the foundation of justice. For Levinas, 'the personal relation is in the rigor of justice which judges me and not in love that excuses me'.[12] Thus, the suggestion is that a romantic relationship would not be able to create the necessarily 'rigorous' conditions needed for ethical relations.

A key aspect of Julian's work as a gigolo has been that he is single and therefore unattached to any individual Other. When he meets Michelle, he is at first slightly bemused by her candid interest in his work, but in the bed scene between them he chats to her intimately and appears to be enjoying having her with him in his apartment – and she tells him she feels they really made love, her implication being that it was not just another of Julian's professional performances. In bringing together Julian and Michelle, a politician's wife unhappy in her marriage, and in transforming Julian from emotionally detached, devoted gigolo to vulnerable lover confused by his feelings for this special woman in his life, *American Gigolo* paradoxically begins to depict the growth of a 'closed society', to paraphrase Levinas's description of a couple. And if the love affair is characterised as something Julian can enjoy, this would constitute a self-satisfying 'rest' rather than an ethical 'restlessness'. As such, we could say that Julian appears to be losing his rigour as he falls for one person and forsakes the equality of caring equally for *all* others.

It is important to note, however, that although I have offered a reading of Julian's lifestyle as one of Levinasian devotion to his clients, Julian is portrayed as being somewhat choosy over the terms on which he operates, which goes against the sense in *Otherwise than Being* that we do not choose, that we are elected as hostage to the Other. Julian is therefore, paradoxically, both devoted to the anonymous Other and self-regarding. He can justify being both because his devotion to the Other is dependent on his self-regard. This self-regarding performance of a devoted self has, however, perhaps turned into arrogance. This is conveyed in the first dialogue scene, at Anne's beachfront house, which makes it clear that Julian's relationship with Anne has been difficult for a while. Anne is resentful of Julian's demand that he and she split the takings 60–40 in his favour rather than their usual 50–50 arrangement. Furthermore, she does not like the idea that Julian is not exclusively hers, that he also turns tricks for another procurer, Leon (Bill Duke). Julian is unapologetic, and so even though he and Anne agree that he will meet with a lucrative client, a widow who is flying into Los Angeles that night 'to close a negotiation on her husband's estate', the agreement is not entirely harmonious. A few minutes later, Leon's phone call to Julian in the workout scene establishes that their relationship, too, is somewhat fractured. Leon is calling to ask if Julian will go to Palm Springs to perform a trick (for the Rheimans), and Julian says he is unable to. Leon gets annoyed, and Julian responds with annoyance of his own: 'Who's doing *who* a favour? Who called *who* up begging for a sub?'

After the visit to the Rheimans', Leon gives Julian a warning, 'as a friend', that if his associates ever turn on him, he's 'through'. There is a sense that, although Julian is clearly attractive and ever in demand, there are tensions in his professional life. These negative views of Julian are perhaps best summed up by Detective Sunday (Hector Elizondo), who, looking to take Julian in for the murder of Mrs Rheiman, considers him to be in need of some 'self-improvement'. To be ethical, for Levinas, is not a choice, and Julian's approach to his work is one of *compromised* ethics, as he does not feel obliged to satisfy *all* potential clients.

But what is most important is not how Julian acts, it is what the film has to say about devotion to the Other. Although I claimed before that the film's style and Julian's style in the early stages of the film were as one, as the film proceeds it is as if a divide opens up between Julian's experience and the film's formal presentation of it. The question of ethics in the film, therefore, turns on our assessment of whether the film's *own* performative energies are at the service of an ethical relation or whether they are focused on the pleasure of the couple at the expense of the wider world. It is this matter that I shall now address.

The Film's Style: Abundance and Sparseness

American Gigolo, like many of Schrader's films, has a multi-faceted style. We can note, for example, the ways in which it is heavily influenced by filmic antecedents. Schrader himself has acknowledged a debt to Bernardo Bertolucci, especially in the use of what he calls Bertolucci's 'unmotivated' camera, the camera that seems to move of its own accord rather than being motivated by the movement of a character.[13] More generally, he has explained how, for *American Gigolo*, he wanted to create a different take on Los Angeles, and so 'I went to what I called my new Axis powers, from Munich and Milan, and I got the visual style from Armani and [Ferdinando] Scarfiotti and the music from Giorgio Moroder'.[14] Scarfiotti, who until his death in 1994 was a frequent collaborator of Bertolucci's, worked on *American Gigolo* in the capacity of 'visual consultant', and in the film there are various visual references to one of Bertolucci and Scarfiotti's most renowned collaborations, *Il conformista* (*The Conformist*, dir. Bernardo Bertolucci, 1970), such as the use of Venetian blinds to add dimension to the lighting in several scenes, notably the scene in which Julian searches his apartment in vain for the evidence that has been planted to incriminate him in the Rheiman murder. And it is possible to see the influences of both Ozu and Bresson, two of Schrader's transcendental forebears; for example, Nichols observes how the quiet moments, such as the shots of Julian's apartment, can be read in terms of the codas in Ozu's films,[15] while Schrader has openly acknowledged the influence of Bresson's *Pickpocket* (1959) on the film's ending.[16] David Thomson suggests further influences when he considers *American Gigolo* to be 'like a New Wave film shot in L.A. on an American budget'.[17] Indeed, the wealth of film references in *American Gigolo* is itself redolent of the delight the French New Wave displayed in intertextuality. And, in containing so much intertextuality, the style marks itself out as distinct from Julian's singular, and hardly cineliterate, experience. Thus, we cannot say that *American Gigolo*'s style is a 'pure' style in the manner of an Ozu or a Bresson film; rather, it is a contaminated style that, intentionally or not, pushes the film in the direction of a postmodernist approach to storytelling that makes a dissection of the style from an ethical standpoint far from straightforward.

In my discussion of *American Gigolo* so far, I have mentioned sequences that convey a performative alignment with Julian's experience and others that observe him from a more detached distance. One example is the dressing scene I mentioned briefly earlier, in which Julian, getting ready for a date, lays out his clothes on the bed while singing along to a song ('The Love I Saw in You Was Just a Mirage', performed by Smokey Robinson and the Miracles). Whereas he was not able to hear 'Call Me' over the opening credits but somehow seemed to convey that he *could* hear it, now he does hear the music – this song is within the diegesis: he sings along to it, and we see him snap off the stereo as he goes to answer the door. And yet, although the scene is edited with a sense of synchronisation between the action and the music (albeit with some filmic sleight of hand in which the music plays without any jumps while the time it takes Julian to get into his shirt is slightly elided), the effect is more one of observing Julian's enjoyment of the song and creation of himself for his evening out (as seen in his singing and shoulder-wiggling and in his assured selection of an outfit from among a number of attractive options) rather than performing that style itself. Thus, where the opening credits sequence is an example of how the film synthesises style and content (Performativity$_1$), moments such as the dressing scene take a more objective look at style *within* content (Performativity$_2$).

The question of division in the style is, however, difficult to sustain. As we saw with regard to *Je Pense à Vous* and *La Promesse*, an attempt to distinguish between 'performative' style and 'constative' style will miss the nuance of Austin's argument, which is that the constative is not separate from the performative but, as Petrey says, a 'subcategory' of it.[18] In this regard, it is fruitful to consider *American Gigolo* in relation to Schrader's theory of transcendental style as put forth in *Transcendental Style in Film*.

Schrader has said, in acknowledging how the film's ending relates to *Pickpocket*, that *American Gigolo* is a film that 'otherwise bore no evidence of transcendental style'.[19] But I would argue that there are transcendental energies – such as moments of sparseness – on display elsewhere in the film. The presentation of the décor in Julian's apartment, for example, is reminiscent of some of the specific detail (pots, blinds) in Ozu interiors. The fragmentation of a love-making scene between Julian and Michelle into close shots of sections of their bodies delivers something akin to the fragmentation of the main character's hand movements in a pickpocket scene in *Pickpocket*. Even Julian's initial meeting with Michelle creates a disparity with the everyday through its sound mix, which artificially drops all other ambient sound to a minimum so as to render the dialogue exchange between Julian and Michelle almost abstract, and thus inspiring contemplation. Moments such as these contrast with the more 'abundant' pleasures of the driving scenes, of some of Julian's larking about, and of the sensual emphasis placed on clothes on the human form. Analysing *American Gigolo* from the perspective of transcendental style enables us to locate the film's relative, and often competing, energies, and this will allow us to assess how to read Julian's narrative trajectory towards accepting Michelle's love.

In its initial formulation as posited by Schrader, transcendental style, when successful, offers to the viewer an experience of the Transcendent, that is, the Wholly Other, by turning experience into form through the emotional 'cul-de-sac' initiated by stylistic stasis.[20] This stasis is the culminating effect of a style that, across a film, moves from abundance to sparseness. The removal of commonly used stylistic elements, a hallmark of transcendental style, goes some way towards returning film to a position anterior to the 'ontology' of conventional filmic approaches to representation. We can consider the irresolution of stasis in transcendental style to be somewhat akin to the irresolution of the Saying as performed in *Otherwise than Being*: if the style is precise and consistent, illocutionary purpose and perlocutionary response will align. As we saw in the Introduction, Schrader has written about the power of transcendental style to turn experience into form. If this form were to be deployed to Levinasian ends, it may result in a powerful expression of responsibility for the Other.

As I argued earlier, Julian turns himself into a form so as to serve the needs of his clients. And to some extent, the film's style performs Julian's dedication. Key to the success of transcendental style, however, is the question of consistency. And in *American Gigolo*, there is no clear division between the abundant and the sparse, no clear indication that the film has committed itself to either an emotionally realistic depiction of character or a rigorous deployment of transcendental style. Nichols contends that the film does not commit fully to conveying the Transcendent and that '*Gigolo*'s camera style seems to owe far more to Bertolucci than to the quiet, simple style of Ozu and Bresson'.²¹ Thus, it is more apt, for this film at least, to compare Schrader to the third director he discusses in *Transcendental Style in Film* – Dreyer. Schrader says,

> For a film-maker, the selection of the transcendental style is not an easy one. A filmmaker truly devoted to expressing the Transcendent on film must not only eschew the more superficial elements of his personality and culture, but he must also sacrifice the vicarious enjoyments that cinema seems uniquely able to provide, empathy for character, plot, and fast movement.²²

And he says of Dreyer that he 'never totally yielded to the transcendental style; he respected it, pioneered many of its techniques, gradually came to use it more and more, but was never willing to completely forsake the expressive, psychological techniques at which he was also expert'.²³ Schrader's achievement in *American Gigolo* is also one that never totally yields, never totally commits to the performative depiction of Julian's stylish ethics – that, like Dreyer, Schrader never devotes himself to transcendental style in full, at least not in this film. (By contrast, *First Reformed* is an example of a film in which Schrader does attempt a total commitment to the disruption of the everyday by stylistic stasis.) Nichols says that

> [t]he abundant means of *American Gigolo* . . . suggest, together with Schrader's other work, that he may be better equipped to convey a powerful sense of the paradoxes facing the solitary hero who stands above the need for the gifts of others, the defiant man of willful self-control . . . than he is capable of giving expression to the transcendent.²⁴

Thus, the film would appear to reflect a version of transcendental style allied to other, more audience-friendly elements.

Given that the film's presentation of Julian does not amount to a sustained performance of selflessness but instead veers between the abundance of the film's indulgence and the sparseness of a more transcendental style, what can we make of these tensions? We can say with assurance that in this film, Schrader's aesthetic is such that quietude and a static camera represent intimacy and love. This does not negate the exuberance of the opening sequence and other elaborately stylised sequences but it does present the more intimate moments in some sort of opposition to them. The ambiguity of Julian's desire becomes an ambiguity of the film itself that the viewer may try to resolve.

Accepting Intimacy

The ultimate ambiguity of *American Gigolo* concerns its ending. Julian has resisted intimacy as far as he can resist it, not least because he wishes to spare Michelle the public and political embarrassment, and private anguish, that would occur if their affair were exposed. Accordingly, he also rejects Michelle's offer of an alibi that could absolve him of the charges against him, and, after he is unable to save the only person – Leon – who might testify to his innocence, he appears resigned to his fate. Then, an event occurs that brings relief and pardon to Julian, as well as love, if he can accept it: Michelle goes to the authorities and, lying to them, tells them that Julian was with her on the night of the Rheiman murder. In the final scene, she meets Julian in the visiting room. Through the glass partition, he asks her why she provided the alibi for him. She replies, 'I had no choice. I love you.' Julian, his face marvelling at what she has done, says to her, 'My God, Michelle, it's taken me so long to come to you' (a tribute to the final line spoken in *Pickpocket*). He then leans his head against the glass, which is the only thing separating him from the caress of Michelle's hand (Figure 7.5).

Nichols believes that the final scenes are filmed in a sparse style that contrasts sharply with the abundance that came before.[25] While I do not wholly agree with this assessment, as I consider there to be elements of abundance and sparseness throughout, it is fair to say that, after Leon's accidental death, the film fixes on a distilled style for its last few minutes. Julian is in jail on remand, and the final scenes of the film are all set in

Figure 7.5 Julian accepting Michelle's love.

interiors – the visiting room where he is being held, the interview room where he shows he has nothing more to say to the authorities, the office where Michelle arrives to provide an alibi for him. In narrative terms, we recognise Julian as a self-sufficient character learning that in order to be close to another person, you have to surrender control, you have to open yourself to them. Nichols notes that the film has earlier 'open[ed] up the psychopathic edge to an ethics no longer firmly anchored to a timeless first principle but instead built on discipline, denial, and services that can be bought and sold . . . Dedication, commitment, service – they become misplaced. Lofty goals are replaced by lesser ones.'[26] Perhaps, therefore, Julian's growing ability to express love indicates an increasing openness to alterity through the otherness of a specific Other, and a concomitant reclaiming of behaviour as ethical. But in ethical terms, this loss of control results in a loss of commitment to an ethical way of life, if to love one person above all is to situate one Other as being more important than all the other others. We could say, then, that the film too loses something of its complicity in Julian's stylish behaviour and becomes instead a more subdued record of Julian's actions so as to perform for us his loss of an ethical drive.

Many commentators have noted the alternative, seemingly contradictory, views within the film; for example, Robert T. Eberwein has said that '[i]t is difficult to view the film purely in the terms in which Schrader conceived of it – as a story about someone unable to receive love . . .',[27] and Thomson has called it 'a deeply ambiguous film'.[28] Nichols says of the film that 'what is most intriguing is . . . teasing out the (contradictory) tension between material conditions and transcendental resolutions to which [Schrader] gives compelling expression'.[29] We may feel that the film achieves a transcendent 'grace note', in Kouvaros's words,[30] or that Julian's good ethical work has fallen away. If *American Gigolo* culminates in a sparseness that attempts the stasis of transcendental style so as to transform experience into form, then there is a gap between Julian's trajectory as protagonist and ours as viewers. To be ethical in Levinasian terms is a lonely business; Julian has sustained such an approach for a long time and now he has met someone and fallen in love. The film therefore shows how he is warmed up, diverted by Michelle, and how he finds he can enjoy responding to her. As a result, he gains something – but his clients lose out.

Through its ambiguity, *American Gigolo* leaves the issue unresolved. Morgan says that 'Levinas asks us to think of our everyday life as a kind of sleep or delirium. This is the life of ordinary experience, relationships, language, thought, and desire . . . In the midst of ordinary experience, our life takes on an ethical character, an ethical orientation or definition.'[31] This could describe Julian's devotion to his clients but also his response to the unique Other that is Michelle. *American Gigolo* ultimately places the onus on its viewers to determine what Julian gains and what he loses ethically when he accepts Michelle's love. For me, what proves conclusive is the love between the couple, conveyed through the tenderness of the ending. But I also feel that the film's early sequences of music, movement, style, and rhythm, their performance of Julian's swagger, remain as echoes resounding throughout the film, a reminder of the exhilaration available to the self who is devoted to the service of anonymous others.

CHAPTER 8

Levinasian Limits of Performativity in *Mishima: A Life in Four Chapters*

Mishima: A Life in Four Chapters, Schrader's fifth film as a director, focuses, like *American Gigolo*, on a protagonist who lives his life according to a fastidiously maintained sense of style. But whereas Julian's focus softens, over the course of *American Gigolo*, into something like love or human intimacy with another person, Mishima's sense of style comes to play an ever more central role in his identity, culminating in an act of personal expression that brings his life to an abrupt end. *Mishima: A Life in Four Chapters* represents the first time that Schrader has, as a director, taken as a subject a real-life figure: its protagonist is the celebrated Japanese author Yukio Mishima, whose literary career in the 1940s, 1950s and 1960s brought him great acclaim, and whose suicide in 1970, in a shocking act of public *seppuku* (a samurai death by self-inflicted disembowelment), brought him notoriety thereafter.

As *Mishima: A Life in Four Chapters* centres on the life story of a real-life figure, this means the film can be classed as a biopic. Because of this, the film prompts Levinasian questions that are especially pertinent to the biopic genre. In exploring Schrader's approach to the subject matter, I shall consider the disjuncture between the unknowable Levinasian Other and the biopic, which, we might say, aims to clarify the essence of a person's life, which, from a Levinasian standpoint, suggests a totalising tendency.

Mishima as a Biopic: Death as a Starting Point

The biopic takes many forms, but it is always, in Belén Vidal's helpful definition, 'a fiction film that deals with a figure whose existence is documented in history, and whose claims to fame or notoriety warrant the uniqueness of his or her story'.[1] One approach to the genre is to begin the film at the end of the subject's life, so as to set the scene, and then to jump back to tell the story chronologically. *Gandhi* (dir. Richard Attenborough, 1982), for example, begins with Mahatma Gandhi's assassination and funeral, before flashing back to find him as a young man being thrown off a train for refusing to move from the whites-only carriage; *Lawrence of Arabia* (dir. David Lean, 1962) opens with T. E. Lawrence's death in a motorcycle accident, followed by his funeral, before jumping back to when he was a young clerk stationed in Cairo and given the mission that will see him embark on the Middle East campaign for which he became famous. A slight variation on this approach is when a biopic does not depict a subject's death but nevertheless begins towards the end of the significant portion of the life story. For example, in *Yankee Doodle Dandy* (dir. Michael Curtiz, 1942), which is based on the life of the American songwriter and showman George M. Cohan, the story is framed around a meeting Cohan has with President Franklin D. Roosevelt at the White House: Cohan's reminiscences to the president about his life form the basis of the film's structure, which proceeds to show us the events he recounts. Similarly, in *Raging Bull* (dir. Martin Scorsese, 1980) – co-written by Schrader and Mardik Martin – we first meet Jake LaMotta when his glory days as a boxer are behind him: he is performing as a nightclub act, and as he rehearses his routine in his dressing-room mirror, we flash back to a point early in his boxing career; by the film's end, we have returned to the dressing room, having seen the course of events that have taken his life through many ups and downs to land him at this moment. There are also biopics that tell a story of a 'continual present' juxtaposed with an earlier time frame to present a rounded portrait of a figure and to give a sense of how the past and the present are connected. *The Last Emperor* (dir. Bernardo Bertolucci, 1987) starts in the middle of the story, with the former emperor of China, Pu Yi, arriving at a Communist prison in 1950: the film then flashes back to when Pu Yi, at the age of three, became the last emperor of China, while also continuing the story of the adult Pu Yi's incarceration and Communist 'rehabilitation'. More recently, *The Social Network* (dir. David Fincher, 2010), which we may consider a biopic of Mark Zuckerberg, is structured around two parallel, chronological stories: how Zuckerberg, as a Harvard student, comes to found Facebook, and how he later comes to be fighting two lawsuits against former business associates.

The perspective taken by *Mishima: A Life in Four Chapters* contains elements of the above approaches. The real-life subject had died in 1970, which means that, by the time the film was being made in the mid-1980s, the film could 'know about' his death. At the same time, the film is narrated by the Mishima character, which gives a sense that he is looking back on, and interpreting, his own life. And then there is a sense of parallel stories, as the depiction of Mishima's final day is juxtaposed with flashbacks to his earlier life and – a third strand – recreations of extracts from three of his novels, which add another dimension to this portrait of an artist. But *Mishima* is also crucially different from the other examples mentioned here. Those films, despite variations, have in common a relatively straightforward approach to filmmaking and storytelling, as if the dramatisation of the life in question will lead to its being understood by all. Their structures are fairly easy to follow, meaning that the variations in difficulty are due to the events being recounted and the significance attached to them. *Mishima* is rather more complex, both in its structure and in its film style, and a key reason for this is its starting point, the particularity of Mishima's final day and his death. These opening elements in the film are key aspects of what I am reading as the film's performance of Mishima's obsession with death. This performativity on the film's part brings into being, as we shall see, the film's point of view with regard to its subject: it will ensure that Mishima the artist is explained while Mishima the man remains unknowable. It is through this that the film will perform the impossibility of knowing an Other, and thus the burden of the self's inescapable responsibility.

On 25 November 1970, Mishima, accompanied by members of his private army, the Shield Society, travelled to the Tokyo headquarters of the Japan Ground Self-Defense Force, took control, and demanded an opportunity to address the assembled troops. Once Mishima had finished his address, he committed *seppuku*. After he had performed this act, one of his associates beheaded him, to complete the ritual. It was an act towards which Mishima had been building for many years, and it shocked and baffled both Japan and the wider literary world.

Such was the effect of Mishima's suicide that it is hard to read anything about Mishima that does not, in some sense, place it in the foreground. For example, John Nathan begins his acclaimed 1974 biography of Mishima as follows: 'Yukio Mishima the novelist chose to die a fanatic's death, and the most Japanese death imaginable.'[2] Meanwhile, the first chapter of Henry Scott Stokes's book on Mishima, also from 1974, starts like this:

> Yukio Mishima rose early on the morning of November 25, 1970. He shaved slowly and carefully.
> This was to be his death face. There must be no unsightly blemishes.[3]

And here is the first line of Damian Flanagan's 2014 biography: 'When one comes to write of Yukio Mishima, Japan's first internationally renowned literary superstar, nearly always one starts with death.'[4] Mishima's death – and especially the *way* in which he committed suicide – is therefore often the standard starting point for assessments of his life. Accordingly, the film begins on this final day and returns to it at the start of each chapter, with the fourth chapter being almost entirely devoted to it. The first three chapters, meanwhile, investigate elements of Mishima's life – his childhood, his wish to fight and die for his country, his homosexual leanings, his writing career, his obsession with helping Japan recover its former military glory and national pride, and his desire to transcend what he refers to in the film as the 'deceitfulness' of words and the limitations of the body. But Mishima's suicide occupies such a central position in interpretations of his life and work, it both clarifies his output and, paradoxically, complicates interpretations of it.

There is a further level of significance to the particular *way* in which Mishima chose to commit suicide. It appears he saw the manner of his death – and the notoriety it would bring him – as the culmination of his life's desire to transcend the role of the writer and become a man of action. Thus, although he was known primarily as a writer, an actor and a filmmaker, it is also possible to see him as a performance artist of sorts. Mishima's dissatisfaction with words and his desire to turn them into action is reminiscent of the concerns of Levinas's essay 'Reality and its Shadow', in which, as we have seen, Levinas criticises artworks as being antithetical to ethics because art freezes the image and therefore prevents ethical action. I am not suggesting that Mishima's desire for action is in itself a conscious engagement with Levinasian ethics. Rather, I want to discuss how Mishima's life and actions pose questions for the film's approach to this material. Given that his life and work can be said to have dramatised the struggle between art and action, Mishima's story raises the issue of performativity of the self within society – and the film tacitly explores how best to convey that performativity filmically.

An Overtly Structured Film

Perhaps the first impression created by the film is a strong sense of its formal design. As its title indicates, the film is divided into four chapters. Each chapter – lasting approximately a quarter of the film's running time – consists of three levels of narrative, with a different film style for each level: a naturalistic colour depiction of Mishima's final day, black-and-white flashbacks to his early life, and extravagantly designed and colourful recreations of his writings, specifically segments from three of his novels. The four chapters are: 1) 'beauty' (featuring extracts from *Temple of the Golden Pavilion*); 2) 'art' (*Kyoko's House*); 3) 'action' (*Runaway Horses*); and 4) 'harmony of pen and sword'. The film makes this structure clear from the outset: the first thing we see after the end of the opening credits sequence is a list of the four chapters, presented starkly in white against a black screen (Figure 8.1). Schrader has said of the chapter titles:

> Some people find [them] pretentious, but they were only meant to be helpful. I found, when I first screened it, that when I didn't put the titles on, people didn't understand what the point was. So I give an entire table of contents to the movie at the beginning . . . The fact that you see the list and know what's happening makes the list a handbook for watching this kind of film.[5]

The 'kind of film' to which Schrader refers is a film that aspires to high art while dealing with very demanding subject matter. Schrader has been explicit about his intentions to make a demanding film: Mishima the man, says Schrader, 'had some very peculiar ideas, a few of which I address . . . They are rarefied, obscure but artistic ideas and the film goes right to the heart of them. There's no way you can talk about such things and make it an easy watch.'[6] And yet Schrader does make it easier for us by way of these elements. If the chapter titles in *Mishima* – each one individually and starkly presented after the four titles have been collected together on the 'contents page' – act to help orient us in relation to the film's material and themes, the effect is one of overt clarity that anchors the film's organising principles from the outset.

As well as the clarity and anchoring provided by the chapter structure, there is the voiceover, spoken in the first person by the character of Mishima himself. The voiceover initially comes in during the early

Figure 8.1 Making the structure clear from the outset: the four chapters.

sequence showing Mishima dressing in his house on the morning of his final day. While the film's dialogue is predominantly in Japanese, the voiceover is in English, and is spoken by American actor Roy Scheider.[7] The voiceover adds to the sense of formal, and omniscient, design, as it is so evidently laid over the action we are seeing, and therefore serves to work as directorial intervention, a layer between us and the diegesis.

Another key structuring device for the film is its music. The film features a score by classical composer Philip Glass, who at that point was relatively new to films but who had already received acclaim for his music for the poetic feature film *Koyaanisqatsi* (dir. Godfrey Reggio, 1982). Over the opening credits of *Mishima*, the music, with its finely modulated balance of restraint and exuberance, its tense strings and tolling bells, announces the film as something of an 'event movie', preparing us for the astonishing story to come, while offering an intriguing tonal mix of minimalism and excess. Schrader uses Glass's music centrally and forcefully in *Mishima*; as such, it is a far cry from the more subdued uses of music encountered in the films of Schrader's chosen transcendental directors.[8] In the recognisable Glass style, these themes are very often structured around incessantly repeated cells of music that seem to move to their own rhythm rather than necessarily commenting upon Mishima's situation. The music therefore can come across as being in some senses independent of the story, rather than truly responding to it. This, however, would be to attempt to suggest a neat division between the score and the rest of the film. Such a division does not exist: the inclusion of Glass's score means it is an integral part of the film and therefore conditions the reading of the film as a whole. To that end, we can note the role the music plays in binding together the different strands of the film's narrative – the 'present' of the film's final day, the flashbacks and the dramatisations of the novels. The music's recurring leitmotifs across varied instrumentations and orchestrations help to create a whole out of the film's disparate, if interconnected, narrative elements. And this binding quality can be read as reflecting the film's performance of how Mishima reflects on and organises the details of his own life story even as he lives it.

On top of these considerations is the sense of *Mishima* being, thematically, very much a Schrader film. The subject matter of *Mishima* reflects interests already present in the work of Schrader. Schrader has said that he wanted to make a film about someone who commits suicide and that he had originally thought to make a film about Hank Williams before he realised that it was Mishima's life that interested him.[9] Furthermore, Japan had already featured in Schrader's work: with his brother Leonard, he had written a screenplay called *The Yakuza*, a gangster story set in Japan that became a 1974 film with a further screenplay credit to Robert Towne and direction by Sydney Pollack, and, prior to that, Schrader's interest in Japanese film and culture had been evident from his study of Ozu's work in *Transcendental Style in Film,* as we have seen. As for the manner of Mishima's life and death, this relates to issues of performativity of identity that I have looked at already in *American Gigolo* as well as in a number of other films in this book, principally *Le Fils, Maîtresse, Reversal of Fortune,* and *Terror's Advocate.* As a film character, Mishima continues the line of Schrader protagonists whose obsession with their own bodies is an integral part of who they are: Travis in *Taxi Driver,* Julian in *American Gigolo,* Irena in Schrader's horror film remake *Cat People* (1982)[10] and, to a certain extent, Jake in *Raging Bull.* Mishima's bodily obsession is not just a question of narcissism – it is an expression of his desire to merge his intellectual life with his desire for action, and more specifically his desire to see Japan abandon the compromises wrought on the country in the wake of its defeat in the Second World War and return it to its former national and military glory. Mishima's bodybuilding, his training in swordplay, his ownership of his own private army – all are inextricably linked with his writings on the themes of nationhood, sexuality and death. In many ways, therefore, Mishima is a typical Schrader subject. We might say that Mishima the man and Schrader the filmmaker are a perfect match, the material allowing Schrader to make a film very much in keeping with his previously demonstrated interests while also permitting him to turn his talents to this historical figure.

Stylistically, too, *Mishima* contributes to the sense of there being a recognisable Schrader style, at least as far as this period of his work is concerned. Just as we saw difficulties in considering *American Gigolo* an example of the 'pureness' of transcendental style, so *Mishima* offers many of the same challenges. Stylistically, it is, like the earlier film, full of what, in transcendental terms, would be considered 'abundance' – or at least a controlled abundance. We can consider *Mishima* to be, after *American Gigolo* and *Cat People,* the third in an unofficial trilogy of films, made one after the other, in which Schrader merges narratives about bodily obsession, limitation and transformation with supremely expressive visual and aural styles comprising rich, colourful lighting and décor, energetic – and often elaborate – camera movements and very driven, ostentatious music.[11] Another hallmark of the Schrader style in *Mishima* is his command of intertextuality by shooting the biographical material in a manner that reflects the preeminent Japanese filmmaking styles of the corresponding periods. Thus, Mishima's early life is filmed in a carefully framed monochrome style redolent of Ozu's work in the 1940s and 1950s, while later passages are shot in a slightly looser style as if akin to Japanese New Wave directors of the 1960s such as Shôhei Imamura, Nagisa Ôshima, and Hiroshi Teshigahara. Schrader also provides references to his own films. For example, *Mishima* and *American Gigolo* both feature shots of the main character's clothes laid out on a bed (Figure 8.2), followed soon after by a shot of him looking at himself in a mirror (Figure 8.3); Kouvaros notes: 'The meticulous manner in which these characters prepare to dress suggests not only a state of heightened self-consciousness but also a desire to re-create the self through the perfecting of certain roles.'[12] The two films also include

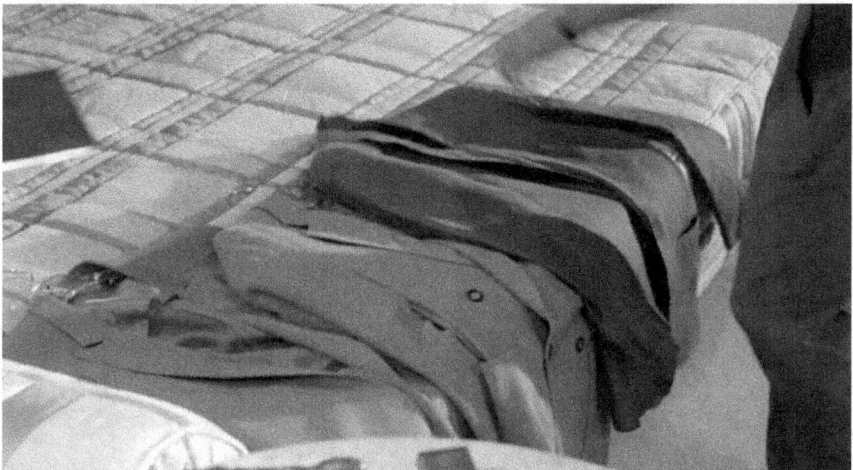

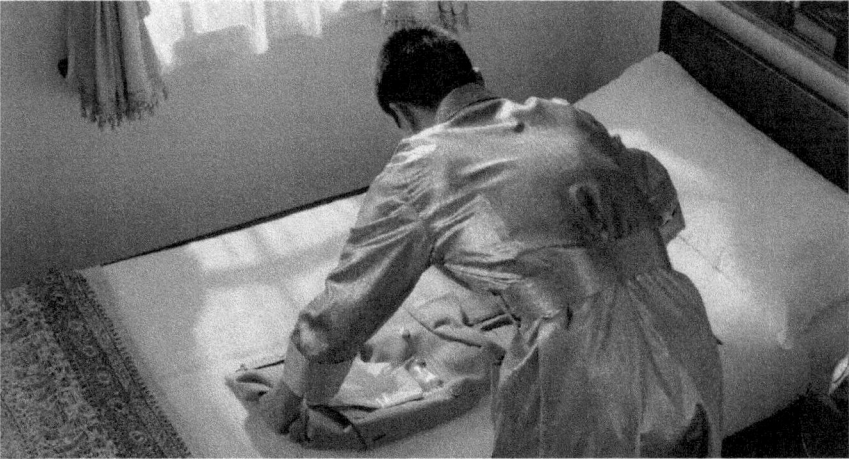

Figure 8.2 *American Gigolo* and *Mishima*: laying out clothes on a bed.

Figure 8.3 *American Gigolo* and *Mishima*: getting dressed in the mirror.

shots involving shadows created by Venetian blinds (Figure 8.4).[13] Overall, *Mishima* is perhaps the apex of a formalism towards which the earlier Schrader films were moving.

We may feel that, with its overt structure, its stylistic abundance, and its intertextuality, *Mishima*'s film style achieves an omniscience in respect of its subject and thereby resists getting close to offering a performance of the preoccupations of its protagonist. But in the murkiness of the division between the constative and the performative, there is not ultimately a clear-cut distinction to be made between performativity and omniscience;

Figure 8.4 *American Gigolo* and *Mishima*: Venetian blinds.

rather, the film's pointed formalism serves to enact the dual purposes of telling the story of Mishima's life and performing his own preoccupations with structure and artistic expression.

Performing Mishima through Structure and Style

With its two-hour running time, its contents page, and its four chapters each lasting approximately thirty minutes, *Mishima* is structured with something approaching mathematical rigidity, and this serves, initially, to suggest a distance from the events being depicted. We could consider it absurd that a film could, in two hours, presume to come close to capturing the essence of a life lived over forty-five years (any life, not just one as immediately striking as Mishima's), with all the experiences, ideas and ideologies that develop over the course of that lifetime. It is a crucial strategy, however, that the film is structured around the events of Mishima's final day. Given that, near the start of the film, we see Mishima get up, have some breakfast while looking at the newspaper and then leave the house to head to the Army Headquarters, and given that historically he and his accompanying members of the Shield Society arrived at the Army HQ at 11:00 and that Mishima and his acolyte had committed *seppuku* by about 12:20,[14] we could consider the final-day events of the film to be depicted almost in real time, which would mean we could say that the film we are watching is Mishima's own version of his life story unspooling in his head in real time as he carries out the actions of his final day. In the light of this, *Mishima* is working on at least two levels: as a film omnisciently portraying a character living by way of a highly structured and organised performance of his own life and work and as a performative depiction of that subject's highly structured approach.

We can read this performativity in, for example, the colour schemes as conveying the different weights that Mishima himself gives to his life. Thus, the black and white of the past represents his imprisoning private and public life within the confines of Japanese history and even within the confines of its art (and, more specifically, its films), the colour in the staged extracts of the novels represents the unbridled creativity of the writer, and the naturalistic colours of the 'final day' sequences represent Mishima's own harmonisation of the two. The starkness of the biographical history and the kaleidoscopic bloom of his art merge into what he has set out to do on what he has planned to be the last day of his life. The voiceover, too, is readable both as an omniscient viewpoint and as Mishima himself speaking to us (or even as a voice that we can hear as *our* voice). And the on-screen text about Mishima's life that opens the film both gives a sense of the story's already being in the past and announces a sense of reputation that could have been written by the self-dramatising Mishima himself.

The film, however, depicts Mishima's own wariness of the power of words. He articulates their failure truly to represent him. For example, during the scene on his final day in which he addresses the assembled troops and they jeer him, we cut to images of him flying in a jet, and as we see this, his voiceover explains that '[t]he closed cockpit and outer space were like the spirit and body of the same being. Here I saw the outcome of my final action. In this stillness was a beauty beyond words. No more body or spirit, pen or sword, male or female.' We see his face encased in the helmet, his point of view showing the clouds rushing by, while Glass's music acts like a funereal reverie, and we can appreciate what this means for Mishima: to be free of his body, which has for so long been a source of anxiety for him, and to be free of words, of the imprisoning desire to write, to transform experience into form – words being both his saving grace and evidence of life's inadequacy. And yet it is formal elements that help us to feel Mishima's desire to escape his own formalism. We know he is feeling what he is feeling because he tells us in voiceover and because we see the visuals depicting the clouds. Matthew Stone says, 'The terms of the said, or the essence of being, which allow a subject to represent itself do not provide access to an authentic mode of existence, but grant intelligibility at the price of veiling the otherwise-than-being.'[15] Mishima is unable to escape his own nature, and the film performs that introspection to show it as an encumbrance; it holds him back, even as it helps him define himself more than anything. Thus, throughout the film, spellbinding sequences and moments of visual splendour are always tempered by the adjacency of severe introspection. Mishima's attachment to the idea of identifying who he is and what his work stands for makes him a prisoner of his own identity.

If, however, this sounds like a concrete depiction of Mishima as a complete person, I want to guard against this. Saxton addresses the question of the representation of otherness on film in relation to the intangible Levinasian notion of the face of the Other:

> If the face of the Other eludes representation and cannot be encountered in images, if it expresses the Second Commandment as well as the Sixth, how could a visual medium reveal alterity or call us to responsibility in the manner described by Levinas? Is it possible to conceive of ways in which cinema might expose us to this face without 'defacing' or 'effacing' it – without reducing it to an object of perception? Is the prohibition against representation signified by the face not always already violated as images of the other are captured on celluloid or translated into digital data?[16]

In asking of an ethical style that it give us a filmic encounter with the Other, we can feel how much more effectively it can do this through fragmentation than through cohesion. Accordingly, we can consider the way in which the film serves to fragment the figure of Mishima by incarnating him in several guises and identities throughout the film. Like Schroeder's *Reversal of Fortune*, *Mishima* features three strands, which come together in a fourth strand – that of the film as a whole. But whereas in *Reversal of Fortune* the three strands represent three different characters, in *Mishima* the three strands are all part of the portrait of one character. In *Reversal of Fortune* the three strands are visually distinct but not in too pronounced a fashion; in *Mishima*, they are overtly distinct, as demonstrated by, for example, the transition from colour to black and white near the start to indicate the transition from the final day to Mishima's childhood, and by the overt artifice of the sets used in the novel dramatisations, in particular the set that moves apart on visible runners as Osamu (Kenji Sawada) lies on the floor in a scene from *Kyoko's House* and the various shots of sets from above. These overt shifts in narrative strand are in keeping with the film's dissection of Mishima through scenes from his childhood, his novels and the last day of his life. These have an effect of presenting different versions of Mishima as a figure in the film (Figure 8.5). As an adult, he is played by Ken Ogata, who features in the 25 November 1970 sequences as well as in the flashback scenes in chapters two, three and four. In chapter one, Mishima is played at age five by Yuki Nagahara, at ages nine to fourteen by Masato Aizawa and at ages eighteen to nineteen by Gô Rijû. Additionally, there are the male protagonists in the segments from the three novels: Mizoguchi (Yasosuke Bando) in *Temple of the Golden Pavilion*, Osamu in *Kyoko's House* and Isao (Toshiyuki Nagashima) in *Runaway Horses*. In its fragmenting of the protagonist figure into characters that illustrate different aspects of his life, therefore, *Mishima* is perhaps a precursor of a film such as *I'm Not There.* (dir. Todd Haynes, 2007), which takes an unorthodox approach to its own real-life subject, Bob Dylan. *I'm Not There.* uses six different characters (or 'multiple avatars', in Vidal's words)[17] – none of them called 'Bob Dylan' – to represent different aspects of the Dylan

Figure 8.5 Mishima as an adult, as a boy, as an adolescent, as a young man; Mizoguchi; Osamu; Isao. (*continued*)

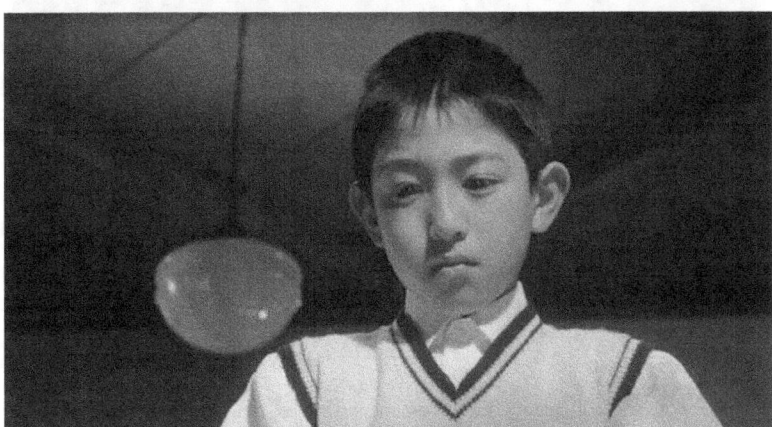

Figure 8.5 (*continued*) Mishima as an adult, as a boy, as an adolescent, as a young man; Mizoguchi; Osamu; Isao. (*continued*)

Figure 8.5 (*continued*) Mishima as an adult, as a boy, as an adolescent, as a young man; Mizoguchi; Osamu; Isao.

persona and legend known to audiences. Through this, the film manages to achieve perhaps more insight into the figure of Dylan than a conventionally structured biopic would have achieved, because its approach invites the viewer to assemble the biographical figure through unobvious means. Similarly, in *Mishima* the inclusion of not just Mishima at different ages but also three of the protagonists from his novels enables Schrader to hint at an overall character who is both overtly and subtly beyond the film's grasp. This distance that the film creates from its real-life subject is a Levinasian move: it reinforces the otherness that no portrait can hope to unlock. It is this Levinasian point that I shall consider in my concluding comments on this film.

Levinasian Limits of Filmic Performativity

Consider again the disclaimer that opens Schroeder's *Terror's Advocate*: 'This film is the director's point of view on Jacques Vergès, which may differ from the opinions of people interviewed in it.' Although it is a documentary rather than strictly speaking a biopic, the film nevertheless covers several decades in the life and career of Vergès, its central figure, and so the disclaimer takes on the role of an admission not just of partiality but also of general limitation: it makes explicit that this is the work of a film director, with all the compromises that implies. *Mishima* does not include a similar, explicit on-screen disclaimer to this effect, but, due to its title as well as its title cards that present the 'contents page' and then the four chapters in turn, the film can be said to announce its intentions as a partial, and highly structured, approach to Mishima's life. This position saves the film from having to try to fulfil some objective sense of completeness or authoritativeness. Schrader has noted in interview the gap between Mishima's life and the film's presentation of it:

> Mishima was infuriatingly contradictory. By the time he could understand anything he was interested in, he had already written or said the opposite, so his entire work and his life remain a conundrum. Part of the fun of cracking such a life is fitting his puzzle into your solution. Mishima was the problem, but the solution is admittedly mine. It does not propose to be the last word on Yukio Mishima; it just opens a lot of doors.[18]

Indeed, we hear the idea of a contradiction used in the voiceover twice early on in the film. As Mishima dresses in the film's opening sequence on the morning of what we will come to understand to be the last day of his life, the first lines of the voiceover are: 'All my life I have been acutely aware of a contradiction in the very nature of my existence. For forty-five years I struggled to resolve this dilemma by writing plays and novels. The more I wrote, the more I realised mere words were not enough. So I found another sort of expression.' This is a reference to, and a foreshadowing of, the events of that last day, in which he set out to achieve a 'harmony of pen and sword', as the film's fourth chapter terms it. A short while later in the film, we see the young Mishima at school, wrestling with a schoolyard bully, and his voiceover tells us: 'In my earliest years I realised life consisted of two contradictory elements. One was words, which could change the world. The other was the world itself, which had nothing to do with words.' He goes on to say that '[f]or the average person, the body precedes language. In my case, words came first.' Kouvaros sees this performative quality in the film's approach to its subject. He notes: 'Instead of simply telling the story of Mishima's life, Schrader's film approximates a form that embodies its contradictions. The relationship between the film and its subject is not simply imitative but also performative . . .'[19]

It is in this way that *Mishima* demonstrates how a film can represent the irreducible alterity of the Other, even within the ostensibly elucidatory mode of the biopic. While it can look at first as though the film presents its subject with an omniscience that feels antithetical to the non-fixity of the Saying, we can see how Schrader's artistic control of the material is testament to the gap between the filmed subject and the historical figure. Perpich says that Levinas's statements in *Otherwise than Being* 'explicitly compromise themselves with being in order to "say" an otherwise than being';[20] similarly, we can read *Mishima* as successfully performing its own inability to unlock the mystery of the Other. The gap between the filmed subject and the historical figure serves to preserve the otherness of Yukio Mishima. The subject is a man who is both unknowable and knowable – unknowable because, as he himself says, words are inadequate, and knowable in that he ensures, through his structured approach to his own life and work, that he becomes a character for other people. And the film, in presenting his story in such a structured fashion, honours Mishima's own performance of his life while preserving his otherness. As such, Schrader has made, in *Mishima*, a Levinasian film.

CHAPTER 9

Passivity and Responsibility in *The Comfort of Strangers, Dominion: Prequel to the Exorcist* and *Adam Resurrected*

One of the most challenging aspects of Levinas's ethics is the notion of the self's responsibility to the Other being something the self does not choose, *cannot* choose. Levinas says,

> Responsibility for the other, in its antecedence to my freedom, its antecedence to the present and to representation, is a passivity more passive than all passivity, an exposure to the other without this exposure being assumed, an exposure without holding back, exposure of exposedness, expression, saying. This exposure is the frankness, sincerity, veracity of saying.[1]

Part of Levinas's project in *Otherwise than Being* is to demonstrate the importance of this absolute passivity to our understanding of the ethical relation. For Levinas, the self is a hostage to the Other and cannot avoid this status, which is that of the exposedness of the Saying 'offering itself even in suffering'.[2] If the self is always a hostage to the Other, always responsible for the Other, even before consciousness – 'non-voluntary – the sacrifice of a hostage designated who has not chosen himself to be hostage, but possibly elected by the Good, in an involuntary election not assumed by the elected one'[3] – then we have to face the idea that the Other who holds us hostage might make the most demanding, barbaric, impossible, destructive calls on our hostage status and we will still be ethically disposed to offer ourselves in substitution for the Other. In this regard, I now wish to focus on the idea of passivity as a principal component of Levinasian responsibility for the Other and to consider Schrader's work in the light of this.

We have seen in *American Gigolo* and *Mishima: A Life in Four Chapters* how Schrader's use of style places those films somewhere between being performative encapsulations of their protagonists' states of mind and being more distanced portraits of these crisis-ridden men. But Schrader's work does not just deploy heightened uses of style such as we have seen so far. He has also explored his preoccupations with more stylistic moderateness, and I shall explore this in order to show how his work often signals an understated awareness of the effects of passivity on the human spirit. The films that I analyse in this chapter – *The Comfort of Strangers*, *Dominion: Prequel to the Exorcist* and *Adam Resurrected* – focus on protagonists who are passive in their wants, desires and relationship with life, and who, in different ways, are each brought into ethical encounters with severe and demanding otherness. There are malign forces in these three films, forces bent on destruction: a murderous Italian aristocrat in *The Comfort of Strangers*, the formidable power of Satan in *Dominion* and insanity as a legacy of Nazism in *Adam Resurrected*. It is because of these malign forces that the films elucidate a powerful sense of the passivity of the self as hostage to the Other. In each of the films, Schrader deploys a directorial style that is somewhat less elaborate than the styles he deployed in *American Gigolo* and *Mishima: A Life in Four Chapters*; as such, he enables passivity to emanate from the films in relatively uncluttered ways that serve as different – and differently effective – types of textual performance from those earlier works. What Schrader's direction shows in these films is that passivity is a necessary component of ethical engagement, and that passivity itself is perhaps the most demanding aspect of Levinas's ethics.

Passively Performing a Levinasian Sacrifice in *The Comfort of Strangers*

The Comfort of Strangers, which is based on a 1981 novel by Ian McEwan, has four principal characters, in the form of two couples: Colin (Rupert Everett) and Mary (Natasha Richardson), a young couple holidaying in Venice, and Robert (Christopher Walken) and Caroline (Helen Mirren), an older couple who live in the same city.[4] The film's screenplay, by Harold Pinter, sticks closely to the events of the novel, with only a small number of variations. Although populated for the most part with just the aforementioned characters, *The Comfort of Strangers* contains a large number of interlocking themes and ideas, including the relations between men and women, the influence of the past on the present, the forcefulness of a certain type of masculinity that desires to subjugate women, the masochism in (some) women in the face of this, and the strange mindset people get into when on holiday. The film does justice to each of these themes but I wish to privilege one particular reading here – namely, that the role Colin occupies as sacrificial lamb in Robert and Caroline's physical and psychological games has much to say about the way the Levinasian responsibility for an Other might play out when taken to its extreme (that is, in the giving of one's life for another). I wish therefore to discuss the film from the position of Colin's being the central character who gives himself totally to the call of an Other (Robert). Schrader has stated that Colin 'is the battleground over which the drama takes place'.[5] This sense of being 'fought over' highlights an aspect of Colin's character that I feel goes hand in hand with his openness to substitution for an Other: his passivity. The other characters are able to fight over Colin precisely because he is not assertive or active enough to withstand the tug of war they play out with him as its rope. Thus, as well as being a study in responsibility and substitution, Colin is a study in the passivity of the ethical subject.

In *Otherwise than Being*, Levinas, in describing sensibility as being a result of the breaking up of the ego, uses versions of the phrase 'a passivity more passive than all passivity' three times in one and a half pages, to describe sensibility, responsibility, and the Saying.[6] He talks of patience, and of how the ego's identity is defeated, with the attendant passivity resulting in the 'trauma of accusation suffered by a hostage to the point of persecution'.[7] We can think about Colin's experience in *The Comfort of Strangers* in this way; indeed, the film takes him beyond persecution to annihilation. To be sure, passivity in Levinas is not the passivity of doing nothing. Passivity brings about exposure and thus responsibility, and the exposedness of responsibility that comes with this passivity 'is not the work of negation, and no longer belongs to the order of being'.[8] What I want to interrogate with regard to *The Comfort of Strangers* is the effect of this responsibility on the self – whom in this case I am defining as Colin.

What both the novel and the film demonstrate is that Colin, through a certain lack of definition – and self-definition – as to who he is and what he wants, is 'available' to an Other. Colin is shown to be indecisive, in his feelings towards Mary and in other aspects of his life. In Levinasian terms, this suggests two contradictory things: an inward-looking personality, paralysed by solipsism, and a personality that shuns egoism and self-interest and is therefore available (unwittingly perhaps) for the fantasies and demands of another. Where Julian in *American Gigolo* and Mishima in *Mishima: A Life in Four Chapters* are both characters in search of self-determination, Colin in *The Comfort of Strangers* does not appear to want to place his hand on the tiller of his own life. To use a Venetian metaphor, he is more gondola than gondolier.

The persecution of Colin is already under way by the time we first meet him and Mary in the film: it becomes clear very early on that someone (who, it is soon revealed, is Robert) is surreptitiously taking his photograph (Figure 9.1). By contrast, the novel gives the reader this information only in the order in which Colin and Mary discover it, and so there is a greater sense in the novel than there is in the film of Colin walking into a trap, rather than being already entrapped. That said, there is a very early moment of typically McEwanesque offhand ominousness in the novel

Figure 9.1 Colin and Mary are unaware that a stranger is photographing them.

when, during a languid passage in which Colin and Mary are described getting ready to go out for the evening, it is casually mentioned that they got ready with such care that it was 'as though somewhere among the thousands they were soon to join, there waited someone who cared deeply how they appeared'.[9] The subtlety of this interjection, the way in which it could simply be intended to evoke the holidaymaker's fantasy of belonging in an unfamiliar but pleasurable environment, is such that the idea of an invasion of Colin and Mary – and, as it will turn out, Colin especially – by a local is ready to take hold of us as the story unfolds.

In the film, Colin's passivity is conveyed also by the directing style, which appears to align itself, at least at first, with the controlling arrogance of Robert and his self-mythologising. The opening of the film is shot in a very overt style: the camera glides and tilts smoothly through Robert's palazzo, the mise en scène spacious and opulent, while we hear Robert's voice on the soundtrack beginning the story of his father, a story he will later tell to Colin and Mary when he first takes them to his favourite bar. This opening is suggestive of Robert's personality, as he gives us a dreamy take on his own existence, his domestic arrangements, his private life, his world. At the same time, the film's style comes across as being laid over the narrative. This is, of course, the case: the narrative could have been presented through an infinite number of stylistic choices. Every film, as I noted when discussing the Dardennes, has a particular approach, a particular style, and those stylistic choices help make the narrative what it is. This is one sense in which all films are performative: how they present their worlds determines the worlds they bring into being. *The Comfort of Strangers*, therefore, proceeds intriguingly, partly as an evocation of Robert's narration and partly as a very controlled director's take on the material. Either way, the style does not favour Colin, who has two personalities dominating him – that of Robert and that of the film's directing.

As I have noted, however, Schrader's directing in *The Comfort of Strangers* is not as overtly stylised as his work in *American Gigolo* or *Mishima: A Life in Four Chapters*. By this I mean that the direction does not feel aligned with a particular aesthetic or philosophical approach to its characters and story, as with the energies brought to the stories of Julian Kay and Yukio Mishima. The intertextuality afforded by Schrader's cinephilia is also largely absent from *The Comfort of Strangers*, notwithstanding the immense history of Venice on-screen. Rather, the film's opulent opening serves to work most powerfully as a structuring device that resonates throughout the rest of the film without the need for a particularly forceful directing style.

The decision to open the film with the start of Robert's story about his father is the most significant structural departure from the novel. In the novel, Robert's story about his father is a narrative device; it is a story the reader needs to know in order for the threat against Colin to be imaginable (and therefore gripping), and Robert tells Colin and Mary the whole story at length in the bar on the night he has met them. By introducing the start of Robert's story as a voiceover during the film's opening credits, Pinter and Schrader have taken some of the pressure off the later bar scene; more crucially, however, they have found a cinematic counterpart to McEwan's early ominous hint in the novel of a sort of persecution already under way. Schrader has said that Pinter's adaptation, in bookending the film with Robert's confession, brings to the fore the idea of the past as being a continual burden on the present, and he says that he sees Robert as someone who lives in the past.[10] This is thematically important as it indicates the depth of Robert's pathology and thus the immensity of what Colin is up against. The decision also makes Robert more central than he is in the book – a centrality enhanced by the casting of Christopher Walken, at that time the biggest name among the film's actors and concomitantly the one who received top billing. For Rupert Everett as Colin, therefore, Walken's casting as Robert is perhaps a third dominant personality for him to contend with.

But although the novel and the film set the scene for Colin's persecution in different ways, in both cases Colin does not know what he is getting himself into. In narrative terms, his passivity works on the story ironically, in that it causes things to happen. He and Mary first encounter Robert in the street because they are lost, looking for somewhere to eat in one of Venice's back alleys after dark. In that labyrinthine environment, it is easy to imagine why they would be beguiled by the offer of a stranger, a local, to point them towards somewhere to get some food and something to drink. In the bar, Colin listens to Robert's story, but he does not have the history of Robert's behaviour, and he cannot know Robert's intentions. Dramatically, this illustrates Levinas's sense that the linking in subjectivity of the self and the Other 'signifies an allegiance of the same to the other, imposed before any exhibition of the other, preliminary to all consciousness'.[11] The Other cannot be known by the self, because the Other does not show any identity ('who as other will not identify himself with anything').[12] I am reading identity here as 'knowability' – Colin knows Robert to a superficial degree, but not to a degree consonant with being aware of the enormity of Robert's ethical demand on him. If Colin did know Robert to this extent, the moment when Robert punches Colin in the stomach would not be as much of a surprise to him. And if Colin knew Robert to that extent, it may be that he would decide, on his and Mary's return from the Lido, not to go up to Robert and Caroline's apartment once more. When Mary asks Colin, 'Do you want to go up?', Colin replies, 'Well, she's seen us. We can't very well be rude', and so they gravitate towards the apartment (Figure 9.2). In that reasonable, even kindly – and passive – response, Colin unwittingly declares his openness to the Other's ethical call: without realising it, or at least without acknowledging it – and without doing anything to stop it – Colin is hostage to Robert and Caroline, and he will pay the ultimate price for it.

The film, however, treats this chain of events with something approaching serenity. In both McEwan's and Schrader's work, there is a fascinating

Figure 9.2 Colin and Mary wonder whether to go up to Robert and Caroline's apartment.

tension between order and disorder, between control and abandon. McEwan has spoken of his interest in the rational in fiction,[13] and for all his famed dwelling on the grotesque and the obscene in much of his fiction, he is a highly ordered writer. With regard to Schrader's work, we have seen how in *American Gigolo* the style performs both Julian's perspective and a more detached *depiction* of a man wanting, and needing, to be rescued by the love of a woman, and how in *Mishima* the overarching structuring principle – the 'life in four chapters' – at once performs Mishima's own desire to control his own life and offers a more detached directorial viewpoint. In *The Comfort of Strangers*, although the gliding camerawork and opulent design give the film an ornate and in a sense stylised mise en scène, there is also a more relaxed rhythm to the film – as though Schrader's style is itself enjoying a holiday – that makes the drama unfolding in Robert's palace feel somewhat small-scale, and which has the effect of underplaying any sense of moral outrage as the story reaches its horrifying climax. This is also indicative of the way in which the film has not, ultimately, aligned us with Robert or Caroline's perspective either – if it had, it would bring us closer to the sexual release they feel upon the killing of Colin. Instead, Schrader's direction is almost offhand in the way in which it encapsulates the terrible events that result in Colin's death. It makes no attempt to explain why Colin does not put up more of a fight against Robert, or why he walks into his trap. As such, Colin's passivity comes across very powerfully. The bleak fact of the climax is that Colin loses his life in the service of another. And I am reading this sacrifice as Levinasian in its selfless responsibility that exhibits what Levinas means by 'exposedness to the other where no slipping away is possible'.[14]

Levinasian Passivity Arising from Failure in *Dominion: Prequel to the Exorcist*

From Colin's ultimate sacrifice, I now want to consider a film in which a passive character is roused to a confrontation with an Other of immense, indeed supernatural, power. This is Father Merrin's encounter with Satan in *Dominion: Prequel to the Exorcist*. *Dominion* is probably Schrader's most notorious film, but its oddities and generic 'failures' are revealing of his sensibilities as a director and of what I am reading as Levinasian non-fixity in his work. When Schrader was hired to direct a screenplay by William Wisher Jr and Caleb Carr for a prequel to the classic horror film *The Exorcist* (dir. William Friedkin, 1973), commentators wondered whether such a notably intellectual and individualistic filmmaker, who over the preceding decade had struggled at times to secure first financing and then distribution for his films, could take on the task of helming a big-budget, studio-produced film and deliver a crowd-pleaser. The answer, in industrial terms, was that he could not: the studio, Morgan Creek, upon viewing a rough cut of Schrader's film, deemed it not good enough to release. Schrader was dismissed from the production and the film was remade, with director Renny Harlin at the helm, and released as *Exorcist: The Beginning* (dir. Renny Harlin, 2004). Eventually, Morgan Creek permitted Schrader to complete his version, and it received a limited release in 2005.[15] Neither of the films was much liked, but Kouvaros has noted how '[v]iewed side by side, the differences between the two films provide a useful glimpse into Schrader's approach to drama'.[16] Rather than take a side-by-side view of the two films here, I shall consider *Dominion* on its own terms in order to point to ways in which reading it as a Schrader film both reveals its strengths and draws out its performative effects. Through this, we will see how *Dominion* speaks to the notion of ethical passivity.

One of the key features of Schrader's approach in this film is his attachment to the idea of passive central characters. Kouvaros, in an interview with Schrader, has raised some important points:

> On one level, this term [passivity] defines them well enough. But, on another level, it really doesn't do justice to the kinds of emotions with which these characters are struggling or their sense of melancholy or introspection. It's almost as if 'passivity', especially in an American context, is a bad word. It's something an actor or spectator doesn't want to find in a character: 'He or she was too passive . . .' Whereas, in your films you have taken that negative stance and turned it into a chance to really explore all these other dimensions.[17]

This quote shows the negative attitudes, in some people's eyes, to the notion of passivity, and how Schrader turns it on its head. Schrader discusses with Kouvaros the fact that the part of Merrin was offered to Liam Neeson but that Neeson turned it down because he felt that Merrin was too passive.[18] In Stellan Skarsgård, Schrader found an actor who could perform the passivity of Merrin. Hence, in the film, Merrin is taciturn and downcast; Skarsgård barely opens his mouth when he speaks, and his range of facial expressions is deliberately restricted (Figure 9.3). There are a number of scenes in which we watch him reacting to and absorbing events, passively bearing the pain of things that are happening. For example, in the scene in which he first sees the mysterious boy Cheche (Billy Crawford) on the hill and then registers his disappearance, the camera captures Skarsgård absorbing the sight of Cheche and considering the mystery that surrounds him. Also, in the scene in the tent with the nurse, Rachel (Clara Bellar), Merrin sees the numbers on Rachel's forearm and the weary wariness in Skarsgård's face registers that she was in a concentration camp. It is a reminder of the

Figure 9.3 Stellan Skarsgård as the melancholy Father Merrin.

war and thus of the terrible incident in Merrin's past under Nazi occupation in Holland in 1944, the scene with which the film opens. Schrader has explained that he likes Skarsgård as an actor in part due to his introspective quality.[19] Skarsgård's performance reveals how introspectiveness on-screen – while initially coming across as self-regarding – can develop into a passivity that can create a sense of a turning-away from the self towards others. The borderline blankness of many of Skarsgård's expressions and the somewhat unvarying tone of his voice are aspects of what we might consider to be an Ozuesque or Bressonian approach to performance. Schrader notes in *Transcendental Style in Film* how Ozu and Bresson '[b]oth strove to eliminate any expression from the actor's performance . . . Both used repeated rehearsals to "wear down" any ingrained or intractable self-expression, gradually transforming fresh movement into rote action, expressive intonation into bland monotone.'[20] The desired result is to assimilate the performance into the film's overall style so as to move beyond any expressiveness that would detract from the film's significance. Although the style of *Dominion* is not designed to work in the same 'transcendental' way Schrader argues for in respect of Ozu and Bresson, the film, like much of Schrader's work, contains traces of that sensibility. As such, Skarsgård's performance helps to bring into being a contemplativeness in the film as a whole. Thus, while *Dominion*'s critical and commercial performance fell far short of the illustrious original *Exorcist* film, it nevertheless gains in this contemplative quality, which makes possible a calm dissection of the hysterias of the indigenous population, the British ruling class and the demon. *Dominion* performs a steely, single-minded devotion to various alterities that achieves a Levinasian absence of self-centredness.

It is important to note, however, that Merrin is not himself choosing such a path consciously. There is a dichotomy at the heart of his character: he is a passive man who feels strong emotions. For example, in the climactic encounter in the film between Merrin and the demon, the demon calls Merrin 'a passionate man' and tells him that his guilt is too much to bear. In defining Merrin as passionate, the demon is wishing to claim Merrin as self-serving, someone who wants to follow his appetites and not worry about others. The demon says, 'There is one thing you can do. You can cease to care.' Merrin replies, 'That is your offer?' And the demon says, 'I offer freedom.' What the demon is offering, of course, is freedom from Merrin's guilt over the deaths he witnessed, and was powerless to prevent, in Holland in the Second World War. Although Merrin would like to be released from this guilt, he is resistant to the demon's offer – a sign that despite his scepticism he still believes deep down in the good work he is trying to do. Passion, as it works for Merrin, is the opposite of passion as the demon sees it: what the demon sees as Merrin's passion for his own pursuits can be reconfigured to become Merrin's passion for helping others, a passive, unsatisfiable Levinasian passion for opening himself up to being a hostage to the Other and to all others. If this is Merrin's calling, it is, in a sense, his triumph over the demon. Peperzak has suggested that '[t]he human Other is the surprise for which we can live and die without losing the meaning of existence. It is possible to suffer for Others without falling into a kind of masochism.'[21] Merrin, despite his own downheartedness, has discovered within himself that his devotion to others is alive and well, and this, in its torturing way, gives him the strength to continue to do his good work.

Merrin is therefore unwilling to give himself over to the demon, to do the devil's bidding, as it were. In the scene in which Merrin puts on his priest's cassock and prays, he says: 'Absolve me of my sins and purify me. Purify me for this task.' A problem with trying to construct a *pure* reading of Merrin as open to alterity is that, as the source of the evil events is revealed to be Satan, the drive is then to destroy Satan. Satan is evidently one Other to which Merrin is not prepared to be a hostage. His climactic confrontation with the demon is successful to the extent that the evil spirit is driven from Cheche, but Merrin does not vanquish the demon entirely. They both know they will meet again (which we will see, or rather have already seen, in the 1973 *Exorcist* film) and in the last shot of *Dominion*, which Schrader has acknowledged was modelled on the famous final shot of *The Searchers* (dir. John Ford, 1956),[22] Merrin exits through a doorway and walks into the far distance, out into the world as an outcast – one of Schrader's wanderers – to do the Lord's work (Figure 9.4).

Figure 9.4 Merrin goes out to do the Lord's work.

Merrin's lonesome calling brings us back to the 'sense of melancholy or introspection' mentioned by Kouvaros. For me, *Dominion*'s own style performs – brings into being – a concomitant sense of melancholy or perhaps especially introspection, in that the film's halting relationship with the standard generic pleasures of the horror film prompts a state of reflection that enables us to think about the ethical issues in the film – similar, perhaps, to O'Shaughnessy's sense of 'engaged yet resistant spectatorship' that, as we have seen, he promotes with regard to the Dardennes' work.[23] Thus, our *disengagement* from this genre film for its evasions *as* a genre film can instigate an *introspective involvement* with the issue of disaffection that Merrin is experiencing. This introspection enables us to see the spread of Christianity (as represented by Father Francis, played by Gabriel Mann), the odiousness of colonialism (as represented by the portrayals of the British characters) and the fearsomeness that attaches itself to a convenient local Other (as represented by Cheche) for the damage they all do in the Kenyan village featured in the story.

What the film achieves, then, is a strong sense of scepticism, both through Schrader's direction and through Skarsgård's suffering performance as Merrin, poised as he is between passivity and activity with their attendant virtues. The sense of passivity and its ethical effect perhaps comes across most forcefully not through Schrader's film style per se but through its recording of Skarsgård's internalised performance as the lethargic, disaffected priest. To borrow from Levinas, we might say that Skarsgård's passivity as a performer radiates a 'relaxation more serious than being'.[24] Skarsgård's passivity creates a type of sinkhole in the film, a vortex into which action, machismo and cliché all tumble, and it is perhaps above all through his performance that the film becomes an active purveyor of a Levinasian passivity. It is another example of how Schrader's use of a more relaxed directing style brings into being a powerful sense of passivity roused into ethical engagement.

Activity Replaced by Passivity in *Adam Resurrected*

Where Skarsgård's performance in *Dominion* turns Merrin's scepticism inwards, Jeff Goldblum as the asylum patient Adam Stein in *Adam Resurrected* gives a performance of such engaging extrovertedness that it shows very clearly how Adam *externalises* his dissatisfaction with the world, transmuting it into play, grotesquerie and, literally, clowning around. If this suggests a strong sense of 'action', of Adam working to change his circumstances, this is not how the story plays out. Adam, ostensibly different from Merrin, shares with him a lack of interest in what he might aspire to be or hope to get from life. Both men are toiling away in their familiar territories (Merrin's archaeological dig, Adam's incarceration in the asylum), and both will only grow through gradually trying to help a young innocent (Cheche in *Dominion*, David [Tudor Rapiteanu] in *Adam Resurrected*). Merrin and Adam are therefore, when we first meet them, both essentially *passive* characters – characters not consciously driven to action that would hope to change anything. Adam is a character very much in his own world – indeed, master of his own world. He has a madness, or a mania, and this both sustains him and keeps him from a life of complete freedom; in the asylum, he is a sort of star but this status also restricts him. When he encounters David, a new inmate, the question begins to emerge as to what Adam can do for someone else and how this relates to what he is doing for, and to, himself. It is, of course, a question with a Levinasian dimension. I want to consider *Adam Resurrected* as a film that centres on the dangerous rootlessness of Adam's self-determining performativity and how this rootlessness gradually gives way to a passivity he finds within himself and which initiates a new-found devotion to David as Other.

As we have seen, performativity brings into being what it purports to announce or describe. Adam in *Adam Resurrected* is a character caught in what appears to be a perpetual performance of identity, and as the story unfolds, this performance of identity is seen to be a response to the suppressed horrors that Adam, a Jew, experienced during the Second World War. In the film, adapted by Noah Stollman from a 1968 novel by Yoram Kaniuk,[25] the year is 1961, and when we first meet Adam he is a tenant in a house in Tel Aviv. Within the film's first few minutes, however, Adam is returned to an asylum in the desert. The asylum contains Jewish survivors of the Holocaust and Adam is something of a star patient, enjoying a benevolent relationship with the chief doctor (Derek Jacobi) and a sexual relationship with one of the nurses (Ayelet Zurer). Flashbacks reveal Adam to have been a successful stage performer in the theatres of between-the-wars Berlin, and we see Adam drawing on this same instinct for extrovertedness in the asylum. The difference is that we can now observe his performing, his need to be the life and soul of the institutional party, through the knowledge of the horrific time he underwent under Nazi rule. This gives his present-day clowning around the flavour of a mask he wears not to entertain but to put a barrier between his public self and his private trauma. He is no longer performing primarily to entertain others (although other patients in the institute do appear to be entertained by him), but to cover up, even for himself, the horrors he carries within himself.

The arrival at the institute of David, a disturbed boy behaving like a dog, disrupts Adam's carefully maintained masquerade (Figure 9.5). As

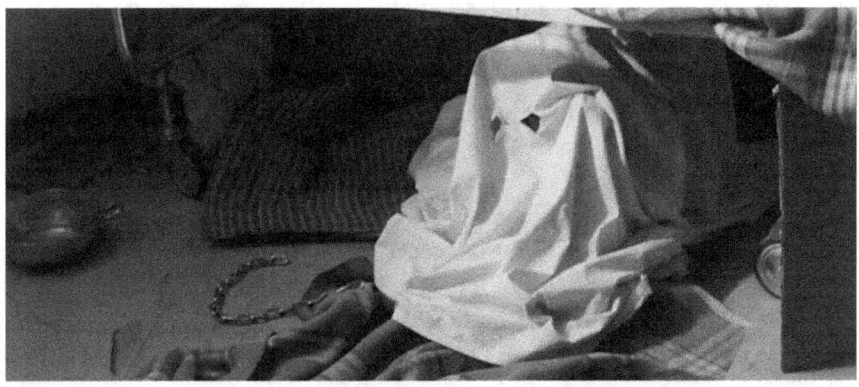

Figure 9.5 David looks out from under his sheet; Adam looks back at him.

Schrader explains, now there is someone who reminds Adam of himself; this awakens in Adam an involuntary confrontation with the past.[26] Adam's commitment to performance and the film's fluid capturing of it will combine to perform the dangerous rootlessness of his psychotic state, a rootlessness that is the prelude to the waiting passivity that Adam will come to access and that will enable him to turn towards the Other.

Adam, with his talent for performing, is used to putting on a performance for others – turning his experience into form, as Schrader might say of him. And as a performer, Adam experiences the pain of having his performing talents turned against him. In further flashbacks we see Adam, along with his wife and daughter, taken to a concentration camp during the war; there, Adam comes face to face with Klein (Willem Dafoe), whom he has formerly encountered at one of his theatrical shows and who is now the camp commandant. In the camp, Adam finds that Klein wants him to entertain him, to make Klein's job more palatable. Adam is forced to act as a dog in Klein's quarters. Adam survives by serving Klein, although Adam's wife perishes in the camp and his daughter will commit suicide after the war. Back in the present at the asylum, Adam slowly befriends David, who lives chained, barely clothed, and with unkempt long hair, who eats from a bowl and who barks rather than speaks. But as Adam's efforts to help the boy begin to yield positive results, Adam begins to feel traumatised anew. As Schrader notes, some of Adam's behaviour is difficult to explain and the film does not try to explain it; there is a sense, however, in which, in seeing the boy begin to 'improve' and become more socialised, Adam finds that he too needs to work through his own unresolved past in which he was forced to act as a dog.

This working through is inextricable from Adam's 'performing' of himself. Schrader's comments on how he worked with Goldblum on the role show an acute sensitivity to the needs of the film. For Schrader, to have an actor continually on-screen risks overexposure – the audience can get sick of seeing the actor so much. Therefore, Schrader tells the actor that one thing to counteract this is to be sure not to dominate *every* scene, and instead to give away some of the scenes to other actors; the actor can do this, believes Schrader, because their continual presence in the film means they are always the overriding focus of attention anyway. Also, Schrader believes that the actor cannot simply do the same thing all the time but must break up the monotony of being in every scene by being *different* from scene to scene. Schrader calls his films 'monocular', the protagonist of the monocular film being a complex figure with many sides to their character, and he charts with the actor the different 'characters' that the actor will play, enabling them together to plan the variety across the film.

If Adam is made up of lots of different characters, this places him alongside other multi-faceted Schrader characters who are seen to be struggling to reveal their true selves, such as Julian Kay, Yukio Mishima, Patty Hearst in *Patty Hearst* (dir. Paul Schrader, 1988) and Bob Crane in *Auto Focus* (dir. Paul Schrader, 2002). But whereas those other characters spend much of their time wrestling with a public persona that is at odds with what they privately want – hence, in the case of Julian and Mishima, the focus on their 'uniforms', as with Merrin's priest's robes in *Dominion* – Adam lives almost entirely under the gaze of those around him (and hence is by default in a performing mode for others) and yet seemingly does not want anything. His actions are in the service of a perpetual present; unlike the standard Hollywood protagonist, he has no overtly stated 'goal'. As such, he is a character unfulfilled by activity. And the events of the story will deliver an opportunity for him to achieve a kind of 'resurrection' through his passive devotion to an Other.

How this sense of performance within the film colludes with film style determines how effectively the theme comes across. Schrader has explained that he adopted a different style for *Adam Resurrected* from the films he had made before. He says that for years he had been 'perfecting a classical Hollywood style': this included a graceful use of the camera, matching edits that never cross the 180-degree line, beautiful lighting, images always in focus, using as few shots as possible and avoiding repeating shots. Schrader says, 'Over the years I had developed all these rules for how you shoot a proper film', but he states that once he had started breaking those rules on this film he found it harder and harder to work out why they were considered so important in the first place. On this film, Schrader started to use shaky cam, multiple cameras, extreme close-ups, and zooms. Also, he realised that a faster editing pattern was emerging: he was editing more within a scene because, as he explains, shooting with multiple cameras gives you more footage to choose from, and also because faster editing is part of this new style. The style is therefore quite a significant departure from the styles that Schrader deployed in films such as *American Gigolo* and *Mishima: A Life in Four Chapters*. But the uses of style I have charted in the Schrader films I have discussed illustrate the ways in which style is deployed in multi-faceted ways in his work. As with the Dardennes, in their subtly evolving style, and as with Schroeder, with his refusal of a singular style, Schrader allows his approach to style to be flexible so as to remain responsive to the needs of the story, and this avoids a congealment of the thematisations of the Said.

Accordingly, the style of *Adam Resurrected*, with its fluid and agitated concentration on Adam, proves effective because it brings us closer to

Adam's torment. The film's rather abstract use of the asylum proves important in this regard. As Edward Gallafent has suggested, *Adam Resurrected* is disturbing partly because having the asylum in the desert precludes a reading of the film as a satire on society: very often in films – a key example being *One Flew Over the Cuckoo's Nest* (dir. Miloš Forman, 1975) – we have the sense that the institution is a microcosm of society and it is we who are mentally disturbed, but in *Adam Resurrected*, the remoteness of the asylum from civilisation asserts the notion that it is *not* we who are mentally disturbed, it is the patients in the asylum, and so we may find we look on in horror at their actions and dilemmas.[27] The asylum in *Adam Resurrected* is not portrayed as a threat; the overriding threat to Adam comes from within himself, and it is what he will do about that trauma that forms the dramatic thrust of the story. But the asylum's remoteness adds to the sense of rootlessness in Adam's life and ensures that he will continue to be stranded unless or until he can find a new state of being. His encounter with David will initiate that new state; the shock, to him, of the encounter is that of his own active selfhood being shocked into passivity in the face of the ethical call of an Other.

This shock leads to both the film's climactic event and, most crucially, its haunting final scene. Adam's resurrection comes about when he storms out into the desert and imagines a confrontation with Klein, whom he vanquishes in a disavowal of the guilt Klein wishes him to feel. He is then reunited with David, now able to take the steps of a biped creature rather than being on all fours; man and boy hug in the desert, and with that hug it is as though Adam embraces the trauma of his responsibility for the Other, his own effort at selflessness that has now enabled the boy to be freed from his dog-like state. But the film ends not on this optimistic note but on a quieter, final scene of Adam's passivity, and I believe this encapsulates the film's value as a performance of the selflessness of Levinasian passivity. Schrader has discussed how he did not want to end the film on the hug between Adam and David; his pragmatic approach suggests how storytelling itself conforms to a need in audiences for films not to be too euphoric or too indulgent. Instead, there is another ending to come – what Schrader calls its epilogue. We see David, now a regular-looking boy with short hair and regular boy's clothes and able to walk perfectly well without assistance, leaving the asylum and being driven away to live with a kindly relative. And we find Adam back in Tel Aviv, 'presumably sane', says Schrader, 'but he's not that happy about it'. The film's final shot is of Adam, seated in his apartment in Tel Aviv, staring into the middle distance, reflecting, as his voiceover reflects, on what has happened and what his situation is now

Figure 9.6 Adam contemplates the future.

(Figure 9.6). This image of contemplation replaces the earlier seesawing between euphoria (when Adam is in control of his performance of self) and despair (when he loses the thread of that performance). Schrader, as we have seen, has said that transforming one's own experience into form enables others to benefit from that experience. If I can read the ending of *Adam Resurrected* as a latter-day stylistic gesture towards the transcendental endings Schrader discusses in his analyses of the films of Ozu and Bresson, any explosion of feeling at the end of the film is likely to be a muffled explosion. What is experienced is not a glimpse of the Wholly Other but a concentrated image of passivity – not the passivity of complacency, but a passivity that, when performed, opens a door to selflessness. The value of the final scene, and above all the final shot, is that it seals a sense of Adam's being a passive character. This is a triumph of Levinasian engagement over the self-determined frenzy that Adam was enacting earlier in the story. By concluding the film on this note, Schrader asserts the value of passivity.

Adam's survival is therefore different from that of Merrin in *Dominion*: Merrin knows he will go out into the world and become an exorcist – it has become his mission – whereas Adam has come through an ordeal but is not left with a sense of what he might turn to next or where his life might be going. And yet Adam, like Merrin, is newly alive – resurrected. In this sense, Colin in *The Comfort of Strangers* is something of an aberration, because he is the one protagonist who dies, who pays the ultimate price for an openness to alterity. All three films, however, through a complex interplay of theme and film style, perform a Levinasian passivity. In doing so, they show how the struggle between acting for oneself and remaining passive enough to act for another is a condition in which Levinasian ethical engagement can emerge.

Conclusion: Levinasian Films in the World

In this book, I have discussed films that, through their styles, perform aspects of a Levinasian ethical philosophy. We have seen in Part I that the films of the Dardenne brothers that I have considered here are depicting the principal Levinasian themes as articulated in *Otherwise than Being*: responsibility for the Other (such as Igor's promise to Hamidou in *La Promesse*), the self's status as hostage to the Other (such as Olivier's association with Francis in *Le Fils*) and the goodness of substituting oneself for the Other (such as Samantha's caring for Cyril in *The Kid with a Bike*). And I have discussed how the films use style in a similar way to how Levinas deploys language: to circumvent established approaches to thinking about relationships and instead to perform the anarchy and non-fixity of the Levinasian Saying, with its powerful sense of responsibility. Performativity theory helps draw out these qualities. By considering these films, and their Levinasian themes and styles, in the light of performativity, we can see how a film, performing an ethical world, can bring that world into being. Where the Dardennes' work is particularly potent in this regard is that, with their films offering such harsh and yet optimistic portrayals of contemporary human social struggle, they invite us to think about how to be optimistic in the face of such harshness. If the audience's responses (the films' perlocutionary effects) align with the films' own ethico-ideological aims (their illocutionary effects), then the result is a product of the power of the films as examples of originary performativity. Just as the United States Declaration of Independence, by purporting to speak on behalf of a certain category of people (the American people), brought that category into being at the very moment in which it spoke of them, so the films, in presenting so persuasively, so performatively, a world in which the Levinasian drive wins out, have the effect of bringing his ethics into being anew, such that we might believe in it as a possibility. The shift from a 'conventional' film (*Je Pense à Vous*) to two overtly performative enactments of Levinasian responsibility (*La Promesse* and *Le Fils*) to a more covertly evocative depiction of a Levinasian ethics of substitution and sacrifice (*The Kid with a Bike*) is indicative of a continuing sense of renewal in the Dardennes' work. This is the filmic Saying in action, the Dardennes presenting the Levinasian ethical relation between characters within the film (Performativity$_2$) and between the film and the viewer (Performativity$_1$) in such ways as to continue to provide us with new and vivid encounters with what lies beyond our expectations.

Part II has shown how Barbet Schroeder's films, while not overtly expressing Levinasian themes, are nevertheless exemplifications of a Levinasian approach to the human subject, being concerned, often, with characters who are in some ways marginalised by society, and presented to us in such a way as to invite an open engagement with these cinematic others. With Schroeder's work, we have weaved through Levinas's philosophy, considering identity and domination (as in Olivier and Ariane's relationship in *Maîtresse*), the ethical and the juridical (as performed by the styles and structures of *Reversal of Fortune* and *Terror's Advocate*) and ethics as first philosophy (as radiating from the way love is filmed in *Our Lady of the Assassins*). We have seen how Schroeder does not deploy as consistent or overt a style as the Dardennes – he has no evident stylistic signature – and nor does he have a persistent and easily identifiable set of thematic preoccupations. His commitment, rather, is to be found in the process of adapting his approach to suit whatever material he is directing. It is this aspect of Schroeder's approach to filmmaking that is especially enabling of a Levinasian reading. The films themselves contain, as I have discussed, their own Levinasian aspects; the effacement of the director's identity is an additional manoeuvre, with Schroeder a representative of Levinasian *dénucléation*, his ego 'cored out'. Levinas says of *dénucléation*, with great assertiveness, 'The passivity or patience of vulnerability has to go that far!'[1] Thus, Schroeder's identity as a filmmaker is, importantly, that he has no clear identity. It makes of him a Levinasian figure, devoid of ego and turned towards the Other. He pursues his ethically and ideologically subversive material with the utmost integrity, open to alterity and determined to enact responsibility for the Other. A study of how Schroeder's work performs what can be read as a Levinasian sense of responsibility and openness to the Other will hopefully add to the appreciation of this veteran director whose films have received so little critical enquiry to date. Schroeder's filmmaking is not explicitly Levinasian like that of the Dardennes, but it has a Levinasian dimension of its own.

In my study of Paul Schrader's work in Part III, I have tackled the contradictions inherent in the films – between selfhood and devotion to Others in *American Gigolo*, between knowability and unknowability of the Other as biographical subject in *Mishima: A Life in Four Chapters* and between activity and passivity in the protagonists of *The Comfort of Strangers*, *Dominion: Prequel to the Exorcist* and *Adam Resurrected* – so as to suggest how contradictions can themselves offer up riches for Levinasian contemplation. Of the directorial achievements that I have chosen to discuss in this book, I decided to discuss Schrader's work last because to read his work as Levinasian requires a different type of ethical engagement from what I have discussed with regard to the Dardennes and Schroeder, one that places more of an onus on the viewer to respond to the sometimes contradictory elements in the films. If Schrader's work feels less overtly Levinasian, it may be because the styles are often, as I noted in the chapter on *American Gigolo*, contaminated styles that include an array of referents that complicate the film's commitment to its subject. Accordingly, the performative nature of Schrader's work is often not overt. But the films are performative in that they seek to communicate ideas and points of view (their illocutionary force) and cannot help but provoke responses (their perlocutionary effects). As we saw earlier, Schrader in his article 'Canon Fodder' champions the film that 'engages him or her in a creative process of viewing' and that leads to a viewer 'making identifications he or she had no intention of making, coming to conclusions the film can't control, reassembling the film in a unique personal way'.[2] Although he is not referring explicitly to his own films, his statement reflects his own achievement as a filmmaker whose work, by way of its contradictions and attendant lack of fixity, can be said to be capable of inspiring Levinasian ethical engagement.

This study of the Dardennes, Schroeder and Schrader in their combination helps open up the different ways in which films can engage with and communicate ethics. My study has sought to make a significant contribution to the study of Levinas and film by linking the performative qualities of Levinas's prose style with the performative qualities of the films in question. Levinas's deployment of a performative language, seen to a degree in *Totality and Infinity* and practised more extensively in *Otherwise than Being*, initiates the reader into a process of identity breakdown – *dénucléation*, the coring out of the ego – leading to ethical epiphany, which is in effect a recognition of what is already there: our pre-existing goodness. Thus, the process is an *uncovering*. The breaking down of identity is also a breaking down of conventional thought. Reading Levinas is both pleasurable and demanding – indeed, it is often pleasurable *because* it is demanding – but being ethical can only be measured in terms of action. This action is at its most powerful when we are responding ethically to the call of an Other whom we cannot know and who demands of us an infinite responsibility. The essence of a performative approach to film, when allied to Levinasian ethics, is that it provides an experience of otherness for the viewer such that the viewer comes away more acutely aware of how life is like for others. The Dardennes, Schroeder and Schrader invite the viewer to leave their expectations and preconceptions at the door; they gently, subtly, *performatively* present filmic experiences that we can consider to be Levinasian. These experiences are significant in the *dénucléation* of the ego. Furthermore, it is hoped that choosing such a disparate group of filmmakers has suggested alternative approaches to our understanding of how Levinas and film intersect. There are many other filmmakers whose work might fruitfully be discussed through the Levinasian lens.

The consideration of performativity in film, and its relation to ethics, offers other further directions for fruitful study. The different levels of performativity – the locutionary, illocutionary and perlocutionary – could unlock previously untapped aspects of films and film culture. These Austinian concepts are not verifiable on film the way they are in spoken or written language. The relation of illocutionary effects to conventionality, for example, is difficult to assess with film, partly because, as Currie has asserted, film is not conventional in the same way as language. As for assessing film's perlocutionary effects, these are likely to be the sum total of the problems associated with assessing film's illocutionary effects *plus* the difficulty of identifying responses to films. I have approached film's performativity through the practice of interpreting films as texts, offering readings, supported through textual analysis, that argue for certain effects. A reception study would be one possible and different future way of approaching the task of ascribing illocutionary and perlocutionary effects to a film because the research framework would serve to place the film within a particular social context, with all the attendant questions of conventions, sociological perspective, and so on. The performative effects of film could also be considered in terms of their propensity for propaganda. Noël Carroll, for example, notes how recalibration 'can be employed by angels or demons'.[3] I have referred to Wilson's work on the 'reading encounter' and suggested that film offers an ethical 'viewing encounter': this can be mapped onto questions of everyday ethics. There will also be value in considering the links between performativity, film and the tenets of political correctness. That term has taken on negative as well as positive connotations ever since its inception, and is in many quarters violently opposed, but in the sense that attitudes, like identities, are performed, there is a potentially ethical benefit in the repetition of politically correct terms, as this repetition might be effective in replacing damaging attitudes with new, progressive ones.

After all, why does Levinas use language the way he does if not to persuade us, somehow, of the veracity of his ethics? What is he doing if not coaxing us into a recognition of how the ethical relation he posits comes to bear on our sense of self? Through performativity theory, we can see how Levinas's mode of expression is an indispensable aspect of his ethics. From there, we can see how a film, too, expresses its own ethics not with the help of its style but *because of* its style. Through Levinasian-performative readings, therefore, we can see ways in which films matter – ways in which they change our world, become part of our lives and our life philosophy.

Performativity thus relates potentially to every area of film. We will recall Petrey's claim that '[t]he punch of speech-act criticism comes less from sensitivity to *certain* kinds of language than from recognition that *all* kinds of language make tangible the network of relationships and agreements in which humans and their signs are always embedded'.[4] Accordingly, any act of filmmaking is a performative act. Performativity theory, rippling outward from the Austinian speech act to significance in literary criticism, performance of identity, and the wider socio-political sphere, does not grant film a legitimacy it otherwise lacks *in relation to* the real world; rather, it recognises film's status *within and as part of* the world. Performativity theory helps us to think about the continual, irrefutable presence of film within the contexts of our world. And in these films directed by the Dardennes, Schroeder and Schrader, as we have seen, that presence is ethical, in ways that reflect Levinas's analysis of the self's responsibility for the Other.

Notes

Introduction

1. Paul Schrader, *Transcendental Style in Film: Ozu, Bresson, Dreyer – With a New Introduction: Rethinking Transcendental Style* (Oakland: University of California Press, 2018 [original edition first published: 1972]), p. 77.
2. Ibid., pp. 79–80.
3. Ibid., p. 80.
4. Emmanuel Levinas, *Otherwise than Being or Beyond Essence*, trans. Alphonso Lingis (Pittsburgh: Duquesne University Press, 2008 [1981; original language publication: 1974]), p. 49. Emphasis in original.
5. See ibid., especially Chapter IV: 'Substitution', pp. 99–129.
6. Ibid., p. 48.
7. Ibid., p. 74.
8. Ibid., p. 6.
9. Ibid., p. 5.
10. Ibid., p. 26.
11. Emmanuel Levinas, 'Reality and its Shadow', in Emmanuel Levinas, *Collected Philosophical Papers*, trans. Alphonso Lingis (Pittsburgh: Duquesne University Press, 2006 [1987; original language publication of essay: 1948]), pp. 1–13.
12. See ibid., for example, the section 'The Meanwhile', pp. 8–11.
13. Reni Celeste, 'The Frozen Screen: Levinas and the Action Film', in Sarah Cooper (ed), 'The Occluded Relation: Levinas and Cinema', Special Issue, *Film-Philosophy*, Vol. 11, Issue 2, August 2007 <https://www.euppublishing.com/doi/abs/10.3366/film.2007.0008> (last accessed 31 January 2019), pp. 15–36; p. 19.
14. Sarah Cooper, 'Introduction: The Occluded Relation: Levinas and Cinema', in Sarah Cooper (ed), 'The Occluded Relation: Levinas and Cinema', Special Issue, *Film-Philosophy*, Vol. 11, Issue 2, August 2007, <https://www.euppublishing.com/doi/abs/10.3366/film.2007.0006> (last accessed 31 January 2019), pp. i–vii; p. i.

15. Emmanuel Levinas, *Totality and Infinity: An Essay on Exteriority*, trans. Alphonso Lingis (Pittsburgh: Duquesne University Press, 2007 [1969; original language publication: 1961]). See in particular the section 'Ethics and the Face', pp. 194–219.
16. Sarah Cooper, *Selfless Cinema?: Ethics and French Documentary* (London: Legenda, 2006).
17. Libby Saxton, 'Blinding Visions: Levinas, Ethics, Faciality', in Lisa Downing and Libby Saxton, *Film and Ethics: Foreclosed Encounters* (Abingdon and New York: Routledge, 2010), pp. 95–106; p. 97.
18. Libby Saxton, 'Fragile Faces: Levinas and Lanzmann', in Sarah Cooper (ed.), 'The Occluded Relation: Levinas and Cinema', Special Issue, *Film-Philosophy*, Vol. 11, Issue 2, August 2007 <https://www.euppublishing.com/doi/abs/10.3366/film.2007.0007> (last accessed 31 January 2019), pp. 1–14; p. 12.
19. Sarah Cooper, 'Mortal Ethics: Reading Levinas with the Dardenne Brothers', in Sarah Cooper (ed.), 'The Occluded Relation: Levinas and Cinema', Special Issue, *Film-Philosophy*, Vol. 11, Issue 2, August 2007 <https://www.euppublishing.com/doi/abs/10.3366/film.2007.0011> (last accessed 31 January 2019), pp. 66–87; p. 83.
20. Michele Aaron, *Spectatorship: The Power of Looking On* (London: Wallflower Press, 2007), p. 112.
21. Doug Cummings, 'The Brothers Dardenne: Responding to the Face of the Other', in Kenneth R. Morefield (ed.), *Faith and Spirituality in Masters of World Cinema* (Newcastle upon Tyne: Cambridge Scholars Publishing, 2008), pp. 91–103; John W. Wright, 'Levinasian Ethics of Alterity: The Face of the Other in Spielberg's Cinematic Language', in Dean A. Kowalski (ed.), *Steven Spielberg and Philosophy: We're Gonna Need a Bigger Book* (Lexington: The University Press of Kentucky, 2008), pp. 50–68.
22. Robert Bernasconi and Simon Critchley, 'Editors' Introduction', in Robert Bernasconi and Simon Critchley (eds), *Re-Reading Levinas* (London: The Athlone Press, 1991), pp. xi–xviii; p. xii.
23. See, for example, Colin Davis, *Levinas: An Introduction* (Cambridge and Malden: Polity Press, 1996), pp. 63–9, and Seán Hand, *Emmanuel Levinas* (Abingdon and New York: Routledge, 2009), pp. 46–7.
24. Jacques Derrida, 'Violence and Metaphysics: An Essay on the Thought of Emmanuel Levinas', in Jacques Derrida, *Writing and Difference*, trans. Alan Bass (Abingdon: Routledge, 2001 [1978; original language publication of book: 1967; original publication of essay: 1964]), pp. 97–192.
25. Ibid., p. 189.
26. Davis, *Levinas: An Introduction*, p. 73.
27. Diane Perpich, *The Ethics of Emmanuel Levinas* (Stanford: Stanford University Press, 2008), p. 118.
28. Quoted in Tamra Wright, Peter Hughes and Alison Ainley, 'The Paradox of Morality: An Interview with Emmanuel Levinas', trans Andrew Benjamin

and Tamra Wright, in Robert Bernasconi and David Wood (eds), *The Provocation of Levinas: Rethinking the Other* (London and New York: Routledge, 1988), pp. 168–180; p. 176.
29. See Adriaan T. Peperzak, 'Preface', in Adriaan T. Peperzak (ed.), *Ethics as First Philosophy: The Significance of Emmanuel Levinas for Philosophy, Literature and Religion* (New York and London: Routledge, 1995), pp. ix–xiii, and Perpich, especially 'Introduction: But is it *Ethics?*', pp. 1–16.
30. Peperzak, 'Preface', p. xi.
31. Levinas, *Otherwise than Being*, n.p. (dedication page).
32. Ibid., p. 5.
33. Ibid.
34. Ibid., p. 64.
35. See, for example, ibid., pp. 136–40.
36. Adriaan Theodoor Peperzak, *Beyond: The Philosophy of Emmanuel Levinas* (Evanston: Northwestern University Press, 1997), p. 67. Emphases in original.
37. Levinas, *Otherwise than Being*, p. 184.
38. Emmanuel Levinas, *Existence and Existents*, trans. Alphonso Lingis (Pittsburgh: Duquesne University Press, 2008 [1978; original language publication: 1947]).
39. Lisa Downing and Libby Saxton, *Film and Ethics: Foreclosed Encounters* (Abingdon and New York: Routledge, 2010).
40. Jinhee Choi and Mattias Frey (eds), *Cine-Ethics: Ethical Dimensions of Film Theory, Practice, and Spectatorship* (Abingdon and New York: Routledge, 2014). See, especially, Jinhee Choi and Mattias Frey, 'Introduction', pp. 1–14, and, in particular, pp. 2–10.
41. Robert Sinnerbrink, *Cinematic Ethics: Exploring Ethical Experience through Film* (Abingdon and New York: Routledge, 2016).
42. J. L. Austin, *How to Do Things with Words: The William James Lectures delivered at Harvard University in 1955 – Second Edition*, J. O. Urmson and Marina Sbisà (eds) (Oxford and New York: Oxford University Press, 1975 [original edition first published: 1962]).
43. Ibid., pp. 5–6.
44. Ibid., p. 6. Emphasis in original.
45. Ibid., pp. 1–3.
46. Ibid., pp. 6–7.
47. See, for example, ibid., Lecture II, 'Conditions for Happy Performatives', pp. 12–24.
48. Ibid., pp. 2–3.
49. See, for example, ibid., p. 40.
50. Ibid., pp. 163–4.
51. Jacques Derrida, 'Signature Event Context', trans Samuel Weber and Jeffrey Mehlman [1977], in Jacques Derrida, *Limited Inc*, Gerald Graff (ed.) (Evanston: Northwestern University Press, 1988 [original language publication: 1972]), pp. 1–23.

52. See Jeffrey T. Nealon, *Alterity Politics: Ethics and Performative Subjectivity* (Durham, NC and London: Duke University Press, 1998), especially pp. 21–3.
53. Sedgwick discusses these authors in, for example, Eve Kosofsky Sedgwick, *Epistemology of the Closet* (Berkeley and Los Angeles: University of California Press, 1990).
54. Sandy Petrey, *Speech Acts and Literary Theory* (New York and London: Routledge, 1990).
55. For a good example of performance theory tackling issues of performativity, see Andrew Parker and Eve Kosofsky Sedgwick (eds), *Performativity and Performance* (London and New York: Routledge, 1995).
56. Judith Butler, *Gender Trouble: Feminism and the Subversion of Identity* (New York and London: Routledge, 1990); Judith Butler, *Excitable Speech: A Politics of the Performative* (New York and London: Routledge, 1997).
57. See Nealon, *Alterity Politics*, pp. 21–30.
58. James Loxley, *Performativity* (Abingdon and New York: Routledge, 2007).
59. Levinas, *Totality and Infinity*, p. 199.
60. Michael L. Morgan, *Discovering Levinas* (New York: Cambridge University Press, 2007), p. 125.
61. Ibid., p. 131.
62. Perpich, 'Introduction: But is it *Ethics?*', p. 16.
63. Davis, *Levinas: An Introduction*, p. 91. Emphasis in original.
64. Perpich, *The Ethics of Emmanuel Levinas*, p. 118.
65. Paul Davies, 'On Resorting to an Ethical Language', in Adriaan T. Peperzak (ed.), *Ethics as First Philosophy: The Significance of Emmanuel Levinas for Philosophy, Literature and Religion* (New York and London: Routledge, 1995), pp. 95–104; p. 103.
66. Ibid., p. 104. Emphasis in original.
67. Davies, 'On Resorting to an Ethical Language', p. 104.
68. Sam B. Girgus, 'Beyond Ontology: Levinas and the Ethical Frame in Film', in Sarah Cooper (ed.), 'The Occluded Relation: Levinas and Cinema', Special Issue, *Film-Philosophy*, Vol. 11, Issue 2, August 2007 <https://www.euppublishing.com/doi/abs/10.3366/film.2007.0012> (last accessed 31 January 2019), pp. 88–107; p. 96.
69. Hagi Kenaan, *The Ethics of Visuality: Levinas and the Contemporary Gaze*, trans. Batya Stein (London and New York: I. B. Tauris, 2013), p. 105.
70. Alphonso Lingis, 'Translator's Introduction', in Emmanuel Levinas, *Otherwise than Being or Beyond Essence*, trans. Alphonso Lingis (Pittsburgh: Duquesne University Press, 2008 [1978; original language publication of book: 1974]), pp. xvii–xlv; p. xviii.
71. Kenaan, *The Ethics of Visuality*, p. 106.
72. Loxley, *Performativity*, p. 2.
73. Christian Metz, 'The Cinema: Language or Language System?', in Christian Metz, *Film Language: A Semiotics of the Cinema*, trans. Michael Taylor

(New York: Oxford University Press, 1974 [original language publication of book: 1971; original language publication of essay: 1964]), pp. 31–91.
74. Ibid., p. 41.
75. Ibid.
76. See, for example, Metz, 'The Cinema', pp. 89–91.
77. Gregory Currie, 'The Long Goodbye: The Imaginary Language of Film' [1993], in Noël Carroll and Jinhee Choi (eds), *Philosophy of Film and Motion Pictures: An Anthology* (Malden, Oxford, and Carlton: Blackwell Publishing, 2006), pp. 91–9.
78. Ibid., p. 92.
79. Ibid., p. 93.
80. Ibid., p. 96.
81. Ibid., p. 97.
82. Ibid., p. 96. Emphasis in original.
83. V. F. Perkins, *Film as Film: Understanding and Judging Movies* (Harmondsworth: Penguin, 1991 [1972]), p. 21.
84. Currie, 'The Long Goodbye', p. 97.
85. For an overview of Classical Hollywood Cinema that is itself classic, see David Bordwell, Janet Staiger and Kristin Thompson, *The Classical Hollywood Cinema: Film Style & Mode of Production to 1960* (London: Routledge, 1988).
86. James Monaco, *How to Read a Film: Movies, Media, and Beyond – Fourth Edition* (Oxford and New York: Oxford University Press, 2009 [original edition first published: 1977]), p. 72. Emphasis in original.
87. Austin, *How to Do Things with Words*, p. 94.
88. Ibid., p. 57.
89. Liza Bakewell, 'Image Acts', *American Anthropologist*, New Series, Vol. 100, No. 1, March 1998, pp. 22–32.
90. Ibid., p. 22.
91. Ibid., p. 30.
92. Ibid., p. 27.
93. Ibid., p. 29.
94. Ibid., p. 30.
95. Lars Sætre, Patrizia Lombardo and Anders M. Gullestad (eds), *Exploring Textual Action* (Aarhus and Copenhagen: Aarhus University Press, 2010).
96. J. Hillis Miller, 'Performativity$_1$/Performativity$_2$', in Lars Sætre, Patrizia Lombardo and Anders M. Gullestad (eds), *Exploring Textual Action* (Aarhus and Copenhagen: Aarhus University Press, 2010), pp. 31–58.
97. Svend Erik Larsen, '"Speak Again. Speak Like Rain" – The Mediality of Performance', in Lars Sætre, Patrizia Lombardo and Anders M. Gullestad (eds), *Exploring Textual Action* (Aarhus and Copenhagen: Aarhus University Press, 2010), pp. 59–82; p. 80. Emphases in original.
98. See Bill Nichols, *Blurred Boundaries: Questions of Meaning in Contemporary Culture* (Bloomington and Indianapolis: Indiana University Press, 1994),

especially Chapter 5, 'Performing Documentary', pp. 92–106, and see Stella Bruzzi, *New Documentary – Second Edition* (Abingdon and New York: Routledge, 2006 [original edition first published: 2000]), especially Chapter 6, 'The Performative Documentary', pp. 185–218.
 99. Nichols, *Blurred Boundaries*, p. 95.
100. Ibid., p. 100.
101. Ibid., p. 102.
102. Bruzzi, *New Documentary*, p. 186.
103. Ibid.
104. Ibid.
105. Cooper, 'Mortal Ethics', p. 66.
106. Ibid. p. 75.
107. Dominic Michael Rainsford, 'Tarkovsky and Levinas: Cuts, Mirrors, Triangulations', in Sarah Cooper (ed.), 'The Occluded Relation: Levinas and Cinema', Special Issue, *Film-Philosophy*, Vol. 11, Issue 2, August 2007 <https://www.euppublishing.com/doi/abs/10.3366/film.2007.0014> (last accessed 31 January 2019), pp. 122–43; p. 125.
108. Simon Critchley, 'To Be or Not to Be is Not the Question: On Beckett's *Film*', in Sarah Cooper (ed.), 'The Occluded Relation: Levinas and Cinema', Special Issue, *Film-Philosophy*, Vol. 11, Issue 2, August 2007 <https://www.euppublishing.com/doi/abs/10.3366/film.2007.0013> (last accessed 31 January 2019), pp. 108–21; p. 119.
109. Ibid., p. 117.
110. Asbjørn Grønstad, *Film and the Ethical Imagination* (London: Palgrave Macmillan, 2016), p. 7.
111. Kristin Lené Hole, *Towards a Feminist Cinematic Ethics: Claire Denis, Emmanuel Levinas and Jean-Luc Nancy* (Edinburgh: Edinburgh University Press, 2016), p. 104.
112. Alexandre Astruc, 'The Birth of a New Avant-Garde: La Caméra-Stylo' [original language publication 1948], trans. unattributed, in Peter Graham and Ginette Vincendeau (eds), *The French New Wave: Critical Landmarks* (London: BFI/Palgrave Macmillan, 2009), pp. 31–6.
113. Bakewell, 'Image Acts', p. 24.

Part I Introduction

1. Luc Dardenne, *Au dos de nos images (1991–2005) suivi de* Le Fils, L'Enfant *et* Le Silence de Lorna *par Jean-Pierre et Luc Dardenne* (Paris: Éditions du Seuil, 2008 [original publication, without *The Silence of Lorna*: 2005]); Luc Dardenne, *Au dos de nos images II (2005–2014) suivi de* Le Gamin au vélo *et* Deux jours, une nuit *par Jean-Pierre et Luc Dardenne* (Paris: Éditions du Seuil, 2015). The title *Au dos de nos images* can be translated as *On the Back of Our Images*. All translations from these two books are my own.

2. 'Levinas a écrit dans *Difficile liberté* que l'âme n'est pas possibilité d'immortalité (la mienne) mais impossibilité de tuer (autrui). L'art est reconnu par beaucoup comme une manifestation de notre possibilité d'immortalité, comme dur désir de durer, comme anti-destin. Pourrait-il être une modalité de l'institution de l'impossibilité de tuer? . . . Regarder l'écran, le tableau, la scène, la sculpture, la page, écouter le chant, la musique, ce serait: ne pas tuer.' Dardenne, *Au dos de nos images (1991–2005)*, p. 42.
3. 'J'ai suivi ses cours et c'est quelqu'un que je continue de lire. Cela a été un choc de découvrir ses textes, sa réflexion sur le visage comme commandement de ne pas tuer.' Jacques Morice, 'Le pari des frères Dardenne: "Filmer le bien en action"', Télérama, 21 May 2011 <http://www.telerama.fr/cinema/le-pari-des-freres-dardenne-filmer-le-bien-en-action,68933.php> (last accessed 31 January 2019). My translation.
4. Luc Dardenne, *Sur l'affaire humaine* (Paris: Éditions du Seuil, 2012). The title can be translated as *On the Human Affair* or *On Human Affairs*.
5. See, for example, Cooper, 'Mortal Ethics'; Sarah Cooper, '"Put Yourself in My Place": *Two Days, One Night* and the Journey Back to Life', in John Caruana and Mark Cauchi (eds), *Immanent Frames: Postsecular Cinema between Malick and von Trier* (Albany: State University of New York Press, 2018), pp. 229–44; Cummings, 'The Brothers Dardenne'; Martin O'Shaughnessy, 'Ethics in the Ruin of Politics: The Dardenne Brothers', in Kate Ince (ed.), *Five Directors: Auteurism from Assayas to Ozon* (Manchester and New York: Manchester University Press, 2008), pp. 59–83; Robert Sinnerbrink, 'Melodrama, Realism, and Ethical Experience (*Biutiful*, *The Promise*)', in *Cinematic Ethics: Exploring Ethical Experience through Film* (Abingdon and New York: Routledge, 2016), pp. 139–64; Sam B. Girgus, 'Existence and Ethics in the Dardenne Brothers' *Two Days, One Night* (2015)', in *Time, Existential Presence, and the Cinematic Image: Ethics and Emergence to Being in Film* (Edinburgh: Edinburgh University Press, 2018), pp. 78–98; Joseph Mai, *Jean-Pierre and Luc Dardenne* (Urbana, Chicago and Springfield: University of Illinois Press, 2010); Philip Mosley, *The Cinema of the Dardenne Brothers: Responsible Realism* (New York and Chichester: Wallflower Press/Columbia University Press, 2013); Olivier Ducharme, *Films de Combat: La résistance du cinéma des frères Dardenne* (Montreal: Varia, 2017); Jacqueline Aubenas (ed.), *Jean-Pierre & Luc Dardenne* (Brussels: Diffusion, 2008).
6. Mai, *Jean-Pierre and Luc Dardenne*, p. x.
7. Mosley, *The Cinema of the Dardenne Brothers*, p. 14.
8. Ibid., p. 13.

Chapter 1

1. For other, largely convergent, considerations of the stylistic failures of this film, see Mai, *Jean-Pierre and Luc Dardenne*, pp. 36–40; Mosley, *The Cinema*

of the Dardenne Brothers, pp. 73–4; and O'Shaughnessy, 'Ethics in the Ruin of Politics', p. 67.
2. See, for example, Dardenne, *Au dos de nos images (1991–2005)*, pp. 13–14 and 17.
3. 'Pourquoi avons-nous fait ce film?' Ibid., p. 14.
4. See, for example, ibid., pp. 13–14.
5. 'Emmanuel Levinas est mort durant notre tournage. Le film doit beaucoup à la lecture de ses livres. Son interprétation du face-à-face, du visage comme premier discours. Sans ces lectures, aurions-nous imaginé les scènes de Roger and Igor dans le garage, d'Assita et Igor dans le bureau du garage et dans l'escalier de la gare? Tout le film peut-être vu comme une tentative d'arriver enfin au face-à-face.' Ibid., p. 56.
6. Damian Cox and Michael P. Levine, *Thinking through Film: Doing Philosophy, Watching Movies* (Chichester: Wiley-Blackwell, 2012), p. 257.
7. Lieve Spaas, *The Francophone Film: A Struggle for Identity* (Manchester and New York: Manchester University Press, 2000), p. 41.
8. O'Shaughnessy, 'Ethics in the Ruin of Politics', p. 61.
9. Mai, *Jean-Pierre and Luc Dardenne*, p. xv.
10. Ibid., pp. 66–7.
11. Ibid., p. 52.
12. Ibid., p. xv.
13. Cooper, 'Mortal Ethics', p. 66.
14. Spaas, *The Francophone Film*, p. 40.
15. Mai, *Jean-Pierre and Luc Dardenne*, p. 60.
16. Syd Field's many books begin with *Screenplay: The Foundations of Screenwriting – Newly Revised and Updated* (New York: Delta, 2005 [original edition first published: 1979]). Robert McKee sets out his approach principally in Robert McKee, *Story: Substance, Structure, Style, and the Principles of Screenwriting* (London: Methuen, 1999 [1997]).
17. Something that is especially charming and accessible about Austin's lectures is that he breaks these distinctions down himself. As Sandy Petrey nicely observes, '[t]he result is a mesmerizing demonstration of how to do things with a mind as well as a seminal description of how to do things with words'. Petrey, *Speech Acts and Literary Theory*, p. 22.
18. Austin, *How to Do Things with Words*, p. 145.
19. Ibid., p. 4.
20. Petrey, *Speech Acts and Literary Theory*, p. 89. Emphases in original.
21. See, for example, ibid., p. 153.
22. Mai, *Jean-Pierre and Luc Dardenne*, p. 34.
23. Mosley, *The Cinema of the Dardenne Brothers*, p. 74.
24. Wouter Hessels, '*Rosetta*', in Ernest Mathijs (ed), *The Cinema of the Low Countries* (London: Wallflower Press, 2004), pp. 238–47; p. 240.
25. Martin O'Shaughnessy, *The New Face of Political Cinema: Commitment in French Film since 1995* (New York and Oxford: Berghahn Books, 2007), pp. 51–3.

26. Richard A. Cohen, 'Translator's Introduction' [1987], in Emmanuel Levinas, *Time and the Other and Additional Essays*, trans. Richard A. Cohen (Pittsburgh: Duquesne University Press, 2008 [original language publication of essay *Time and the Other*: 1947]), pp. 1–27; p. 11.
27. 'Tout style est une caricature, une resemblance à soi-même, un destin, une momification, une victoire du nécrophile qui se tient en nous toujours prêt à refroidir ce qui bouge, ne trouve pas sa forme, son image.' Dardenne, *Au dos de nos images (1991–2005)*, p. 26.

Chapter 2

1. Emma Wilson, *Sexuality and the Reading Encounter: Identity and Desire in Proust, Duras, Tournier, and Cixous* (Oxford: Clarendon Press, 1996), p. 3.
2. Ibid. p. 6.
3. Ibid. Emphasis in original.
4. Davis, *Levinas: An Introduction*, p. 110. Emphasis in original.
5. Mai, *Jean-Pierre and Luc Dardenne*, p. x.
6. Levinas, *Otherwise than Being or Beyond Essence*, p. 26.
7. Cox and Levine, *Thinking through Film*, p. 190.
8. Ibid., p. 259.
9. Ibid., p. 258.
10. R. D. Crano, '"Occupy without Counting": Furtive Urbanism in the Films of Jean-Pierre and Luc Dardenne', *Film-Philosophy*, Vol. 13, Issue 1, April 2009 <http://www.film-philosophy.com/2009v13n1/crano.pdf> (last accessed 31 January 2019), pp. 1–15; p. 13.
11. Cooper, 'Mortal Ethics', p. 75.
12. 'Le film, c'est le personnage, c'est l'acteur, c'est Olivier Gourmet . . .' Dardenne, *Au dos de nos images (1991–2005)*, p. 123.
13. Mai, *Jean-Pierre and Luc Dardenne*, p. 72.
14. Richard Rushton, 'Empathic Projection in the Films of the Dardenne Brothers', *Screen*, Vol. 55, Issue 3, 1 September 2014, pp. 303–16; p. 310. Emphases in original.
15. Daniel Frampton, *Filmosophy* (London: Wallflower Press, 2006), p. 146.
16. Mai, *Jean-Pierre and Luc Dardenne*, p. 87.
17. Crano, '"Occupy without Counting"', p. 2.
18. Ibid., p. 3. Emphases in original.
19. Cooper, 'Mortal Ethics', p. 74.
20. Jacques Derrida, 'Declarations of Independence', trans Tom Keenan and Tom Pepper [1986], in Jacques Derrida, *Negotiations: Interventions and Interviews, 1971–2001*, Elizabeth Rottenberg (ed.) (Stanford: Stanford University Press, 2002 [original language publication: 1984]), pp. 46–54; p. 48.
21. Ibid., p. 49.
22. Ibid., p. 49. Translations in original.
23. Ibid., p. 49. Emphasis in original.

24. Ibid., p. 49. Emphases in original.
25. Loxley, *Performativity*, pp. 102–3.
26. Derrida, 'Declarations of Independence', pp. 51–2. Emphases in original.
27. Jacques Derrida, *Specters of Marx: The State of the Debt, the Work of Mourning and the New International*, trans. Peggy Kamuf (New York and Abingdon: Routledge, 1994 [original language publication: 1993]), pp. 36–7. Emphasis in original.
28. Mosley, *The Cinema of the Dardenne Brothers*, p. 14.
29. Cooper, 'Mortal Ethics', p. 85.
30. Ibid., p. 66.
31. Ibid., p. 72.
32. Wilson, *Sexuality and the Reading Encounter*, p. 3.
33. For this formulation, I am indebted to an observation about a different film in V. F. Perkins, 'Where is the World? The Horizon of Events in Movie Fiction', in John Gibbs and Douglas Pye (eds), *Style and Meaning: Studies in the Detailed Analysis of Film* (Manchester: Manchester University Press, 2005), pp. 16–41, which inspired it; see pp. 19–20.
34. Levinas, *Otherwise than Being*, p. 15.
35. Ibid.
36. Levinas, *Totality and Infinity*, p. 197.
37. 'Olivier, en ne tuant pas Francis, est le père qui permettra peut-être à Francis de renouer avec la vie.' Dardenne, *Au dos de nos images (1991–2005)*, p. 116.

Chapter 3

1. *Chacun son cinéma* was commissioned on the occasion of the sixtieth anniversary of the Cannes Film Festival, and is composed of thirty-four short films by leading international directors.
2. 'On hésite. Devons-nous faire ce film avec le garçon? Ne sommes-nous pas pris dans une forme dont nous n'arrivons pas à sortir, dont nous n'osons pas sortir? Je ne sais plus. On verra.' Dardenne, *Au dos de nos images II*, pp. 25–6.
3. '[Q]uelque chose doit changer dans notre cinéma. Je pressens que l'année qui vient ne va pas être de tout repos. Si notre cinéma devient plus narratif, si nous filmons plus une intrigue (et ses sous-intrigues) qu'un personnage, comment ne pas perdre la vibration du plan?' Ibid., p. 104.
4. Mosley, *The Cinema of the Dardenne Brothers*, p. 123.
5. Benoît Dillet and Tara Puri, 'Left-over Spaces: The Cinema of the Dardenne brothers', *Film-Philosophy*, Vol. 17, Issue 1, December 2013 <https://www.euppublishing.com/doi/abs/10.3366/film.2013.0021> (last accessed 31 January 2019), pp. 367–82; p. 367.
6. 'Nous tournerons en Kodak 35 mm. Il y aura sans doute moins de nervosité que dans nos mouvements avec la caméra super 16 mm. Une inertie plus grande qui devrait aller dans le sens de ce que nous voulons filmer: l'observation

de Lorna, l'enregistrement de son comportement, de sa présence difficile à cerner, à sentir. Pour la regarder, il ne faut pas se laisser prendre dans ses mouvements, ne pas mimer son énergie, il faut garder une distance et donc moins bouger avec elle.' Dardenne, *Au dos de nos images II*, p. 86.
7. Hand, *Emmanuel Levinas*, p. 53.
8. Robert Pippin, 'Psychology Degree Zero? The Representation of Action in the Films of the Dardenne Brothers', *Critical Inquiry*, Vol. 41, Summer 2015, pp. 757–85; p. 764.
9. Butler, *Excitable Speech*, p. 69. Emphasis in original (although Butler also elsewhere uses the term without the emphasis).
10. See Derrida, 'Signature Event Context', especially pp. 7–12.
11. See Loxley, *Performativity*, p. 132.
12. Butler, *Excitable Speech*, p. 100.
13. 'Interview with Jean-Pierre and Luc Dardenne', Press kit, *The Kid with a Bike* <https://encodeur.movidone.com/getimage/rsnrvhlSdgp5qtsUk4Ov4-LdPJw5tY9rH53UAs_lqO8kJPjJIJHgs9li5pSUo0Nr3YxyJU-4zGf8GvOWFm8dz7USaf9qUMgjtcYHRRUTi2nyJq9iNd6lZTI7-rbTwav1RF_vh9vk1pic6aWvcbwgQ8xvAyshux5AV4yTEEedtEPuqoqKXzydSIa7_6Wmgdve8c1s2AIv9YDN4HR5WBpHhaD2> (last accessed 31 January 2019), pp. 4–5.
14. Levinas, *Otherwise than Being*, p. 51.
15. 'Il n'y a aucune réponse (certainement pas la réponse psychologique du style: elle a perdu un enfant dans le passé ou elle ne peut en avoir un) et c'est précisément cela le film: empêcher la formulation d'une réponse qui délivrerait le spectateur de cette question: «Pourquoi accepte-t-elle cet enfant?» . . . En livrant le spectateur à ce comportement mystérieux de Samantha, nous espérons le conduire jusqu'à ce qu'il accepte pour lui-même, comme pour Samantha, qu'il n'y a d'autre motivation qu'avoir été face à la souffrance de Cyril.' Dardenne, *Au dos de nos images II*, p. 158.
16. 'Interview with Jean-Pierre and Luc Dardenne', p. 4.
17. Ibid.
18. Levinas, *Otherwise than Being*, p. 115.
19. Richard Rushton, 'Empathic Projection in the Films of the Dardenne Brothers', p. 310.
20. Ibid., p. 306. Emphases in original.
21. O'Shaughnessy, 'Ethics in the Ruin of Politics', p. 61.

Part II Introduction

1. Dominique Bax and Cyril Béghin (eds), *Théâtres au cinéma – Tome 23: Barbet Schroeder* (Bobigny: Collection Magic Cinéma, 2012); Jérôme d'Estais, *Barbet Schroeder: Ombres et clarté* (La Madeleine: LettMotif, 2017). All translations from these books are my own.

2. David Thomson, *The New Biographical Dictionary of Film – Sixth Edition* (New York: Alfred A. Knopf, 2014 [original edition first published: 1975]), p. 939.
3. 'Ma carrière cinématographique n'a pas d'orientation, de direction unique. J'aime changer à chaque film, prendre un chemin tout à fait différent de celui qui à précédé. Mon objectif est de surprendre. Cela ne me plairait pas d'être catalogué . . .' Quoted in 'Tout Barbet Schroeder', Press kit, *Théâtres au cinema: 23e festival à Bobigny* <http://www.theatresaucinema.fr/images/pdf/dpresse2012.pdf> (last accessed 31 January 2019), pp. 3–5. My translation.
4. 'Partir de ce que l'on connaît pour aller vers l'inconnu. . . . Toujours changer. De pays, de style, de genre. Redémarrer à zéro.' D'Estais, *Barbet Schroeder*, p. 43.
5. Levinas, *Otherwise than Being*, p. 49.

Chapter 4

1. For an excellent distilled look at this period in Hollywood history, see Mark Harris, *Pictures at a Revolution: Five Movies and the Birth of the New Hollywood* (New York: The Penguin Press, 2008). For a classic take on the 'Movie Brat' era, see Peter Biskind, *Easy Riders, Raging Bulls: How the Sex-Drugs-and-Rock 'n' Roll Generation Saved Hollywood* (New York: Simon & Schuster, 1998). For an impressionistic account of the proliferation of international cinemas in the 1960s, see Peter Cowie, *Revolution!: The Explosion of World Cinema in the 60s* (London: Faber and Faber, 2004).
2. There are many significant films that could be mentioned. Among the most high-profile, I suggest, are: for sex and nudity, *Jag är nyfiken – en film i gult* (*I Am Curious [Yellow]*, dir. Vilgot Sjöman, 1967), *Last Tango in Paris* (dir. Bernardo Bertolucci, 1972), and *L'Empire des sens* (*Empire of the Senses* a.k.a. *In the Realm of the Senses*, dir. Nagisa Oshima, 1976); for drugs, *The Trip* (dir. Roger Corman, 1967), *Easy Rider* (dir. Dennis Hopper, 1969), and Schroeder's *More*; for violence, *Bonnie and Clyde* (dir. Arthur Penn, 1967), *The Wild Bunch* (dir. Sam Peckinpah, 1969), and *Taxi Driver* (dir. Martin Scorsese, 1976); for sexual violence, *Straw Dogs* (dir. Sam Peckinpah, 1971), *A Clockwork Orange* (dir. Stanley Kubrick, 1971), and *Salò o le 120 giornate di Sodoma* (*Salò, or the 120 Days of Sodom*, dir. Pier Paolo Pasolini, 1975).
3. 'Gérard avait dit: "Il faut que nous sortions nos imperméables et nos parapluies tellement on va recevoir de crachats." Et cela s'est avéré. Les gens étaient tres choqués . . .' Quoted in Élisabeth Lequeret, '"Comme des explorateurs": Entretien avec Bulle Ogier', in Dominique Bax and Cyril Béghin (eds), *Théâtres au cinéma – Tome 23: Barbet Schroeder* (Bobigny: Collection Magic Cinéma, 2012), pp. 34–6; p. 35.
4. 'Comme *La Vallée*, comme *Général Idi Amin Dada*, *Maîtresse* recommence *More*. Galerie à monstres? Descente aux enfers? En apparence, oui, pour ceux qui se contentent des apparences. Ce qui n'est pas le cas de Schroeder. Il s'acharne à fouiller sous l'apparence pour déterrer les racines humaines.' Jean-Louis Bory, 'Les flics d'Ariane' [1976], in Dominique Bax and Cyril

Béghin (eds), *Théâtres au cinéma – Tome 23: Barbet Schroeder* (Bobigny: Collection Magic Cinéma, 2012), p. 86; p. 86.
5. See 'Domestic Masochism: Barbet Schroeder's *Maîtresse*', *Maîtresse*, Blu-ray/DVD (BFI, spine number: BFIB1041, 2012).
6. Levinas, *Otherwise than Being*, p. 26.
7. Pippin, 'Psychology Degree Zero?', p. 764.
8. I made an earlier version of this argument about the break-in and the torch light in my comments as an interviewee in 'Domestic Masochism'.
9. Russell Campbell, *Marked Women: Prostitutes and Prostitution in the Cinema* (Madison: University of Wisconsin Press, 2006), p. 224.
10. Crano, '"Occupy without Counting"', p. 6. Emphasis in original.
11. Levinas, *Totality and Infinity*, p. 213.
12. Peperzak, *Beyond: The Philosophy of Emmanuel Levinas*, p. 127. Emphases in original.
13. See Levinas, *Totality and Infinity*, pp. 212–14.
14. John Simon, 'Movies – A Kiss For Cinderella', *New York Magazine*, 15 November 1976, pp. 117–19; p. 119.
15. Elliott Stein, '*Maîtresse*', <http://www.criterion.com/current/posts/309-maitresse> (last accessed 31 January 2019).
16. I make a similar observation in 'Domestic Masochism', as part of my discussion of the non-judgemental camera style in the film.
17. Quoted in Stein, '*Maîtresse*'.
18. Lisa Downing, 'Re-viewing the Sexual Relation: Levinas and Film', in Sarah Cooper(ed.),'TheOccludedRelation:LevinasandCinema',SpecialIssue,*Film-Philosophy*,Vol. 11, Issue 2, August 2007 <https://www.euppublishing.com/doi/abs/10.3366/film.2007.0010> (last accessed 31 January 2019), pp. 49–65; p. 58. Emphasis in original.
19. Ibid., pp. 63–4.
20. Hand, *Emmanuel Levinas*, p. 43.
21. Levinas, *Otherwise than Being*, p. 185.
22. '*Maîtresse* est le film d'un vertige absolu. On est à mille lieux de la petite performance bourgeoise, d'un cinéma qui voudrait choquer. Le film cherche autre chose: une compréhension intime de la mécanique masochiste. Le résultat passe par une intelligence d'un jeu qui se placerait par-delà la morale.' Philippe Azoury, 'Trois Bulle(s)', in Dominique Bax and Cyril Béghin (eds), *Théâtres au cinéma – Tome 23: Barbet Schroeder* (Bobigny: Collection Magic Cinéma, 2012), pp. 37–8; p. 38.
23. Quoted in Bette Gordon, 'Barbet Schroeder', *BOMB*, Issue 32, 1 July 1990 <https://bombmagazine.org/articles/barbet-schroeder/> (last accessed 31 January 2019).
24. Cooper, 'Mortal Ethics',, p. 72.
25. See 'Interview du réalisateur', *La Vierge des Tueurs*, DVD (StudioCanal, spine number: 196 627-2, 2002). This is a French DVD release of *Our Lady of the Assassins*; the interview is in English.

26. Emmanuel Levinas, 'Everyday Language and Rhetoric without Eloquence', in Emmanuel Levinas, *Outside the Subject*, trans. Michael B. Smith (London: The Athlone Press, 1993 [1987; original language publication of essay: 1981]), pp. 135–43; p. 142.
27. Levinas, *Otherwise than Being*, pp. 56–7.
28. In 'Domestic Masochism' I offer similar comments (albeit without the Levinasian dimension) on how we can read in Schroeder's films an attempt to remove the notion of direction.
29. Levinas, *Otherwise than Being*, p. 46.
30. Gary Indiana, 'Barbet and Koko: An Equivocal Love Affair' <http://www.criterion.com/current/posts/430barbet-and-koko-an-equivocal-love-affair> (last accessed 31 January 2019).
31. For a very good discussion on this topic, see John Springhall, 'Censoring Hollywood: Youth, Moral Panic and Crime/Gangster Movies of the 1930s', *The Journal of Popular Culture*, Vol. 32, Issue 3 <http://onlinelibrary.wiley.com/doi/10.1111/j.0022-3840.1998.3203_135.x/pdf> (last accessed 31 January 2019), pp. 135–54.
32. James M. Cain's novel *The Postman Always Rings Twice* (New York: Alfred A. Knopf, 1934) has been filmed by directors Tay Garnett (1946) and Bob Rafelson (1981) and unofficially as *Ossessione* (*Obsession*, dir. Luchino Visconti, 1943).
33. 'À la différence de ce qui se passe avec la drogue dans *More*, le prosélytisme est pratiquement impossible en matière de masochisme si l'on n'a pas déjà cela en soi; et, alors que la drogue peut être montrée comme symbole de destruction, dans *Maîtresse* il aurait été malhonnête de faire jouer ce role au masochisme. C'est d'ailleurs pour cette raison que j'ai été amené à modifier un premier stade du dénouement où l'accident suicidaire du couple aboutissait à sa destruction concrète, ce qui introduisait en outre an aspect moral alors que cette dimension ne se trouvait absolument nulle part ailleurs, et qu'il était important pour moi de faire un film òu la morale n'entre d'aucune façon . . .' Quoted in Guy Braucourt, '*Maîtresse*' [1976], in Dominique Bax and Cyril Béghin (eds), *Théâtres au cinéma – Tome 23: Barbet Schroeder* (Bobigny: Collection Magic Cinéma, 2012), p. 85; p. 85.

Chapter 5

1. See Levinas, *Totality and Infinity*, pp. 82–101.
2. Emmanuel Levinas, 'The Rights of Man and the Rights of the Other', in Emmanuel Levinas, *Outside the Subject*, trans. Michael B. Smith (London: The Athlone Press, 1993 [original language publication of book: 1987; original language publication of essay: 1985]), pp. 116–25.
3. Ibid., p. 117.
4. Ibid.
5. Ibid., p. 125.

6. Desmond Manderson, 'Introduction', in Desmond Manderson (ed.), *Essays on Levinas and Law: A Mosaic* (Basingstoke: Palgrave Macmillan, 2009), pp. 3–17; 3.
7. Manderson, 'Introduction', p. 4.
8. Nick Smith, 'Questions for a Reluctant Jurisprudence of Alterity', in Desmond Manderson (ed.), *Essays on Levinas and Law: A Mosaic* (Basingstoke: Palgrave Macmillan, 2009), pp. 55–75.
9. Ibid., p. 57.
10. Ibid., p. 58.
11. Hand, *Emmanuel Levinas*, pp. 57–8.
12. Matthew Stone, *Levinas, Ethics and Law* (Edinburgh: Edinburgh University Press, 2018 [2016]), p. 111.
13. Alan M. Dershowitz, *Reversal of Fortune: Inside the von Bülow Case* (Harmondsworth: Penguin, 1991 [1986]). In this discussion, I shall distinguish between the real-life figure and author of the book, whom I shall refer to as Dershowitz, and the character in the film, whom I shall refer to as Alan.
14. Thomas Leitch, *Crime Films* (Cambridge: Cambridge University Press, 2002), p. 245.
15. Thomson, *The New Biographical Dictionary of Film – Sixth Edition*, p. 939.
16. '"fantastique", où la caméra flotte, vole, et réprésente quelque chose comme l'âme de Sunny.' Quoted in Cyril Béghin, 'Autoportraits', in Dominique Bax and Cyril Béghin (eds), *Théâtres au cinéma – Tome 23: Barbet Schroeder* (Bobigny: Collection Magic Cinéma, 2012), pp. 6–19; p. 12.
17. 's'appliquait aux différentes versions des événements. Comme des fictions de cinéma: c'était pour moi du Douglas Sirk, une idée de luxe et de la beauté. Et il fallait que ce soit accompagné de musique symphonique . . .' Quoted in ibid., p. 12.
18. '[D]ans la réalité de Dershowitz, pas de musique off, juste de vagues échos de radio. On devait être plus "documentaire" dans ces séquences . . .' Quoted in ibid.
19. See Levinas, *Otherwise than Being*, pp. 157–62.
20. Peperzak, *Beyond: The Philosophy of Emmanuel Levinas*, p. 114.
21. Quoted in Dershowitz, *Reversal of Fortune*, p. 88.
22. Quoted in Robert Sklar, 'Justice, Irony, and Reversal of Fortune: An Interview with Barbet Schroeder', *Cineaste*, Vol. 18, No. 2, 1991, pp. 4–7; p. 7.
23. Quoted in ibid.
24. Manderson, 'Introduction', p. 7.
25. 'C'est tout le sens de ces voix off contradictoires, de ces récits dans le récit, de ces flashbacks en volutes, de cette réversibilité du temps fictionnel énoncée par la bouche même du Sunny von Bulow, qui déstabilise en permanence la croyance du spectateur.' Thierry Jousse, 'Les enchaînés' [1991], in Dominique Bax and Cyril Béghin (eds), *Théâtres au cinéma – Tome 23: Barbet Schroeder* (Bobigny: Collection Magic Cinéma, 2012), pp. 121–2; p. 122.
26. Levinas, *Otherwise than Being*, p. 160.
27. Dershowitz, *Reversal of Fortune*, p. 68. Emphasis in original.

28. Leitch, *Crime Films*, p. 254.
29. A sad conclusion to one aspect of the story is that, on 6 December 2008, Sunny von Bülow passed away, having never awoken from her coma.
30. Levinas, *Otherwise than Being*, p. 161.
31. Austin, *How to Do Things with Words*, p. 4, n.2.
32. Peter Travers, '*Reversal of Fortune*', *Rolling Stone*, 17 October 1990, <https://www.rollingstone.com/movies/movie-reviews/reversal-of-fortune-96263/> (last accessed 31 January 2019).
33. Thomson, *The New Biographical Dictionary of Film – Sixth Edition*, p. 939.
34. Irons's performance won him a number of 1990 Best Actor film awards, including the Oscar, the Golden Globe, and awards from the Los Angeles Film Critics Association and the National Society of Film Critics.
35. Leitch, *Crime Films*, p. 245.
36. 'la construction achronologique du film, l'usage des documents d'archives, la mosaïque des témoignages transforment le portrait de l'avocat sulfureux en véritable film d'espionnage politique, aussi palpitant qu'une enquête de politique fiction. Certes, Vergès est un témoin fascinant, d'une intelligence quasi diabolique, mais c'est le montage du film qui lui offre cette densité dans la reflexion historique, par-delà les provocations négationnistes.' Michel Marie, 'Schroeder Nouvelle Vague', in Dominique Bax and Cyril Béghin (eds), *Théâtres au cinéma – Tome 23: Barbet Schroeder* (Bobigny: Collection Magic Cinéma, 2012), pp. 24–6; p. 26.
37. Bruzzi, *New Documentary*, pp. 185–6.
38. Libby Saxton, 'Terms of *Engagement*: Algeria, France and the Middle East in Barbet Schroeder's *L'Avocat de la terreur* and Philippe Faucon's *Dans la vie*', *Modern & Contemporary France*, Vol. 19, No. 2, May 2011, pp. 209–22; p. 212.
39. Levinas, *Otherwise than Being*, p. 54.
40. Peperzak, *Beyond: The Philosophy of Emmanuel Levinas*, p. 128. Emphases in original.
41. Levinas, 'The Rights of Man', p. 117.
42. Derrida, 'Violence and Metaphysics', n.7, pp. 397–8; p. 398.

Chapter 6

1. Levinas, *Otherwise than Being*, p. 58. Emphasis in original.
2. Quoted in Tom Dawson, 'Barbet Schroeder – Legal eagle', *The List*, 22 May 2008, <http://www.list.co.uk/article/8479-barbet-schroeder/> (last accessed 31 January 2019).
3. Richard Dyer, 'Straight Acting' [1990], in Richard Dyer, *The Matter of Images: Essays on Representations – Second Edition* (London and New York: Routledge, 2002 [original edition first published: 1993]), pp. 118–21; pp. 118–19.
4. Ibid., p. 119.
5. 'La majorité ignore la minorité, c'est une loi sociétale. La majorité vit dans l' évidence d'être le tout. Comment pourrait-il en être autrement puisque

toutes les institutions et toutes les coutumes sont son miroir? Rares et précieux sont les individus de la majorité qui trouent le miroir.' Dardenne, *Au dos de nos images II*, p. 33.
6. Quoted in Stephen Moss, 'I Don't Make Moral Judgments', *The Guardian*, 21 October 2004 <https://www.theguardian.com/books/2004/oct/21/bookerprize2004.bookerprize> (last accessed 31 January 2019).
7. Alan Hollinghurst, *The Swimming-Pool Library* (London: Chatto & Windus, 1988); Alan Hollinghurst, *The Folding Star* (London: Chatto & Windus, 1994); Alan Hollinghurst, *The Spell* (London: Chatto & Windus, 1998); Alan Hollinghurst, *The Line of Beauty* (London: Picador, 2004); Alan Hollinghurst, *The Stranger's Child* (London: Picador, 2011); Alan Hollinghurst, *The Sparsholt Affair* (London: Picador, 2017).
8. From 'Interview du réalisateur', *La Vierge des Tueurs*, DVD (StudioCanal, spine number: 196 627-2, 2002).
9. From ibid.
10. Fernando Vallejo, *Our Lady of the Assassins*, trans. Paul Hammond (London: Serpent's Tail, 2001 [original language publication: 1994]).
11. Peperzak, *Beyond: The Philosophy of Emmanuel Levinas*, p. 100.
12. Levinas, *Otherwise than Being*, p. 53.
13. Davis, *Levinas: An Introduction*, p. 73.
14. Levinas, *Otherwise than Being*, p. 57.
15. Noël Carroll, 'Moral Change: Fiction, Film, and Family', in Jinhee Choi and Mattias Frey (eds), *Cine-Ethics: Ethical Dimensions of Film Theory, Practice, and Spectatorship* (Abingdon and New York: Routledge, 2014), pp. 43–56; p. 51.
16. Quoted in Gregg Kilday, 'Boys to Men', *The Advocate*, 11 September 2001, pp. 52–7; p. 56.
17. Gary Needham, *Brokeback Mountain* (Edinburgh: Edinburgh University Press, 2010), p. 33.
18. Ibid., p. 34.
19. Barbet Schroeder, 'Fin de siècle à Medellín, journal de tournage' [2000], in Dominique Bax and Cyril Béghin (eds), *Théâtres au cinéma – Tome 23: Barbet Schroeder* (Bobigny: Collection Magic Cinéma, 2012), pp. 151–61. On equipment, see, for example, pp. 154 and 158. On the threat of kidnapping, on bodyguards, and on youngsters and gangs, see, for example, p. 154.
20. Lingis, 'Translator's Introduction', p. xviii.
21. From 'Interview du réalisateur'.
22. Nicolas Azalbert writes that the moment is 'filmed coldly' ('filmé froidement') in high definition (HD) rather than with the 'aura' ('aura') of 35mm. Nicolas Azalbert, 'Le temps s'envole dans la chambre aux papillons', in Dominique Bax and Cyril Béghin (eds), *Théâtres au cinéma – Tome 23: Barbet Schroeder* (Bobigny: Collection Magic Cinéma, 2012), p. 150; p. 150.
23. From 'Interview du réalisateur'.
24. Robert Bresson, *Notes on Cinematography*, trans. Jonathan Griffin (New York: Urizen Books, 1977 [original language publication: 1975]), p. 41.

25. Levinas, *Otherwise than Being*, p. 69.
26. 'C'est ce qui dérange dans le film: que l'homosexualité soit filmée comme allant de soi. De même que la violence. Cette combinaison, si l'on ajoute la différence d'âge des amants, donne un film tout à fait innocent au premier abord, mais qui se révèle très subversif, à tel point que beaucoup de festivals ont pris peur devant ce film.' Quoted in Michel Ciment, 'Entretien avec Barbet Schroeder: Un auteur en quête de personnages', *Positif*, No. 496, June 2002, pp. 8–13; p. 13. My translation.
27. Levinas, *Otherwise than Being*, p. 117.
28. Peperzak, *Beyond: The Philosophy of Emmanuel Levinas*, p. 178.
29. Levinas, *Otherwise than Being*, pp. 37–8.
30. Peperzak, *Beyond: The Philosophy of Emmanuel Levinas*, p. 178.

Part III Introduction

1. See, for example, the quote in Kevin Jackson (ed.), *Schrader on Schrader & Other Writings – Revised Edition* (London: Faber and Faber, 2004 [original edition first published: 1990]), p. 163.
2. George Kouvaros, *Paul Schrader* (Urbana and Chicago: University of Illinois Press, 2008), p. 5.
3. Levinas, *Totality and Infinity*, p. 77.
4. Quoted in Amy Taubin, *Taxi Driver* (London: BFI Publishing, 2000), p. 17.
5. Levinas, *Otherwise than Being*, p. 49.
6. Kouvaros, *Paul Schrader*, p. 61.
7. Schrader, *Transcendental Style in Film*, p. 19.
8. Paul Schrader, 'Canon Fodder', *Film Comment*, September–October 2006, pp. 33–49; p. 46. To reinforce this point, Schrader also includes a quote by French critic Louis Haugmard from the 1913 publication *The Aesthetic of Cinematography*: 'The charmed masses will learn to not think anymore, to resist all desire to reason and construct: they will know only how to open their large and empty eyes, only to look, look, look.' 'Canon Fodder', p. 49, n.9. We can read Haugmard's words as, among other things, a forerunner of Levinas's arguments against art in 'Reality and its Shadow'.
9. 'Canon Fodder', p. 46.
10. Kouvaros, *Paul Schrader*, p. 3.
11. Quoted in Jackson, *Schrader on Schrader*, p. 166.

Chapter 7

1. Quoted in Jackson, *Schrader on Schrader*, p. 158.
2. For a helpful analysis of this scene that reads it as a subversion of gender codes in Hollywood cinema, see Peter Lehman, '*American Gigolo*: The Male Body Makes an Appearance, of Sorts', in Jeanne Ruppert (ed.), *Gender: Literary*

and Cinematic Representation: Selected Papers from the Eleventh Annual Florida State University Conference on Literature and Film (Gainesville: University Press of Florida, 1994), pp. 8–16.
3. Morgan, *Discovering Levinas*, p. 200.
4. Bill Nichols, '*American Gigolo*: Transcendental Style and Narrative Form', *Film Quarterly*, Vol. 34, No. 4, Summer 1981, pp. 8–13; p. 9.
5. Levinas, *Otherwise than Being*, p. 54.
6. The blog *Movie Tourist* helpfully identifies some of the locations used in *American Gigolo*. See Yuri G., '*American Gigolo* (1980) dir. Paul Schrader', *Movie Tourist*, 4 May 2013 <http://movie-tourist.blogspot.co.uk/2013/05/american-gigolo-1980.html> (last accessed 31 January 2019).
7. For an examination of similar issues related to the interaction of song, character, and film style, see Richard Dyer, *In the Space of a Song: The Uses of Song in Film* (Abingdon and New York: Routledge, 2012), Chapter 8, 'Music and Presence in Blaxploitation Cinema', pp. 156–74, especially p. 158.
8. Emmanuel Levinas, 'The Ego and the Totality', in Emmanuel Levinas, *Collected Philosophical Papers*, trans. Alphonso Lingis (Pittsburgh: Duquesne University Press, 2006 [1987; original language publication of essay: 1954]), pp. 25–45; p. 31.
9. Levinas, *Totality and Infinity*, p. 213.
10. Ibid., p. 265. Emphasis in original.
11. See, principally, Section IV of *Totality and Infinity*, 'Beyond the Face', pp. 249–85. This discussion has inspired negative reactions from some scholars, who have accused Levinas of unthinkingly repeating a complacent patriarchal structure of relations between men and women, with the woman existing to provide for the man erotic interest as well as a welcoming home and a child. Other critics have read Levinas's position in more positive terms; but it remains one of the most contested aspects of Levinas's thought. For a good survey of debates concerning Levinas and the feminine, see B. C. Hutchens, *Levinas: A Guide for the Perplexed* (London and New York: Continuum, 2004), pp. 146–54.
12. Levinas, *Totality and Infinity*, p. 304.
13. Quoted in Jackson, *Schrader on Schrader*, p. 211.
14. Quoted in ibid., p. 158.
15. Nichols, '*American Gigolo*', p. 10.
16. For its declared influence on *American Gigolo*, see, for example, Paul Schrader, 'A Postscript from Paul Schrader', in Bill Nichols, '*American Gigolo*: Transcendental Style and Narrative Form', *Film Quarterly*, Vol. 34, No. 4, Summer 1981, pp. 8–13; p. 13.
17. Thomson, *The New Biographical Dictionary of Film – Sixth Edition*, p. 938.
18. Petrey, *Speech Acts and Literary Theory*, p. 113.
19. Schrader, *Transcendental Style in Film*, p. 22.
20. Ibid., p. 110.
21. Nichols, '*American Gigolo*', p. 11.

22. Schrader, *Transcendental Style in Film*, pp. 134–5.
23. Ibid., p. 135.
24. Nichols, '*American Gigolo*', p. 13.
25. Ibid., pp. 11–13.
26. Ibid., p. 9.
27. Robert T. Eberwein, 'Framing and Representation in *American Gigolo*', in Jeanne Ruppert (ed.), *Gender: Literary and Cinematic Representation: Selected Papers from the Eleventh Annual Florida State University Conference on Literature and Film* (Gainesville: University Press of Florida, 1994), pp. 33–40; p. 36.
28. Thomson, *The New Biographical Dictionary of Film – Sixth Edition*, p. 938.
29. Nichols, '*American Gigolo*', p. 13.
30. Kouvaros, *Paul Schrader*, p. 117.
31. Morgan, *Discovering Levinas*, p. 200.

Chapter 8

1. Belén Vidal, 'Introduction: The Biopic and Its Critical Contexts', in Tom Brown and Belén Vidal (eds), *The Biopic in Contemporary Film Culture* (New York and Abingdon: Routledge, 2014), pp. 1–32; p. 3.
2. John Nathan, *Mishima: A Biography* (New York: Da Capo Press, 2000 [1974]), p. xiii.
3. Henry Scott Stokes, *The Life and Death of Yukio Mishima* (New York: Cooper Square Press, 2000 [1974]), p. 9.
4. Damian Flanagan, *Yukio Mishima* (London: Reaktion Books, 2014), p. 7.
5. Quoted in Karen Jaehne, 'Schrader's *Mishima*: An Interview', *Film Quarterly*, Vol. 39, No. 3, Spring 1986, pp. 11–17; p. 16.
6. Ibid., p. 16.
7. There is also an alternate voiceover in Japanese, spoken by Ken Ogata, originally unreleased but since made available as an option on Criteron's 2008 DVD and 2018 Blu-ray editions of *Mishima: A Life in Four Chapters* (spine number: 432). And there is a third voiceover available, an alternate English-language track recorded as a temp track and included on the 2001 Warner Home Video DVD (spine number: 11530), with the same wording as the Scheider voiceover, and subsequently included on the Criterion edition, too. Various online sources explain the reason for this third version; see, for example, Jamie S. Rich, 'Mishima: A Life in Four Chapters – Criterion Collection' <https://www.dvdtalk.com/reviews/33741/mishima-a-life-in-four-chapters-criterion-collection/> (last accessed 31 January 2019).
8. For Schrader's thoughts on the use of music within transcendental style, see, for example, Schrader, *Transcendental Style in Film*, pp. 42, 89, and 96–7.
9. See 'New Audio Commentary Featuring Schrader and Producer Alan Poul', *Mishima: A Life in Four Chapters*, DVD/Blu-ray (Criterion, spine number: 432, 2008/2018).

10. Schrader's *Cat People* is a remake of *Cat People* (dir. Jacques Tourneur, 1942).
11. Like *American Gigolo* before it, Schrader's *Cat People* benefits from a score by Giorgio Moroder and a hit theme song – in the latter case 'Cat People (Putting Out Fire)', written by Moroder and David Bowie and sung by Bowie.
12. Kouvaros, *Paul Schrader*, p. 2.
13. John Bailey was the cinematographer on both films, as well as on *Cat People* – another detail that binds these three films together stylistically.
14. See Flanagan, *Yukio Mishima*, pp. 7–11.
15. Stone, *Levinas, Ethics and Law*, p. 40.
16. Saxton, 'Blinding Visions', p. 100.
17. Vidal, 'Introduction', p. 15.
18. Quoted in Jaehne, 'Schrader's *Mishima*', p. 14.
19. Kouvaros, *Paul Schrader*, p. 61.
20. Perpich, *The Ethics of Emmanuel Levinas*, p. 110.

Chapter 9

1. Levinas, *Otherwise than Being*, p. 15.
2. Ibid.
3. Ibid.
4. Ian McEwan, *The Comfort of Strangers* (London: Vintage, 2001 [1981]). In the novel, the city is unnamed but its description evokes Venice. In the film, the city is explicitly Venice.
5. Quoted in Jackson, *Schrader on Schrader*, p. 200.
6. Levinas, *Otherwise than Being*, pp. 14–15.
7. Ibid., p. 15.
8. Ibid.
9. McEwan, *The Comfort of Strangers*, p. 3.
10. Jackson, *Schrader on Schrader*, pp. 199–200.
11. Levinas, *Otherwise than Being*, p. 25.
12. Ibid.
13. McEwan discussed this in, for example, *The Book Review Special with Ian McEwan* (London: BBC, broadcast date: 24 August 2012).
14. Levinas, *Otherwise than Being*, p. 50.
15. For more on this debacle, see Jackson, *Schrader on Schrader*, p. xvi, and Kouvaros, *Paul Schrader*, pp. 110–11.
16. Kouvaros, *Paul Schrader*, p. 111.
17. Ibid., p. 139.
18. Ibid.
19. See 'Commentary By Director Paul Schrader', *Dominion: Prequel to the Exorcist*, DVD (Warner Home Video, spine number: Z1 69262, 2005), Jackson, *Schrader on Schrader*, p. 275, and Kouvaros, *Paul Schrader*, p. 139.
20. Schrader, *Transcendental Style in Film*, p. 66.
21. Peperzak, *Beyond: The Philosophy of Emmanuel Levinas*, p. 173.

22. Jackson, *Schrader on Schrader*, p. 282.
23. O'Shaughnessy, 'Ethics in the Ruin of Politics', p. 61.
24. Levinas, *Otherwise than Being*, p. 56.
25. Yoram Kaniuk, *Adam Resurrected*, trans. Seymore Simckes (London: Atlantic Books, 2008 [1971; original language publication: 1969]).
26. See 'Audio Commentary with Director Paul Schrader', *Adam Resurrected*, DVD (Image Entertainment, spine number: ID6286HKDVD, 2009). All of Schrader's comments regarding *Adam Resurrected* are taken from this audio commentary.
27. I am indebted to Edward Gallafent for this idea, which he put to me in conversation.

Conclusion

1. Levinas, *Otherwise than Being*, p. 64.
2. Schrader, 'Canon Fodder', p. 46.
3. Carroll, 'Moral Change', p. 55.
4. Petrey, *Speech Acts and Literary Theory*, p. 89. Emphases in original.

Bibliography

Aaron, Michele, *Spectatorship: The Power of Looking On* (London: Wallflower Press, 2007).

Astruc, Alexandre, 'The Birth of a New Avant-Garde: La Caméra-Stylo' [original language publication 1948], trans. unattributed, in Peter Graham and Ginette Vincendeau (eds), *The French New Wave: Critical Landmarks* (London: BFI/Palgrave Macmillan, 2009), pp. 31–6.

Aubenas, Jacqueline (ed.), *Jean-Pierre & Luc Dardenne* (Brussels: Diffusion, 2008).

Austin, J. L., *How to Do Things with Words: The William James Lectures Delivered at Harvard University in 1955 – Second Edition*, J. O. Urmson and Marina Sbisà (eds) (Oxford and New York: Oxford University Press, 1975 [original edition first published: 1962]).

Azalbert, Nicolas, 'Le temps s'envole dans la chambre aux papillons', in Dominique Bax and Cyril Béghin (eds), *Théâtres au cinéma – Tome 23: Barbet Schroeder* (Bobigny: Collection Magic Cinéma, 2012), p. 150.

Azoury, Philippe, 'Trois Bulle(s)', in Dominique Bax and Cyril Béghin (eds), *Théâtres au cinéma – Tome 23: Barbet Schroeder* (Bobigny: Collection Magic Cinéma, 2012), pp. 37–8.

Bakewell, Liza, 'Image Acts', *American Anthropologist*, New Series, Vol. 100, No. 1, March 1998, pp. 22–32.

Bax, Dominique, and Cyril Béghin (eds), *Théâtres au cinéma – Tome 23: Barbet Schroeder* (Bobigny: Collection Magic Cinéma, 2012).

Béghin, Cyril, 'Autoportraits', in Dominique Bax and Cyril Béghin (eds), *Théâtres au cinéma – Tome 23: Barbet Schroeder* (Bobigny: Collection Magic Cinéma, 2012), pp. 6–19.

Bernasconi, Robert, and Simon Critchley, 'Editors' Introduction', in Robert Bernasconi and Simon Critchley (eds), *Re-Reading Levinas* (London: The Athlone Press, 1991), pp. xi–xviii.

Biskind, Peter, *Easy Riders, Raging Bulls: How the Sex-Drugs-and-Rock 'n' Roll Generation Saved Hollywood* (New York: Simon & Schuster, 1998).

Bordwell, David, Janet Staiger and Kristin Thompson, *The Classical Hollywood Cinema: Film Style & Mode of Production to 1960* (London: Routledge, 1988).

Bory, Jean-Louis, 'Les flics d'Ariane' [1976], in Dominique Bax and Cyril Béghin (eds), *Théâtres au cinéma – Tome 23: Barbet Schroeder* (Bobigny: Collection Magic Cinéma, 2012), p. 86.

Braucourt, Guy, '*Maîtresse*' [1976], in Dominique Bax and Cyril Béghin (eds), *Théâtres au cinéma – Tome 23: Barbet Schroeder* (Bobigny: Collection Magic Cinéma, 2012), p. 85.

Bresson, Robert, *Notes on Cinematography*, trans. Jonathan Griffin (New York: Urizen Books, 1977 [original language publication: 1975]).

Bruzzi, Stella, *New Documentary – Second Edition* (Abingdon and New York: Routledge, 2006 [original edition first published: 2000]).

Butler, Judith, *Gender Trouble: Feminism and the Subversion of Identity* (New York and London: Routledge, 1990).

Butler, Judith, *Excitable Speech: A Politics of the Performative* (New York and London: Routledge, 1997).

Cain, James M., *The Postman Always Rings Twice* (New York: Alfred A. Knopf, 1934).

Campbell, Russell, *Marked Women: Prostitutes and Prostitution in the Cinema* (Madison: University of Wisconsin Press, 2006).

Carroll, Noël, 'Moral Change: Fiction, Film, and Family', in Jinhee Choi and Mattias Frey (eds), *Cine-Ethics: Ethical Dimensions of Film Theory, Practice, and Spectatorship* (Abingdon and New York: Routledge, 2014), pp. 43–56.

Celeste, Reni, 'The Frozen Screen: Levinas and the Action Film', in Sarah Cooper (ed.), 'The Occluded Relation: Levinas and Cinema', Special Issue, *Film-Philosophy*, Vol. 11, Issue 2, August 2007 <https://www.euppublishing.com/doi/abs/10.3366/film.2007.0008> (last accessed 31 January 2019), pp. 15–36.

Choi, Jinhee, and Mattias Frey, 'Introduction', in Jinhee Choi and Mattias Frey (eds), Cine-Ethics: *Ethical Dimensions of Film Theory, Practice, and Spectatorship* (Abingdon and New York: Routledge, 2014), pp. 1–14.

Choi, Jinhee, and Mattias Frey (eds), *Cine-Ethics: Ethical Dimensions of Film Theory, Practice, and Spectatorship* (Abingdon and New York: Routledge, 2014).

Ciment, Michel, 'Entretien avec Barbet Schroeder: Un auteur en quête de personnages', *Positif*, No. 496, June 2002, pp. 8–13.

Cohen, Richard A., 'Translator's Introduction' [1987], in Emmanuel Levinas, *Time and the Other and Additional Essays*, trans. Richard A. Cohen (Pittsburgh: Duquesne University Press, 2008 [original language publication of essay *Time and the Other*: 1947]), pp. 1–27.

Cooper, Sarah, *Selfless Cinema?: Ethics and French Documentary* (London: Legenda, 2006).

Cooper, Sarah, 'Introduction: The Occluded Relation: Levinas and Cinema', in Sarah Cooper (ed.), 'The Occluded Relation: Levinas and Cinema', Special Issue, *Film-Philosophy*, Vol. 11, Issue 2, August 2007 <https://www.euppublishing.com/doi/abs/10.3366/film.2007.0006> (last accessed 31 January 2019), pp. i–vii.

Cooper, Sarah, 'Mortal Ethics: Reading Levinas with the Dardenne Brothers', in Sarah Cooper (ed.), 'The Occluded Relation: Levinas and Cinema', Special Issue, *Film-Philosophy*, Vol. 11, Issue 2, August 2007 <https://www.euppublishing.com/doi/abs/10.3366/film.2007.0011> (last accessed 31 January 2019), pp. 66–87.

Cooper, Sarah, '"Put Yourself in My Place": *Two Days, One Night* and the Journey Back to Life', in John Caruana and Mark Cauchi (eds), *Immanent Frames: Postsecular Cinema between Malick and von Trier* (Albany: State University of New York Press, 2018), pp. 229–44.

Cowie, Peter, *Revolution!: The Explosion of World Cinema in the 60s* (London: Faber and Faber, 2004).

Cox, Damian, and Michael P. Levine, *Thinking through Film: Doing Philosophy, Watching Movies* (Chichester: Wiley-Blackwell, 2012).

Crano, R. D., '"Occupy without Counting": Furtive Urbanism in the Films of Jean-Pierre and Luc Dardenne', *Film-Philosophy* Vol. 13, Issue 1, April 2009 <http://www.film-philosophy.com/2009v13n1/crano.pdf> (last accessed 31 January 2019), pp. 1–15.

Critchley, Simon, 'To Be or Not to Be is Not the Question: On Beckett's *Film*', in Sarah Cooper (ed.), 'The Occluded Relation: Levinas and Cinema', Special Issue, *Film-Philosophy*, Vol. 11, Issue 2, August 2007 <https://www.euppublishing.com/doi/abs/10.3366/film.2007.0013> (last accessed 31 January 2019), pp. 108–21.

Cummings, Doug, 'The Brothers Dardenne: Responding to the Face of the Other', in Kenneth R. Morefield (ed.), *Faith and Spirituality in Masters of World Cinema* (Newcastle upon Tyne: Cambridge Scholars Publishing, 2008), pp. 91–103.

Currie, Gregory, 'The Long Goodbye: The Imaginary Language of Film' [1993], in Noël Carroll and Jinhee Choi (eds), *Philosophy of Film and Motion Pictures: An Anthology* (Malden, Oxford, and Carlton: Blackwell Publishing, 2006), pp. 91–9.

Dardenne, Luc, *Au dos de nos images (1991–2005) suivi de* Le Fils, L'Enfant *et* Le Silence de Lorna *par Jean-Pierre et Luc Dardenne* (Paris: Éditions du Seuil, 2008 [original publication, without *The Silence of Lorna*: 2005]).

Dardenne, Luc, *Sur l'affaire humaine* (Paris: Éditions du Seuil, 2012).

Dardenne, Luc, *Au dos de nos images II (2005–2014) suivi de* Le Gamin au vélo *et* Deux jours, une nuit *par Jean-Pierre et Luc Dardenne* (Paris: Éditions du Seuil, 2015).

Davies, Paul, 'On Resorting to an Ethical Language', in Adriaan T. Peperzak (ed.), *Ethics as First Philosophy: The Significance of Emmanuel Levinas for Philosophy, Literature and Religion* (New York and London: Routledge, 1995), pp. 95–104.

Davis, Colin, *Levinas: An Introduction* (Cambridge and Malden: Polity Press, 1996).

Dawson, Tom, 'Barbet Schroeder – Legal Eagle', *The List*, 22 May 2008 <http://www.list.co.uk/article/8479-barbet-schroeder/> (last accessed 31 January 2019).

Derrida, Jacques, 'Signature Event Context', trans Samuel Weber and Jeffrey Mehlman [1977], in Jacques Derrida, *Limited Inc*, Gerald Graff (ed.) (Evanston: Northwestern University Press, 1988 [original language publication: 1972]), pp. 1–23.

Derrida, Jacques, *Specters of Marx: The State of the Debt, the Work of Mourning and the New International*, trans. Peggy Kamuf (New York and Abingdon: Routledge, 1994 [original language publication: 1993]).

Derrida, Jacques, 'Violence and Metaphysics: An Essay on the Thought of Emmanuel Levinas', in Jacques Derrida, *Writing and Difference*, trans. Alan Bass (Abingdon: Routledge, 2001 [1978; original language publication of book: 1967; original publication of essay: 1964]), pp. 97–192.

Derrida, Jacques, 'Declarations of Independence', trans Tom Keenan and Tom Pepper [1986], in Jacques Derrida, *Negotiations: Interventions and Interviews, 1971–2001*, Elizabeth Rottenberg (ed.) (Stanford: Stanford University Press, 2002 [original language publication: 1984]), pp. 46–54.

Dershowitz, Alan M., *Reversal of Fortune: Inside the von Bülow Case* (Harmondsworth: Penguin, 1991 [1986]).

D'Estais, Jérôme, *Barbet Schroeder: Ombres et clarté* (La Madeleine: LettMotif, 2017).

Dillet, Benoît, and Tara Puri, 'Left-over Spaces: The Cinema of the Dardenne Brothers', *Film-Philosophy*, Vol. 17, Issue 1, December 2013 <https://www.euppublishing.com/doi/abs/10.3366/film.2013.0021> (last accessed 31 January 2019), pp. 367–82.

Downing, Lisa, 'Re-viewing the Sexual Relation: Levinas and Film', in Sarah Cooper (ed.), 'The Occluded Relation: Levinas and Cinema', Special Issue, *Film-Philosophy*, Vol. 11, Issue 2, August 2007 <https://www.euppublishing.com/doi/abs/10.3366/film.2007.0010> (last accessed 31 January 2019), pp. 49–65.

Downing, Lisa, and Libby Saxton, *Film and Ethics: Foreclosed Encounters* (Abingdon and New York: Routledge, 2010).

Ducharme, Olivier, *Films de Combat: La résistance du cinéma des frères Dardenne* (Montreal: Varia, 2017).

Dyer, Richard, 'Straight Acting' [1990], in Richard Dyer, *The Matter of Images: Essays on Representations – Second Edition* (London and New York: Routledge, 2002 [original edition first published: 1993]), pp. 118–21.

Dyer, Richard, *In the Space of a Song: The Uses of Song in Film* (Abingdon and New York: Routledge, 2012).

Eberwein, Robert T., 'Framing and Representation in *American Gigolo*', in Jeanne Ruppert (ed.), *Gender: Literary and Cinematic Representation: Selected Papers from the Eleventh Annual Florida State University Conference on Literature and Film* (Gainesville: University Press of Florida, 1994), pp. 33–40.

Field, Syd, *Screenplay: The Foundations of Screenwriting – Newly Revised and Updated* (New York: Delta, 2005 [original edition first published: 1979]).

Flanagan, Damian, *Yukio Mishima* (London: Reaktion Books, 2014).

Frampton, Daniel, *Filmosophy* (London: Wallflower Press, 2006).

G., Yuri, '*American Gigolo* (1980) dir. Paul Schrader', *Movie Tourist*, 4 May 2013 <http://movie-tourist.blogspot.co.uk/2013/05/american-gigolo-1980.html> (last accessed 31 January 2019).
Girgus, Sam B., 'Beyond Ontology: Levinas and the Ethical Frame in Film', in Sarah Cooper (ed.), 'The Occluded Relation: Levinas and Cinema', Special Issue, *Film-Philosophy*, Vol. 11, Issue 2, August 2007 <https://www.euppublishing.com/doi/abs/10.3366/film.2007.0012> (last accessed 31 January 2019), pp. 88–107.
Girgus, Sam B., 'Existence and Ethics in the Dardenne Brothers' *Two Days, One Night* (2015)', in Sam B. Girgus, *Time, Existential Presence, and the Cinematic Image: Ethics and Emergence to Being in Film* (Edinburgh: Edinburgh University Press, 2018), pp. 78–98.
Girgus, Sam B., *Time, Existential Presence, and the Cinematic Image: Ethics and Emergence to Being in Film* (Edinburgh: Edinburgh University Press, 2018).
Gordon, Bette, 'Barbet Schroeder', *BOMB*, Issue 32, 1 July 1990 <https://bombmagazine.org/articles/barbet-schroeder/> (last accessed 31 January 2019).
Grønstad, Asbjørn, *Film and the Ethical Imagination* (London: Palgrave Macmillan, 2016).
Hand, Seán, *Emmanuel Levinas* (Abingdon and New York: Routledge, 2009).
Harris, Mark, *Pictures at a Revolution: Five Movies and the Birth of the New Hollywood* (New York: The Penguin Press, 2008).
Hessels, Wouter, '*Rosetta*', in Ernest Mathijs (ed.), *The Cinema of the Low Countries* (London: Wallflower Press, 2004), pp. 238–47.
Hole, Kristin Lené, *Towards a Feminist Cinematic Ethics: Claire Denis, Emmanuel Levinas and Jean-Luc Nancy* (Edinburgh: Edinburgh University Press, 2016).
Hollinghurst, Alan, *The Swimming-Pool Library* (London: Chatto & Windus, 1988).
Hollinghurst, Alan, *The Folding Star* (London: Chatto & Windus, 1994).
Hollinghurst, Alan, *The Spell* (London: Chatto & Windus, 1998).
Hollinghurst, Alan, *The Line of Beauty* (London: Picador, 2004).
Hollinghurst, Alan, *The Stranger's Child* (London: Picador, 2011).
Hollinghurst, Alan, *The Sparsholt Affair* (London: Picador, 2017).
Hutchens, B. C., *Levinas: A Guide for the Perplexed* (London and New York: Continuum, 2004).
Indiana, Gary, 'Barbet and Koko: An Equivocal Love Affair' <http://www.criterion.com/current/posts/430barbet-and-koko-an-equivocal-love-affair> (last accessed 31 January 2019).
'Interview with Jean-Pierre and Luc Dardenne', Press kit, *The Kid with a Bike* <https://encodeur.movidone.com/getimage/rsnrvhlSdgp5qtsUk4Ov4-LdPJw5tY9rH53UAs_lqO8kJPjJIJHgs9li5pSUo0Nr3YxyJU-4zGf8GvOWFm8dz7USaf9qUMgjtcYHRRUTi2nyJq9iNd6lZTI7-rbTwav1RF_vh9vk1pic6aWvcbwgQ8xvAyshux5AV4yTEEedtEPuqoqKXzydSIa7_6Wmgdve8c1s2AIv9YDN4HR5WBpHhaD2> (last accessed 31 January 2019), pp. 4–5.

Jackson, Kevin (ed.), *Schrader on Schrader & Other Writings – Revised Edition* (London: Faber and Faber, 2004 [original edition first published: 1990]).

Jaehne, Karen, 'Schrader's *Mishima*: An Interview', *Film Quarterly*, Vol. 39, No. 3, Spring 1986, pp. 11–17.

Jousse, Thierry, 'Les enchaînés' [1991], in Dominique Bax and Cyril Béghin (eds), *Théâtres au cinéma – Tome 23: Barbet Schroeder* (Bobigny: Collection Magic Cinéma, 2012), pp. 121–2.

Kaniuk, Yoram, *Adam Resurrected*, trans. Seymore Simckes (London: Atlantic Books, 2008 [1971; original language publication: 1969]).

Kenaan, Hagi, *The Ethics of Visuality: Levinas and the Contemporary Gaze*, trans. Batya Stein (London and New York: I. B. Tauris, 2013).

Kilday, Gregg, 'Boys to Men', *The Advocate*, 11 September 2001, pp. 52–7.

Kouvaros, George, *Paul Schrader* (Urbana and Chicago: University of Illinois Press, 2008).

Larsen, Svend Erik, '"Speak Again. Speak Like Rain" – The Mediality of Performance', in Lars Sætre, Patrizia Lombardo and Anders M. Gullestad (eds), *Exploring Textual Action* (Aarhus and Copenhagen: Aarhus University Press, 2010), pp. 59–82.

Lehman, Peter, '*American Gigolo*: The Male Body Makes an Appearance, of Sorts', in Jeanne Ruppert (ed.), *Gender: Literary and Cinematic Representation: Selected Papers from the Eleventh Annual Florida State University Conference on Literature and Film* (Gainesville: University Press of Florida, 1994), pp. 8–16.

Leitch, Thomas, *Crime Films* (Cambridge: Cambridge University Press, 2002).

Lequeret, Élisabeth, '"Comme des explorateurs": Entretien avec Bulle Ogier', in Dominique Bax and Cyril Béghin (eds), *Théâtres au cinéma – Tome 23: Barbet Schroeder* (Bobigny: Collection Magic Cinéma, 2012), pp. 34–6.

Levinas, Emmanuel, 'Everyday Language and Rhetoric without Eloquence', in Emmanuel Levinas, *Outside the Subject*, trans. Michael B. Smith (London: The Athlone Press, 1993 [1987; original language publication of essay: 1981]), pp. 135–43.

Levinas, Emmanuel, 'The Rights of Man and the Rights of the Other', in Emmanuel Levinas, *Outside the Subject*, trans. Michael B. Smith (London: The Athlone Press, 1993 [original language publication of book: 1987; original language publication of essay: 1985]), pp. 116–25.

Levinas, Emmanuel, 'Reality and its Shadow', in Emmanuel Levinas, *Collected Philosophical Papers*, trans. Alphonso Lingis (Pittsburgh: Duquesne University Press, 2006 [1987; original language publication of essay: 1948]), pp. 1–13.

Levinas, Emmanuel, 'The Ego and the Totality', in Emmanuel Levinas, *Collected Philosophical Papers*, trans. Alphonso Lingis (Pittsburgh: Duquesne University Press, 2006 [1987; original language publication of essay: 1954]), pp. 25–45.

Levinas, Emmanuel, *Totality and Infinity: An Essay on Exteriority*, trans. Alphonso Lingis (Pittsburgh: Duquesne University Press, 2007 [1969; original language publication: 1961]).

Levinas, Emmanuel, *Existence and Existents*, trans. Alphonso Lingis (Pittsburgh: Duquesne University Press, 2008 [1978; original language publication: 1947]).
Levinas, Emmanuel, *Otherwise than Being or Beyond Essence*, trans. Alphonso Lingis (Pittsburgh: Duquesne University Press, 2008 [1981; original language publication: 1974]).
Lingis, Alphonso, 'Translator's Introduction', in Emmanuel Levinas, *Otherwise than Being or Beyond Essence*, trans. Alphonso Lingis (Pittsburgh: Duquesne University Press, 2008 [1978; original language publication of book: 1974]), pp. xvii–xlv.
Loxley, James, *Performativity* (Abingdon and New York: Routledge, 2007).
McEwan, Ian, *The Comfort of Strangers* (London: Vintage, 2001 [1981]).
McKee, Robert, *Story: Substance, Structure, Style, and the Principles of Screenwriting* (London: Methuen, 1999 [1997]).
Mai, Joseph, *Jean-Pierre and Luc Dardenne* (Urbana, Chicago and Springfield: University of Illinois Press, 2010).
Manderson, Desmond, 'Introduction', in Desmond Manderson (ed.), *Essays on Levinas and Law: A Mosaic* (Basingstoke: Palgrave Macmillan, 2009), pp. 3–17.
Marie, Michel, 'Schroeder Nouvelle Vague', in Dominique Bax and Cyril Béghin (eds), *Théâtres au cinéma – Tome 23: Barbet Schroeder* (Bobigny: Collection Magic Cinéma, 2012), pp. 24–6.
Metz, Christian, 'The Cinema: Language or Language System?', in Christian Metz, *Film Language: A Semiotics of the Cinema*, trans. Michael Taylor (New York: Oxford University Press, 1974 [original language publication of book: 1971; original language publication of essay: 1964]), pp. 31–91.
Miller, J. Hillis, 'Performativity$_1$/Performativity$_2$', in Lars Sætre, Patrizia Lombardo and Anders M. Gullestad (eds), *Exploring Textual Action* (Aarhus and Copenhagen: Aarhus University Press, 2010), pp. 31–58.
Monaco, James, *How to Read a Film: Movies, Media, and Beyond – Fourth Edition* (Oxford and New York: Oxford University Press, 2009 [original edition first published: 1977]).
Morgan, Michael L., *Discovering Levinas* (New York: Cambridge University Press, 2007).
Morice, Jacques, 'Le pari des frères Dardenne: "Filmer le bien en action"', Télérama, 21 May 2011 <http://www.telerama.fr/cinema/le-pari-des-freres-dardenne-filmer-le-bien-en-action,68933.php> (last accessed 31 January 2019).
Mosley, Philip, *The Cinema of the Dardenne Brothers: Responsible Realism* (New York and Chichester: Wallflower Press/Columbia University Press, 2013).
Moss, Stephen, 'I Don't Make Moral Judgments', *The Guardian*, 21 October 2004 <https://www.theguardian.com/books/2004/oct/21/bookerprize2004.bookerprize> (last accessed 31 January 2019).
Nathan, John, *Mishima: A Biography* (New York: Da Capo Press, 2000 [1974]).
Nealon, Jeffrey T., *Alterity Politics: Ethics and Performative Subjectivity* (Durham, NC and London: Duke University Press, 1998).

Needham, Gary, *Brokeback Mountain* (Edinburgh: Edinburgh University Press, 2010).
Nichols, Bill, '*American Gigolo*: Transcendental Style and Narrative Form', *Film Quarterly*, Vol. 34, No. 4, Summer 1981, pp. 8–13.
Nichols, Bill, *Blurred Boundaries: Questions of Meaning in Contemporary Culture* (Bloomington and Indianapolis: Indiana University Press, 1994).
O'Shaughnessy, Martin, *The New Face of Political Cinema: Commitment in French Film since 1995* (New York and Oxford: Berghahn Books, 2007).
O'Shaughnessy, Martin, 'Ethics in the Ruin of Politics: The Dardenne Brothers', in Kate Ince (ed.), *Five Directors: Auteurism from Assayas to Ozon* (Manchester and New York: Manchester University Press, 2008), pp. 59–83.
Parker, Andrew, and Eve Kosofsky Sedgwick (eds), *Performativity and Performance* (London and New York: Routledge, 1995).
Peperzak, Adriaan T., 'Preface', in Adriaan T. Peperzak (ed.), *Ethics as First Philosophy: The Significance of Emmanuel Levinas for Philosophy, Literature and Religion* (New York and London: Routledge, 1995), pp. ix–xiii.
Peperzak, Adriaan Theodoor, *Beyond: The Philosophy of Emmanuel Levinas* (Evanston: Northwestern University Press, 1997).
Perkins, V. F., *Film as Film: Understanding and Judging Movies* (Harmondsworth: Penguin, 1991 [1972]).
Perkins, V. F., 'Where is the World? The Horizon of Events in Movie Fiction', in John Gibbs and Douglas Pye (eds), *Style and Meaning: Studies in the Detailed Analysis of Film* (Manchester: Manchester University Press, 2005), pp. 16–41.
Perpich, Diane, 'Introduction: But is it *Ethics?*', in *The Ethics of Emmanuel Levinas* (Stanford: Stanford University Press, 2008), pp. 1–16.
Perpich, Diane, *The Ethics of Emmanuel Levinas* (Stanford: Stanford University Press, 2008).
Petrey, Sandy, *Speech Acts and Literary Theory* (New York and London: Routledge, 1990).
Pippin, Robert, 'Psychology Degree Zero? The Representation of Action in the Films of the Dardenne Brothers', *Critical Inquiry*, Vol. 41, Summer 2015, pp. 757–85.
Rainsford, Dominic Michael, 'Tarkovsky and Levinas: Cuts, Mirrors, Triangulations', in Sarah Cooper (ed.), 'The Occluded Relation: Levinas and Cinema', Special Issue, *Film-Philosophy*, Vol. 11, Issue 2, August 2007 <https://www.euppublishing.com/doi/abs/10.3366/film.2007.0014> (last accessed 31 January 2019), pp. 122–43.
Rich, Jamie S., 'Mishima: A Life in Four Chapters – Criterion Collection' <https://www.dvdtalk.com/reviews/33741/mishima-a-life-in-four-chapters-criterion-collection/> (last accessed 31 January 2019).
Rushton, Richard, 'Empathic Projection in the Films of the Dardenne Brothers', *Screen*, Vol. 55, Issue 3, 1 September 2014, pp. 303–16.
Sætre, Lars, Patrizia Lombardo and Anders M. Gullestad (eds), *Exploring Textual Action* (Aarhus and Copenhagen: Aarhus University Press, 2010).

Saxton, Libby, 'Fragile Faces: Levinas and Lanzmann', in Sarah Cooper (ed.), 'The Occluded Relation: Levinas and Cinema', Special Issue, *Film-Philosophy*, Vol. 11, Issue 2, August 2007 <https://www.euppublishing.com/doi/abs/10.3366/film.2007.0007> (last accessed 31 January 2019), pp. 1–14.

Saxton, Libby, 'Blinding Visions: Levinas, Ethics, Faciality', in Lisa Downing and Libby Saxton, *Film and Ethics: Foreclosed Encounters* (Abingdon and New York: Routledge, 2010), pp. 95–106.

Saxton, Libby, 'Terms of *Engagement*: Algeria, France and the Middle East in Barbet Schroeder's *L'Avocat de la terreur* and Philippe Faucon's *Dans la vie*', *Modern & Contemporary France*, Vol. 19, No. 2, May 2011, pp. 209–22.

Schrader, Paul, 'A Postscript from Paul Schrader', in Bill Nichols, '*American Gigolo*: Transcendental Style and Narrative Form', *Film Quarterly*, Vol. 34, No. 4, Summer 1981, pp. 8–13.

Schrader, Paul, 'Canon Fodder', *Film Comment*, September–October 2006, pp. 33–49.

Schrader, Paul, *Transcendental Style in Film: Ozu, Bresson, Dreyer – With a New Introduction: Rethinking Transcendental Style* (Oakland: University of California Press, 2018 [original edition first published: 1972]).

Schroeder, Barbet, 'Fin de siècle à Medellín, journal de tournage' [2000], in Dominique Bax and Cyril Béghin (eds), *Théâtres au cinéma – Tome 23: Barbet Schroeder* (Bobigny: Collection Magic Cinéma, 2012), pp. 151–61.

Scott Stokes, Henry, *The Life and Death of Yukio Mishima* (New York: Cooper Square Press, 2000 [1974]).

Sedgwick, Eve Kosofsky, *Epistemology of the Closet* (Berkeley and Los Angeles: University of California Press, 1990).

Simon, John, 'Movies – A Kiss For Cinderella', *New York Magazine*, 15 November 1976, pp. 117–19.

Sinnerbrink, Robert, *Cinematic Ethics: Exploring Ethical Experience through Film* (Abingdon and New York: Routledge, 2016).

Sinnerbrink, Robert, 'Melodrama, Realism, and Ethical Experience (*Biutiful*, *The Promise*)', in Robert Sinnerbrink, *Cinematic Ethics: Exploring Ethical Experience through Film* (Abingdon and New York: Routledge, 2016), pp. 139–64.

Sklar, Robert, 'Justice, Irony, and Reversal of Fortune: An Interview with Barbet Schroeder', *Cineaste*, Vol. 18, No. 2, 1991, pp. 4–7.

Smith, Nick, 'Questions for a Reluctant Jurisprudence of Alterity', in Desmond Manderson (ed.), *Essays on Levinas and Law: A Mosaic* (Basingstoke: Palgrave Macmillan, 2009), pp. 55–75.

Spaas, Lieve, *The Francophone Film: A Struggle for Identity* (Manchester and New York: Manchester University Press, 2000).

Springhall, John, 'Censoring Hollywood: Youth, Moral Panic and Crime/Gangster Movies of the 1930s', *The Journal of Popular Culture*, Vol. 32, Issue 3 <http://onlinelibrary.wiley.com/doi/10.1111/j.0022-3840.1998.3203_135.x/pdf> (last accessed 31 January 2019), pp. 135–54.

Stein, Elliott, '*Maîtresse*' <http://www.criterion.com/current/posts/309-maitresse> (last accessed 31 January 2019).

Stone, Matthew, *Levinas, Ethics and Law* (Edinburgh: Edinburgh University Press, 2018 [2016]).
Taubin, Amy, *Taxi Driver* (London: BFI Publishing, 2000).
Thomson, David, *The New Biographical Dictionary of Film – Sixth Edition* (New York: Alfred A. Knopf, 2014 [original edition first published: 1975]).
'Tout Barbet Schroeder', Press kit, *Théâtres au cinema: 23e festival à Bobigny* <http://www.theatresaucinema.fr/images/pdf/dpresse2012.pdf> (last accessed 31 January 2019), pp. 3–5.
Travers, Peter, '*Reversal of Fortune*', *Rolling Stone*, 17 October 1990 <https://www.rollingstone.com/movies/movie-reviews/reversal-of-fortune-96263/> (last accessed 31 January 2019).
Vallejo, Fernando, *Our Lady of the Assassins*, trans. Paul Hammond (London: Serpent's Tail, 2001 [original language publication: 1994]).
Vidal, Belén, 'Introduction: The Biopic and Its Critical Contexts', in Tom Brown and Belén Vidal (eds), *The Biopic in Contemporary Film Culture* (New York and Abingdon: Routledge, 2014), pp. 1–32.
Wilson, Emma, *Sexuality and the Reading Encounter: Identity and Desire in Proust, Duras, Tournier, and Cixous* (Oxford: Clarendon Press, 1996).
Wright, John W., 'Levinasian Ethics of Alterity: The Face of the Other in Spielberg's Cinematic Language', in Dean A. Kowalski (ed.), *Steven Spielberg and Philosophy: We're Gonna Need a Bigger Book* (Lexington: The University Press of Kentucky, 2008), pp. 50–68.
Wright, Tamra, Peter Hughes and Alison Ainley, 'The Paradox of Morality: An Interview with Emmanuel Levinas', trans Andrew Benjamin and Tamra Wright, in Robert Bernasconi and David Wood (eds), *The Provocation of Levinas: Rethinking the Other* (London and New York: Routledge, 1988), pp. 168–80.

Index

Note: *italic* page numbers indicate figures

À Bout de souffle (*Breathless*), 103
Aaron, Michele, 5
Adam Resurrected, 147, 150, 198–203, 206
   Jeff Goldblum, 198, *199*, 200, *203*
   performativity of identity, 22, 198
   style, 21, 22, 187–8, 201–3
Adorno, Theodor W., 106
Affliction, 147
Aizawa, Masato, 182, *183*
Almendros, Nestor, 91
American Gigolo, 147, 151–69, 170, 177, 178, 179, 205, 226–7n2
   music, 150, 155–7, 158, 160, 164, 229n11
   performativity of identity, 22, 155, 165, 176, 177–8, 189, 201
   style, 22, 150, 155–60, 163–8, 169, 176, 177–8, 187, 188, 191, 193, 201, 206
   transcendental style, 165–8
Amin, Idi, 89, 119, 122
Amnesia, 86
Angels with Dirty Faces, 103
Armani, Giorgio, 152, 157, 163
Arriagada, Jorge, 124, 138
Astruc, Alexandre, 23
Atonement, 91
Attenborough, Richard, 170
Aubenas, Jacqueline, 30
Austin, J. L. *see* performativity
Auto Focus, 201
Avocat de la terreur, L' see *Terror's Advocate*
Azalbert, Nicolas, 225n22
Azoury, Philippe, 101

Babe, Fabienne, 34, 35
Bailey, John, 229n13

Bakewell, Liza, 19, 24
Ballesteros, Anderson, 132, *133*
Bando, Yasosuke, 182, *184*
Barbie, Klaus *see Terror's Advocate*
Barfly, 86
Beckett, Samuel, 21
Beethoven, Ludwig van, 72, 73
Before and After, 86, 119, 141
Bellar, Clara, 194
Bernasconi, Robert, 6
Bertolucci, Bernardo, 91, 103, 163, 166, 171, 220n2
Biskind, Peter, 220n1
Blondie (band), 155, 159
Blue Collar, 150
Bonnie and Clyde, 220n2
Bordwell, David, 213n85
Bory, Jean-Louis, 90
Bouhired, Djamila *see Terror's Advocate*
Boulangère de Monceau, La (*The Bakery Girl of Monceau* a.k.a. *The Girl at the Monceau Bakery*), 86
Bowie, David, 229n11
Breillat, Catherine, 99–100
Bresson, Robert, 1, 22, 141, 164, 166, 195, 203
Brokeback Mountain, 137–8, 141
Brown, Rosellen, 119
Bruzzi, Stella, 20, 121
Busquets, Manuel, 132, *139*
Butler, Judith, 12, 20, 31, 71–2, 82, 140–1

Cagney, James, 103
Cain, James M., 222n32

Campbell, Russell, 95
Carlos the Jackal *see Terror's Advocate*
Caron, Laurent, 78
Carr, Caleb, 193
Carr, Patti, 160
Carroll, Noël, 10, 135–6, 207
Cat People (1942), 229n10
Cat People (1982), 176, 229n10 , 229n11
Cavell, Stanley, 10
Celeste, Reni, 4
Céline et Julie vont en bateau (*Céline and Julie Go Boating*), 86
Chabrol, Claude, 86
Chacun son cinéma (*To Each His Own Cinema*), 69, 218n1
Charles Bukowski Tapes, The, 86
Child, The see Enfant, L'
Choi, Jinhee, 10
Cidade de Deus (*City of God*), 37
Cidade dos Homens (*City of Men*), 137
Cidade dos Homens (*City of Men*) (TV series), 137
Ciment, Michel, 142
Clockwork Orange, A, 220n2
Close, Glenn, 108, *109, 116*
Cohan, George M., 171
Cohen, Richard A., 48
Comfort of Strangers, The, 21, 150, 188–93, 203, 206
  as adaptation of book, 188, 189–90, 191, 192–3, 229n4
  Ian McEwan, 188, 189–90, 191,192–3
  style, 187–8, 190–1, 192–3
  Venice as location, 188, 191, 229n4
conformista, Il (*The Conformist*), 163
Cooper, Sarah, 4, 5, 20–1, 30, 43–4, 54, 57, 60–1, 62, 101
Corman, Roger, 220n2
Cowie, Peter, 220n1
Cox, Damian, 37, 52, 53
Crane, Bob, 201
Crano, R. D., 54, 56–7, 95
Crawford, Billy, 194
Critchley, Simon, 6, 21
Cummings, Doug, 5, 30
Currie, Gregory, 10, 16–17, 207
Curtiz, Michael, 103, 171

Dafoe, Willem, 200
'Dans l'obscurité' (short film), 69

Dardenne brothers, the, 1, 3, 5, 10, 21, 22, 23, 29–82, 85, 88, 91, 92, 95, 101, 105, 130, 143, 147, 150, 151, 190, 197, 204–5, 206, 207, 208
Au dos de nos images (book by Luc Dardenne), 29, 36, 48, 214n1
Au dos de nos images II (book by Luc Dardenne), 29, 70, 214n1
documentary background, 22, 33, 47
evolution of style, 22, 31, 34, 36, 43, 45, 46–7, 48, 52–3, 56, 69–82, 85, 140, 142, 148, 201, 204–5
influence of Levinas, 3, 29, 33, 36
Palmes d'Or, 69
Sur l'affaire humaine (book by Luc Dardenne), 29–30, 215n4
Davies, Paul, 14, 15, 31, 58
Davis, Colin, 6, 14, 50, 135
de France, Cécile *see The Kid with a Bike*
De Sica, Vittorio, 79
Death in Venice, 138
Deleuze, Gilles, 10
Demme, Jonathan, 135
Denis, Claire, 21
dénucléation see Levinas, Emmanuel
Depardieu, Gérard, 89, 90, *93*, 94, *94, 104*
Dequenne, Émilie, 36
Derrida, Jacques, 10, 12
  critique of *Totality and Infinity*, 6, 12, 34
  iterability, 31, 71–2
  Levinas's prose style, 127; *see also* Levinas, Emmanuel
  United States Declaration of Independence, the *see* performativity
Dershowitz, Alan M. *see Reversal of Fortune*
Dershowitz, Elon, 119
Desperate Measures, 86, 141
d'Estais, Jérôme, 86, 87
Deux Jours, une nuit see Two Days, One Night
Di Mateo, Egon, 78
Dillet, Benoît, 70
Dobroshi, Arta, 72
Dominion: Prequel to the Exorcist, 22, 147, 150, 188, 193–8, 201, 203, 206
  as prequel to *The Exorcist*, 193–4, 196
  making of, 193–4
  Stellan Skarsgård, 194–5, *195*, 197–8, *197*
  style, 22, 187–8, 195, 196–8, 203
  subject matter, 147, 188, 193, 194–5, 196, 198

Doret, Thomas, 36, 73, *74*, *77*
Douchet, Jean, 86
Downing, Lisa, 9–10, 99–100
Dozo, Marie-Hélène, 36
Dreyer, Carl Theodor, 1, 22, 166
Ducharme, Olivier, 30
Duke, Bill, 162
Duras, Marguerite, 61
Duroy, Lionel, 123
Dyer, Richard, 130, 137, 142, 227n7
Dylan, Bob, 182, 185

Easy Rider, 220n2
Eberwein, Robert T., 168
Elizondo, Hector, 163
Empire des sens, L' (*Empire of the Senses* a.k.a. *In the Realm of the Senses*), 103, 220n2
Enfant, L', 5, 36, 56, 69–70, 73, 74–5, 81
ethics as first philosophy *see* Levinas, Emmanuel
Everett, Rupert, 188, *190*, 191, *192*
Exorcist, The, 193, 195, 196
Exorcist: The Beginning, 194

face of the Other, the *see* Levinas, Emmanuel
face-to-face encounter, the *see* Levinas, Emmanuel
Falsch, 33
Field, Syd, 44–5
Fille inconnue, La see *The Unknown Girl*
Film, 21
Fils, Le, 31, 36, 50–68, 74, 75, 78, 91, 204
  absence of music, 53–4, 66, 73, 74
  Olivier Gourmet, 51, *53*, 54, 55–6, *62*, *65*
  originary performativity, 31, 58–61, 63, 66, 68
  narrative structure, 51–3, 61, 64–8
  performativity of identity, 54–6, 176
  sound, 53, 68
  style, 21, 80, 51, 52–4, 55–8, 61, 62–3, 69, 71, 75, 76, 80, 81, 82
Fincher, David, 171
First Reformed, 147, 166
Flanagan, Damian, 172
Ford, John, 196
Forman, Milos, 202
Foucault, Michel, 10
Frampton, Daniel, 56, 81
François, Déborah, 36, 75

Frey, Mattias, 10
Friedkin, William, 193
Furlong, Edward, 119

G., Yuri, 227n6
Gallafent, Edward, 202
Gamin au vélo, Le see *The Kid with a Bike*
Gandhi, 170–1
Gandhi, Mahatma, 170–1
Garnett, Tay, 222n32
Gauder, Thomas, 36
Gaviria, Víctor, 136
Général Idi Amin Dada: autoportrait (*General Idi Amin Dada: A Self Portrait*), 86, 89–90, 118, 119, 122
Gere, Richard, 151, *153*, *158*, *159*, *167*, *178*, *179*
Girgus, Sam B., 14, 30
Glass, Philip *see Mishima: A Life in Four Chapters*
Godard, Jean-Luc, 35, 86, 103
Goldblum, Jeff *see Adam Resurrected*
GoodFellas, 91
Gourmet, Olivier, 36, *40*; *see also Fils, Le*
Grønstad, Asbjørn, 21
Gruault, Jean, 35
Gullestad, Anders M., 19

Haddad, Hachemi, 39, *40*
Hagen, Uta, 113
Hagerty, Julie, 108, *109*
Hand, Seán, 71, 100, 106
Hardcore, 150
Harlin, Renny, 194
Harris, Mark, 220n1
Harry, Debbie, 155
Haugmard, Louis, 226n8
Hawks, Howard, 103
Haynes, Todd, 182
Hearst, Patty, 201
Hessels, Wouter, 47
Hole, Kristin Lené, 21
Hollinghurst, Alan, 131, 137, 142, 143
Hopper, Dennis, 220n2
Huffman, Felicity, 111
Hutchens, B. C., 227n11
Hutton, Lauren, 151, *158*

I Think of You see *Je Pense à Vous*
I'm Not There., 182, 185

illocutionary, the *see* performativity
Imamura, Shôhei, 177
Indiana, Gary, 102, 140
Infante, Pedro, 132
Inju, la bête dans l'ombre (*Inju: The Beast in the Shadow*), 86
Irons, Jeremy *see Reversal of Fortune*
Isham, Mark, 114
Italian neorealism, 31, 79

Jackson, Kevin, 149
Jacob, Valentin, 76
Jacobi, Derek, 199
Jag är nyfiken – en film i gult (*I Am Curious [Yellow]*), 220n2
Jagged Edge, 114
Jairo El Sicario (*Sicario*), 136
James, Henry, 12
Jaramillo, Germán, 132, *133, 134, 139, 140*
Je Pense à Vous, 33, 36, 38, 50, 151, 204
 making of, 35, 36
 music, 72, 73
 negative responses, 35, 36, 215–16n1
 Seraing, 34, *35*, 47
 style, 31, 33, 34, 35–6, 43, 44, 46, 47, 69, 70, 164
 subject matter, 34, 35, 38, 47–8
Jesus Christ, 147
Jeune Ahmed, Le, 69
Jousse, Thierry, 112, 113

Kaniuk, Yoram, 198
Karasuma, Setsuko, *179*
Kazan, Nicholas, 107
Kazantzakis, Nikos, 147
Kenaan, Hagi, 14, 15
Kid with a Bike, The, 22, 36, 69, 70, 73–82, 204, 205
 Cécile de France, 73, *77*, 78
 fairytales, 73–4
 music, 73–5
 protagonists, 75–9
 style, 31, 69, 74–5, 75–6, 79–82
Kiss of Death (1995), 86, 141
Koko, le gorille qui parle (*Koko: A Talking Gorilla*), 86, 118
Kouvaros, George, 148, 150, 168, 177, 186, 194, 197
Koyaanisqatsi, 175
Kubrick, Stanley, 220n2

Lacan, Jacques, 10
Ladri di biciclette (*Bicycle Thieves*), 79
Lagerfeld, Karl, 157
LaMotta, Jake, 171, 176
Lanzmann, Claude, 4
Larsen, Svend Erik, 19–20
Last Emperor, The, 171
Last Tango in Paris, 91, 103, 220n2
Last Temptation of Christ, The, 147
Lawrence, T. E., 171
Lawrence of Arabia, 171
Lean, David, 171
Lee, Ang, 137
Lehman, Peter, 226–7n2
Leigh, Mike, 31
Leitch, Thomas, 107, 114, 120
LeRoy, Mervyn, 103
Levinas, Emmanuel
 Being, 6, 9, 15, 20–1, 34, 52, 60, 63, 102, 103, 129, 135, 144, 181, 186, 189, 197
 dénucléation, 8, 9, 63, 118, 152, 205, 206, 207
 Derrida's critique of *Totality and Infinity see* Derrida, Jacques
 ethics as first philosophy, 8, 20, 60, 66, 88, 130, 134–5, 137, 143–4, 205; *see also* pre-original, the
 face of the Other, the, 4–5, 6, 13, 29, 36, 44, 96, 100, 110, 117, 118, 181
 face-to-face encounter, the, 13, 36, 44, 57, 112–13
 gender, 161, 227n11
 hostage status, 5, 9, 13, 37, 53, 63, 123, 148, 162, 187, 188, 189, 192, 196, 204
 influence on Film Studies, 3–6, 9–10, 20–1
 influence on the Dardenne brothers *see* Dardenne brothers, the
 justice and law, 105–7, 110–11, 112–13, 114, 115, 123–4, 127–8, 161–2
 Otherwise than Being or Beyond Essence (book), 2, 3, 4, 5–6, 7–9, 10, 13–15, 17, 20–1, 24, 30, 31, 33, 34, 48, 52, 53, 100, 101, 102, 105, 113, 123, 124, 127, 131, 138, 141, 143, 152, 154, 161, 162, 165, 186, 187, 189, 204, 206
 pre-original, the, 3, 66, 88, 102–3, 114, 131, 135, 144

prose style, 1, 2, 3, 5–6, 7–9, 10, 12, 14–15, 20–1, 24, 30, 34, 106, 113, 124, 126–7, 135, 206
proximity, 3, 5, 8, 48, 52, 64, 79, 114
'Reality and its Shadow' (essay), 3–4, 48, 98, 173, 226n8
Said, the, 8–9, 14–15, 25, 31, 48, 58, 71, 75, 106, 114, 123, 131, 135, 142, 143, 144, 156, 181, 201
Saying, the, 3, 8–9, 13, 14–15, 21, 23, 24–5, 31, 34, 48, 58, 66, 71, 75, 102, 106, 112, 114, 123, 131, 135, 143–4, 148, 165, 186, 187, 189, 204, 205
substitution, 2, 8, 9, 61, 63, 79, 87, 102, 114, 122, 123, 142–3, 187, 189, 205; *see also* the-one-for-the-other
the-one-for-the-other, 8, 9, 61, 63, 71, 79, 114, 122, 142
Totality and Infinity: An Essay on Exteriority (book), 4, 5, 6, 8, 9, 13, 14, 30, 31, 33, 34, 35, 37, 48, 53, 95, 96, 100, 105, 161, 206
Levine, Michael P., 37, 52, 53
Light Sleeper, 147
Lingis, Alphonso, 14–15, 138
Linha de Passe, 137
Little Caesar, 103
Loach, Ken, 31
locutionary, the *see* performativity
Lombardo, Patrizia, 19
Loxley, James, 12, 16, 59

MacCormack, Patricia, 90
McEwan, Ian *see Comfort of Strangers, The*
McKee, Robert, 44–5
Mad Men – 'The Grown-Ups' (TV episode), 86
Mahler, Gustav, 138
Mai, Joseph, 30, 42–3, 44, 47, 51, 54, 56
Maîtresse, 86, 87, 89–104, 110, 136, 140, 153, 157, 161, 205
controversy, 89–90
era of production and release, 89–90, 103, 220n1, 220n2
narrative structure, 90–1, 92, 95–6
performativity of identity, 22, 176
representation of BDSM, 90, 92, 98–101
style, 21, 87, 90–1, 92–4, 96–103, 104, 105, 129,
subject matter, 87, 89, 90, 104, 129

Manderson, Desmond, 106, 112, 120
Mann, Gabriel, 197
Marcoen, Alain, 36
Marie, Michel, 120
Marinne, Morgan, 36, 51, *62*, *65*, 72
Marquand, Richard, 114
Marriott, David, 111
Martin, Mardik, 171
Meirelles, Fernando, 137
Melville, Herman, 12
Mertens, Wim, 73; *see also Je Pense à Vous*
Metz, Christian, 16, 44
Miike, Takashi, 92
Miller, J. Hillis, 19, 20, 52–3
Mirren, Helen, 188
Mishima, Yukio *see Mishima: A Life in Four Chapters*
Mishima: A Life in Four Chapters, 147, 170–86, 189
narrative structure, 171–2, 173–5, 179–80, 193
performativity of identity, 22, 153, 170, 173, 175, 176, 177–9, 180, 186, 193, 201
Philip Glass's music, 175, 181
relation to biopics, 170, 171–2, 206
style, 21–2, 148, 150, 172, 176–85, 186, 187, 188, 191, 201
subject matter, 170, 171, 172–3, 175–6
suicide of Yukio Mishima, 170, 172–3, 176, 180
Yukio Mishima, 150, 170, 171, 174, 175, 176, 179, 180, 181, 185, 186
Monaco, James, 17–18
More, 86, 89–90, 104, 220n2
Morelli, Paulo, 137
Morgan, Michael L., 13, 152, 168–9
Moroder, Giorgio, 155, 159, 163, 229n11
Mosley, Philip, 30, 47, 60, 70
Mosquito Coast, The, 147
Muni, Paul, 103
Murder by Numbers, 86, 141

Nagahara, Yuki, 182, *183*
Nagashima, Toshiyuki, 182, *184*
Nancy, Jean-Luc, 21
Nathan, John, 172
Nealon, Jeffrey T., 12
Needham, Gary, 137, 141
Neeson, Liam, 119, 194

Nichols, Bill, 20, 153, 164, 166, 167–8
Novoa, José, 136

Ôdishon (Audition), 92
Ogata, Ken, *177, 178*, 182, *182*, 228n7
Ogier, Bulle, 89, 92, 98, *99, 104*
One Flew Over the Cuckoo's Nest, 202
originary performativity *see* performativity
O'Shaughnessy, Martin, 30, 41, 47, 81, 197, 215–16n1
Ôshima, Nagisa, 177, 220n2
Ossessione (Obsession), 222n32
Otherwise than Being or Beyond Essence (book) *see* Levinas, Emmanuel
Ouédraogo, Assita, 36, *40*
Ouédraogo, Idrissa, 36
Ouédraogo, Rasmané, 36, *42*
Our Lady of the Assassins, 22, 86, 87, 88, 129–44, 205
   as adaptation of book, 129, 131–2, 137
   Fernando Vallejo, 129, 131
   genre, 136–8, 141
   making of, 138
   music, 138, 140–1
   style, 88, 132–4, 135–6, 141–2, 143, 205
Out 1, 86
Ozu, Yasujirô,1, 22, 164, 165, 166, 176, 195, 203

Pakula, Alan J., 114
Paris vu par . . ., 86
Parker, Andrew, 212n55
Pasolini, Pier Paolo, 220n2
Patty Hearst, 201
Peckinpah, Sam, 220n2
Penn, Arthur, 220n2
Peperzak, Adriaan Theodor, 7, 8, 95–6, 97, 110, 123, 135, 143–4, 196
performativity
   constative, the, 11, 20, 31, 33, 34, 44, 45–6, 47, 48, 50, 59, 113, 164, 178
   illocutionary, the, 11, 12, 18, 43, 45–6, 47–8, 58, 66, 79, 129, 131, 143, 165, 204, 206, 207
   image acts, 19, 24
   iterability *see* Derrida, Jacques
   J. L. Austin, 10–12, 16, 18, 19, 20, 22, 31, 33, 34, 114–5, 164, 207, 208, 216n17
   locutionary, the, 11, 18, 46, 66, 207

originary performativity, 31, 58–60, 63, 66, 68, 72, 148, 204
Performativity$_1$, 19, 20, 31, 53, 117, 155, 164, 205
Performativity$_2$, 19, 20, 31, 52–3, 117, 155, 164, 205
perlocutionary, the, 11, 12, 18, 46, 48, 66, 143, 149, 165, 204, 206, 207
recalibration, 135, 207
resignification, 31, 71–2, 74–5, 82, 140–1, 143
social relations, 12, 13, 16–17, 18, 24, 37, 41, 46, 50, 66, 207, 208
speech acts, 11, 12, 13, 14, 16, 18, 19, 21, 31, 37, 46, 50, 56, 57, 58, 59, 60, 114, 208
United States Declaration of Independence, the, 58–60, 68, 143, 204
Perkins, V. F., 17, 19, 218n33
perlocutionary, the *see* performativity
Perpich, Diane, 6, 7, 13, 14, 37, 53, 186
Petrey, Sandy, 12, 16, 46, 164, 208, 216n17
Philadelphia, 135
Pickpocket, 164, 165, 167
Pinter, Harold, 188, 191
Pippin, Robert, 71, 92
Plantinga, Carl, 10
Pol Pot, 121
Pollack, Sydney, 176
Pollet, Jean-Daniel, 86
Pondeville, Stéphane, 34
Postman Always Rings Twice, The (book), 103, 222n32
Postman Always Rings Twice, The (1946), 222n32
Postman Always Rings Twice, The (1981), 222n32
pre-original, the *see* Levinas, Emmanuel
Presumed Innocent, 114
Promesse, La (The Promise), 10, 33, 36–49, 50, 52–3, 55, 56, 75, 80, 91, 151, 204
   Jérémie Renier, *40*, 42–3, *42*
   making of, 36
   narrative structure, 37–8, 39, 41, 44–5, 46, 52–3
   Seraing, 34, 35, 47
   style, 21, 31, 33, 34, 38–9, 41–2, 43–4, 45, 46–7, 48, 57, 69, 70, 72–3, 74–5, 81, 81–2, 85, 164

Proust, Marcel, 12, 61
Pu Yi (last emperor of China), 171
Public Enemy, The, 103
Puri, Tara, 70

Rafelson, Bob, 222n32
Raging Bull, 171, 176
Rainsford, Dominic Michael, 21
Rapiteanu, Tudor, 198, *199*
'Reality and its Shadow' (essay) *see* Levinas, Emmanuel
Reggio, Godfrey, 175
Renier, Jérémie, 36, 73, 75; *see also Promesse, La*
Renucci, Robin, 34, 35
Resnais, Alain, 35
Reversal of Fortune, 87, 107–18, 119, 120, 127–8, 136, 161, 176, 181–2
  Alan Dershowitz, 107, 118
  as adaptation of book, 107–8
  Claus von Bülow, 22, 107, 118
  Jeremy Irons, 108, *109*, *116*, 117–18, *117*, 224n34
  music, 114
  performativity of identity, 22, 117–18, 176
  style, 21–2, 87, 105, 107, 108–10, 127–8, 129, 205
  Sunny von Bülow, 107, 224n29
Rich, Jamie S., 228n7
Richardson, Natasha, 188, *190*, *192*
Rijû, Gô, 182, *183*
Rivette, Jacques, 35, 86
Robinson, Edward G., 103
Robinson, Smokey, and the Miracles, 164
Rodrigo D: No Futuro (*Rodrigo D: No Future*), 136
Rohmer, Éric, 86
Rolland, Jacques, 48
Rongione, Fabrizio, 72, 76
Roosevelt, Franklin D., 171
Rosetta, 36, 44, 54, 55, 69, 73, 75, 81
Rossellini, Roberto, 35
Rouch, Jean, 86
Rouyer, André, 90
Rushton, Richard, 55–6, 81

Sætre, Lars, 19
Said, the *see* Levinas, Emmanuel
Salles, Walter, 137

Salò o le 120 giornate di Sodoma (*Salò, or the 120 Days of Sodom*), 220n2
Saussure, Ferdinand de, 16
Sawada, Kenji, 182, *184*
Saxton, Libby, 4–5, 10, 121–2, 181
Saying, the *see* Levinas, Emmanuel
Scarface (1932), 103
Scarfiotti, Ferdinando, 163
Scheider, Roy, 175, 228n7
Schneider, Alan, 21
Schrader, Leonard, 175
Schrader, Paul, 1–2, 3, 10, 21–2, 23–4, 147–203, 205–6, 207, 208, 228n8, 229n10–11
  as screenwriter on other directors' films, 147, 171, 175
  on transcendental style, 1–2, 22, 149, 164–6, 175, 176, 195, 203
Schroeder, Barbet, 1, 3, 10, 20, 21, 22, 23–4, 85–144, 147, 148, 150, 157, 181, 185, 201, 205, 206, 207, 208
  as actor, 86
  as producer, 86
  background, 22, 23, 85–6, 131
Sciorra, Annabella, *110*, 111
Sciuscià (*Shoeshine*), 79
Scorsese, Martin, 91, 147, 171, 220n2
Scott Stokes, Henry, 172
Searchers, The, 196
Sedgwick, Eve Kosofsky, 12, 212n55
Shoah, 4–5
Silence de Lorna, Le see Silence of Lorna, The
Silence of Lorna, The, 47, 69, 70, 75
  music, 72–3, 74
  style, 70, 73, 74, 80–1
Silver, Ron, 108, *110*, *116*
Simon, John, 98, 100
Single White Female, 86, 141
Sinnerbrink, Robert, 10, 30
Sirk, Douglas, 108
Sjöman, Vilgot, 220n2
Skarsgård, Stellan *see Dominion: Prequel to the Exorcist*
Smith, Nick, 106, 127
Sobchack, Vivian, 10
Social Network, The, 171
Son, The see Fils, Le
Soupart, Isabella, 61
Spaas, Lieve, 38, 44
speech acts *see* performativity

Spielberg, Steven, 5
Springhall, John, 222n31
Staiger, Janet, 213n85
Stein, Elliott, 99
Steiner, Max, 80
Stevens, Fisher, 111
Stollman, Noah, 198
Stone, Matthew, 107, 181
Storaro, Vittorio, 91
Straw Dogs, 220n2
Streep, Meryl, 119
substitution *see* Levinas, Emmanuel
Suspect, 114

Taxi Driver, 147, 176, 220n2
Terror's Advocate, 86, 118–28, 136, 147, 153
   Carlos the Jackal, 120
   Djamila Bouhired, 120, 124
   documentary, 20, 88, 118, 119–20, 121, 185
   Jacques Vergès, 22, 88, 118, 119, 120, 121–4, 148, 153, 185
   Klaus Barbie, 120, 122–3
   music, 124
   performativity of identity, 22, 121–3, 176
   style, 87–8, 105, 107, 121–2, 124, 126–7, 127, 129, 141, 185, 205
Teshigahara, Hiroshi, 177
the-one-for-the-other *see* Levinas, Emmanuel
Theroux, Paul, 147
Thomas, Daniela, 137
Thompson, Kristin, 213n85
Thomson, David, 86, 107, 113, 115, 164, 168
Tilaï (*The Law*), 36
Totality and Infinity: An Essay on Exteriority (book) *see* Levinas, Emmanuel
Tourneur, Jacques, 229n10
Towne, Robert, 175
transcendental style *see* Schrader, Paul
Travers, Peter, 115
Tricheurs, 86, 118
Trip, The, 220n2

Truffaut, François, 35
Two Days, One Night, 69, 70

United States Declaration of Independence, the *see* performativity
Unknown Girl, The, 69, 70

Vallée, La (*The Valley [Obscured by Clouds]*), 86, 89–90
Vallejo, Fernando *see Our Lady of the Assassins*
van Pallandt, Nina, 155
Vénérable W., Le (*The Venerable W.*), 86, 119
Vergès, Jacques *see Terror's Advocate*
Vidal, Belén, 170, 182
Virgen de los Sicarios, La see Our Lady of the Assassins
Visconti, Luchino, 138, 222n32
von Bülow, Claus *see Reversal of Fortune*
von Bülow, Sunny *see Reversal of Fortune*
Voujargol, Paul, 90

Walken, Christopher, 188, 191
Walker, The, 147
Weir, Peter, 147
Wellman, William A., 103
Wild Bunch, The, 220n2
Williams, Hank, 175
Williams, John, 80
Wilson, Emma, 50–1, 60, 61, 66, 144, 207
Wirathu, Ashin, 119
Wisher Jr, William, 193
Wright, Joe, 91
Wright, John W., 5

Yaaba, 36
Yakuza, The, 175
Yankee Doodle Dandy, 171
Yates, Peter, 114
Young Ahmed see Jeune Ahmed, Le

Žižek, Slavoj, 10
Zuckerberg, Mark, 171
Zurer, Ayelet, 199